KLAUS BARBIE

KLAUS BARBIE

Ladislas de Hoyos

Translated from the French by
Nicholas Courtin

McGraw-Hill Book Company

New York   St. Louis   San Francisco   Bogotá
Guatemala   Hamburg   Lisbon   Madrid   Mexico
Montreal   Panama   Paris   San Juan   São Paulo
Tokyo   Toronto

To Erika, Corinne, Amélie and Charlotte

First McGraw-Hill edition, 1985.

First published in France under the title Barbie by Editions Robert Laffont 1984
First published in Great Britain by W.H. Allen 1985

1 2 3 4 5 6 7 8 9 0 D O C D O C 8 7 6 5

ISBN 0-07-016297-2

LIBRARY OF CONGRESS CATALOGING IN PUBLICATION DATA

Hoyos, Ladislas de, 1939-
   Klaus Barbie.
   Translation of: Barbie.
   1. Barbie, Klaus, 1913-   2. National
socialists—Biography.   3. War criminals—Biography.
4. World War, 1939-1945—France.   5. World War,
1939-1945—Atrocities.   6. France—History—German
occupation, 1940-1945.   I. Title.
DD247.B32H6913   1985   327.1'2'0924 [B]   85-11326
ISBN 0-07-016297-2

Acknowledgements

To THE MANY PEOPLE in France and other countries who have assisted me in my research, opened up their files and helped me gain access to unpublished official archives, I express my sincerest thanks. Without these diplomats, historians, officials in the judiciary and others, my task would not have been nearly so fruitful.

Special thanks are due to Ambassadors Albert Chambon, Dominique Ponchardier, Joseph Lambroschini, Jean-Louis Mandereau and Raymond Césaire, along with Consuls Thérèse de Lioncourt and Paul Colombani, and French Ambassador Jean-Marie Soutou. I am grateful also to Henri Noguères, David Barnouw and other historians, Jean Moulin's secretary Daniel Cordier, Colonel Paul Paillole, Public Prosecutor Paul Brilman and Mr J. J. Koppe of Amsterdam, Serge Barcellini, the local officials of Caluire and Saint-Genis-Laval, and Charles Ronsac for his valuable advice.

I obtained help, too, from Serge and Beate Klarsfeld, Maître Zelmati and Simon Wiesenthal, from the press bureau of the United States Embassy in Paris, and from numerous officials in Bolivia, Peru, the Netherlands, West Germany, Italy and Austria. My respects are due to Mrs Françoise Croizier.

Not forgetting Pascale and Marie-Paule and several others unknown to the public who contributed to my basic purpose – to find out as much as I could about Klaus Barbie and convey this to an international audience.

To the victims, their children,
and their oppressors' children

1

MADAME LISE LESÈVRE, now over eighty, shifted in her chair and her eyes met mine. 'He was sort of whining for his money, because he'd been paid for just one. He said: "I got you two, don't forget." And Barbie gave him more money for the second Jew.'

Lise had prepared a few notes of her own, and her hand quivered slightly as she ran over them. Not that she had forgotten, but she wanted me to have all the details she considered important.

She added: 'That man didn't really need the money for telling the Gestapo about the Jews, you know. He was very smartly dressed.'

Madame Lesèvre fell into Klaus Barbie's clutches at Perrache railway station in Lyons when she was forty-four. She was thirteen years older and rather taller than Barbie, a diminutive SS man who had bought a couple more Jews from the well-dressed stranger.

She remembered Barbie's harsh gaze. 'The Germans arrested me on the platform itself,' she said. 'I had a written message for Didier – that was the name used by Albert Chambonnet, captain in the air force and head of the French Secret Army for Ain, Jura and Saône-et-Loire. I wasn't the only one; they took us with about twenty men to the Gestapo headquarters in the École de Santé Militaire. It was 13 May 1944, and inside the car, a Citroën, I swallowed a few sheets of paper and made the others into tight little balls, which I slipped into my gloves. They took me into a ground-floor room, the Gestapo offices. The room had a picture of Hitler and others in the Reich, his aides. Then they told me: "You are Didier." I said I wasn't. One of them said: "Who is it then?" So I gave the first name that came into my head, the name of the street opposite where I lived, Louis Guérin. Later they tried something on me, wanting to see my reaction: "Guérin's been arrested, they've hanged him." Well, of course, I didn't know whether to laugh or cry.'

The next day, Barbie, in shirt-sleeves, put handcuffs on Lise Lesèvre and hung her up on a hook.

She said: 'They beat me with a cosh, and I kept passing out, but they pulled me round again. After that they handcuffed me again with my hands behind my back, and hit me again. "You'll talk in the end," they said.'

That evening they paraded her husband and youngest boy in front of her. Barbie adopted a reasonable tone: 'Just give us the name and I'll let them go free.' She kept silent and Barbie snapped: 'You see, it's your fault if they stay prisoners.'

Madame Lesèvre spent nineteen days under inter-rogation, nine of them in the torture room, where they forced her to remove all her clothes. When she was naked, Barbie would come in and start hitting her. She said again and again she knew nothing about the Resistance people, the 'terrorists', as Barbie called them. They tied her to a plank and put her in a metal bath filled with ice-cold water. They took hold of her hair and forced her under until she ceased struggling, then they pulled her out, gasping frantically, and poured water into her mouth from an old biscuit-tin as she fought for air. Then they pushed her under again.

Lise told me that even twenty years after the war, she almost fainted every time she saw one of those old iron baths with their splayed legs.

The bath torture failed to loosen her tongue, and Barbie tried another form of persuasion. He would show her other prisoners who were not as obstinate as she was, and had her put in a domed cellar where women and priests were herded together. That made him chuckle, she said. Barbie would walk away along the filthy corridor where men half dead from torture lay on the ground, and would turn them over with his boot. If it was a Jew, he would just walk on the man's face and not look back.

— 2 —

'One day,' the old lady said, 'they took me to an office and pushed me towards the desk. I could see the leather blotter of my boy, Jean-Pierre, and on the wall were the dried thistle he kept in his bedroom, photos of my husband and myself, Jean-Pierre's poems on small sheets of paper. I saw the sheets and recognized them, they had *maman* scribbled everywhere.'

To jog her memory, Barbie had carefully reproduced part of her son's room in his own office. How is it possible to understand a sadist who went to that kind of trouble? Was it solely the creed of Hitler and of the Nazis that made him a torturer?

In order to comprehend the man we must go back to well before the Second World War, to a day when the Butcher of Lyons was confronted with a question that would have made any other man in his position think twice. Klaus Barbie's pen moved to the next line on the printed form. It read: *LEGITIMATE/ILLEGITIMATE*.

Without hesitating he neatly crossed through the first word, leaving the other. For the first time in his life, Warrant Officer Barbie was filling in a questionnaire of that kind, printed in venerable Gothic lettering, and with an oblique stroke of the pen he was admitting that he was a child of love and not necessarily the product of a rational decision – not a confession that could be made lightly at the time.

Genealogically speaking, he had no reason to feel ashamed. But if he wanted to make progress in the SS and keep his nose clean, there was no escaping the questions the word 'illegitimate' would raise. In those days, being a natural child implied unpleasant things, and the Reich would certainly not give him good marks for that. It was also a nuisance in his relationships with his family. This illegitimate young man desperately sought to affirm that he was not inferior just because he had entered this world before his parents had been through the marriage ceremony. As any psychiatrist will agree, that explains a great deal.

Klaus would have liked to clear up this irritating matter with his father, but the old man had died. Barbie Senior had had one major piece of luck in his life. He was the first of seven brothers and sisters, and was the first to elude the back-breaking toil on the farm. He became a schoolmaster at Udler in the woody Eifel country between Koblenz and Trier – and no doubt his position earned him considerable respect in the local community.

Barbie Senior was twenty-five when Klaus was born on 25 October 1913, at Bad Godesberg. (Today this is a wealthy suburb of Bonn derisively called Bad Judesberg, 'the Jews' Mountain', by anti-Semites.) Germany was building up to the First World War, troops were being concentrated on the border in the Saar and compulsory military service had been raised to three years. The nation's finest airship, the Zeppelin *L II*, had exploded during a demonstration flight over Johannisthal.

Klaus's mother was twenty-seven, somewhat older than his father, and the baby was five months old when the wedding took place on 30 January 1914 at Merzig in the Saar – a locality that has known at least five generations of Barbies. Merzig nudges the French border. Metz is only fifty kilometres away.

Anna Hees, Barbie's mother, called the infant Nikolaus, which quickly became contracted to Klaus, the father's name. Klaus Senior had no objection at all, for he had been named after his grandfather, a day labourer, and his great-grandfather, a farmer, and was pleased that the name should continue in the family.

In 1939 Klaus Barbie Junior was to supply his genealogical tree to the Rasse und Siedlungs-Hauptamt SS (RuSHA: Central Service of Race and Settlement), a kind of Ministry of the Aryan Race. This document reveals that as far back as one can trace, all the Barbies were avowed Catholics, both on the paternal and maternal sides. With the advent of the Führer, Klaus Barbie and his fiancée described themselves on official papers as *'Gottgl.'* (Gottgläubig), meaning 'believer'. The Nazis had no time for Christianity; Hitlerism was a creed in itself.

The Barbie and Hees family records show that for generations they came from Saar farming stock. On the maternal side, the Hees, Martens, Wolffs, Hermes, Schneiders, Illigens and other families came from Boverath, Mehren and Kradenbach, villages that came under the rule of France after the 1914–18 war.

Chats with the older villagers in Daun produce only a vague memory of Barbie, he was so little at the time. But when I showed them a photo taken outside the classroom, they remembered his father. Klaus Senior used to box the children's ears when he had had a drink or two . . . He raised goats . . . Every year he would kill a couple of pigs, and for a whole week the children at school would help him turn them into sausages. The oldest boy used to wear a sailor suit; he was brainy and never got into scraps, they said.

His parents moved to Trier at the end of 1925, but the boy went back to the Eifel region every summer, wearing his school cap with coloured stripes that showed which class he was in. Everyone could see how he was getting along at school, whether he went up a class or stayed down – usually it was up.

A local newsman found out that the lad felt the stirrings of a religious vocation; he said he was drawn to theological studies. But later, after he had taken his school-leaving exam, he sent a letter to a girlfriend, in which he made fun of priests and religion. The Nazi indoctrination had already taken root, so much so that one of his first duties in the SS security services was to keep tabs on churches, reporting anything that might be seen as a threat to the Reich and his Führer, which to him were one and the same.

Barbie's father died in October 1933, from a neck tumour according to his son, but the Udler villagers think it was more likely an overdose of the demon drink. Possibly he drank to dull the pain of the wound. The neighbours remember that he was at the school for only six years, until 1925, and that when he was too drunk to take his class his wife Anna would go in his place.

In May 1972, Klaus Barbie told the Brazilian journalist Ewaldo Dantas Ferreira: 'My father was seriously wounded in the First World War. It was a throat wound, near the carotid artery, and he died of it. He played a big part in the struggle against the French occupation, under the leadership of Schlageter*, and set up a group of partisans among the peasants. These groups had no weapons, but they organized passive resistance, sabotaging railway lines, spreading all sorts of propaganda. I remember clearly what my father did: he was caught up in a celebrated clash in the village of Aegeidienberg where the German resistance fighters hit back at those who favoured the Rhineland's separation.'

The roots of Barbie's hatred for the French stem from his father's experiences. Christian Pineau, head of the Libé-Nord Resistance movement, was questioned by Barbie for a period of eleven hours in the Gestapo headquarters in Lyons in 1943. He remembers Barbie's bitter accusation against the French: 'They kept my father prisoner for three years.' The humiliation of the Versailles Treaty added fuel to his hatred.

Barbie was twenty when his father died, and he had yet to pass his school-leaving exam, but six months earlier he had joined the Hitler Youth, as most young men were doing throughout Germany.

France was just a short distance away and yet, on a day in February 1940 when he was asked if he had ever been abroad, he said no.

Barbie wrote out his curriculum vitae for the Gestapo several times. In 1939 he wrote: 'I was born at Godesberg

---

* Schlageter, a leader in the campaign against French rule in the Ruhr, was caught and shot in 1923 at the age of twenty-seven, and became a symbol for the Nazis. It was he, and not Goebbels, as some historians say, who declared: 'When I hear the word "culture", I reach for my revolver.'

on 25 October 1913. Until the age of eleven I attended primary school at Udler/Eifel, where my father taught. At eleven years of age I started my secondary schooling at Friedrich-Wilhelm Gymnasium in Trier. At the end of my secondary education I obtained the *Abitur* [Germany's school-leaving certificate] at Easter, 1934. I then volunteered for the Arbeitsdienst (Labour Service) at Niebüll/Schleswig-Holstein. On returning home I was out of work to begin with, but during this period I led a small group of the Deutsches Jungvolk (German Youth). I performed this activity from April 1933 onwards, when I joined the HJ (Hitler Youth). Meanwhile I was a volunteer in the Trier Central Section of the NSDAP (Nazional Sozialist Deutsche Arbeits Partei – the Nazi party). There I had my first contacts with the Sicherheitsdienst (SD–Security Service) of the SS in early 1935. In September 1935 I was taken on full time at the Central Bureau of the SD. In October 1936 I was transferred to the head of this service in the Western Section of the SS.'

There is nothing spectacular about Barbie's progress. He was ambitious, no doubt, but he took his time. He had nothing in the way of vocational training behind him, and his father's death meant he did not go to university. Nor did he enter any of the six schools run by the SS: Bad Tölz, Braunschweig, Bern, Forst, Bernau and Dachau. This was no obstacle, for he found a new interest in life, hob-nobbing with the Trier police. His ambition was to become a kind of supercop.

In another curriculum vitae dated 12 February 1940, he noted that he had not been to university because of a lack of funds. He gave details of his political work: 'My political activity began with my joining the Hitler Youth in April 1933. After six months' service I was selected as head of the Deutsches Jungvolk. As a result of my work with the local section of the NSDAP in Trier, I was in touch with the Security Service, where I initially acted in a voluntary capacity. I applied for membership and was recruited.' So we have it from Barbie himself that he volunteered for his career.

In 1935, Gestapo chief Himmler said: 'The SD unmasks the adversaries of the National Socialist idea and guides the duties of the police. The SD will police the minds of people, it will be an instrument for taking the measure of and controlling thought.' But Barbie did not rush things, he took no short cuts to promotion.

From 28 May to 1 November 1934, Barbie completed a five-month period of voluntary labour in the Hitler Youth. Then he joined the SS; he was not even twenty-two. The Schutzstaffeln (the SS) were the summit of the pyramid, the ultimate goal, representing security and power. On 1 October 1935, Barbie was allotted the number 272284, which was stated at the top of all his official documents, and sometimes appeared next to his signature.

Rudolph Pechel, founder of the *Deutsche Rundschau (German Review)*, has said: 'All the SS men have this in common: cold eyes like those of fish, reflecting a complete absence of inner life, a complete lack of sentiments.'

Other victims of Nazism were to assert that the SS were a bunch of dissatisfied and frustrated failures of every kind. Historians concerned more with the origin of the SS than with its record judge that there were as many criminals and loud-mouthed brutes among them as there were idealists and romantics. Whichever category Barbie falls into, he could hardly be called a romantic.

With implacable logic, Barbie joined the Nazi party (NSDAP) on 1 May 1937, four days after the German planes bombed Guernica in Spain. He liked to pick the first of the month for new beginnings; it was so much neater and tidier. His party card bore the number 4583085. For those interested in the details of Barbie's career, this number was to prove as important as the SS number. From 5 September to 3 December 1938, Barbie was in the Reich infantry, which provided him with an alibi for Crystal Night, the first major attack on a Jewish community. Then he began another job as reporter with the SD under the number II/122-123, Central Düsseldorf Sector. SS boss Heinrich Himmler had decided to keep tabs on the private lives of the faithful, and at this time the staff at RuSHA carefully noted Barbie's engagement to Fräulein Regina Willms. Regina Willms, second of four children, was a loyal Nazi with party card number 5429240. She looked after children at the Nazi Party nursery in Düsseldorf, and showed a gift for painting and music. Before they could marry and have children, the Barbies had to submit to a medical examination, a kind of purity detector. Under an Interior Ministry decree of 5 August 1938 the élite dictatorial regime required couples not only to take the medical exam but to fill in detailed and far-reaching questionnaires, to trace their family history as far back as the sixty-third generation in some cases (for senior officers) with the object of establishing beyond doubt the immaculate condition of the Aryan race. All this took more than a few hours. The bureaucrats were fastidious, especially since Klaus Barbie had applied for financial benefit. The medical check could not be done by any doctor, he had to be a Nazi doctor. Moreover, the SS wanted references from superiors and guarantees of good moral standing. In all, forty-six separate documents were needed.

One of the questionnaires informed the applicant: 'There is no need for concern of any kind if it is necessary to mention a relation who has a hereditary taint. The information provided will serve only to determine the worst taints . . . This is to protect the SS member himself from the possibility of passing on defects to his children.'

So we find a long and highly detailed medical record in the RuSHA file on Barbie. It is most instructive. On 9 March 1939, Dr A. Hoffman, sworn doctor domiciled at Düsseldorf, Spielbergstrasse 4, inscribed his comments on the untarnished nature of the applicant. Medical Report No. 115607, six pages long, sets out to assure the regime that Barbie is neither a half-breed, gypsy, Russian, Pole, Communist, homosexual, pervert, madman, nor possessed of any Jewish antecedents. Klaus Barbie was inspected from top to toe, and for our edification we learn that baby Klaus came into this world completely normal, and the fact that he arrived out of wedlock had no effect on his physical make-up. He did not wet the bed, the report states, was walking at the age of one year, and began talking at eighteen months – in short he was the perfect SS baby.

His forebears were investigated for alcoholism, drying-out treatments, jail sentences, multiple births and suicides. Only one grandparent was still alive, and he was eighty. The others died of influenza, stoppage of the bowels, and one, at the age of forty-five, of pneumonia. Klaus had a brother who died of heart failure at eighteen.

As an adolescent, the report goes on, Barbie went in for athletics, swimming and fencing. On the intellectual side, he did four years at primary school, went through high school without repeating a single year, got his *Abitur* certificate, and continued as described above. Our budding SS man did not smoke, drank hardly anything in the way of alcohol, and lived with his mother.

We also learn that the applicant for marriage was 5 feet 7 inches tall, 2 feet 9 inches when seated on the ground. Hitler's scientists overlooked nothing, it seems. He weighed just over 10 stone, which was exactly right for his age (twenty-five). His chest measurement was 34/36 inches (breathing in/breathing out) and his head measurement was 22½ inches – useful information when they ordered his cap. Dr Hoffmann marked him down as slim and well proportioned, with a good upright walk and firm belly. As to colouring, his complexion was pink-white (*rosigweiss*), his eyes grey-blue, his hair fair with a tendency to light brown. Barbie's cheekbones did not protrude and there was no Mongolian crease to the eyes. Racial type: 'Nordic'. RuSHA must have been proud of their man.

A look inside the Barbie mouth revealed that he had thirty-two perfectly healthy teeth. His fiancée's record was not so good, because on the same day it was discovered that Fräulein Willms had seven fillings, three capped premolars and two others missing.

Hair coverage of Klaus Barbie was normal with no pigmentation anomalies; his mucous membranes functioned normally. Backbone, chest, cranium were OK. The applicant's vision was 20/20 in each eye, he did not squint, he identified all colours correctly. He had no diction problems either, and his hearing was just as perfect since he could hear a murmur at six yards, a faculty that would prove extremely useful in the future. His lungs were in good order, his heartbeat was a strong 72 per minute. Blood pressure was normal. No sugar or albumin in the urine; genitalia OK. Procreative capacity was 'normal, according to the examination'. Blood analysis showed no anomalies and all the reflex tests proved normal.

Did he give the impression of being a trustworthy and genuine sort of person? Yes, said the Nazi doctor. Was a specialist consultant to be called in? No need. And the doctor concluded with the verdict: 'Suitable for marriage'. Barbie was free to reproduce for the race.

To sum up, Klaus Barbie might have been a little blonder and somewhat taller – he would then have been the perfect SS man depicted on the Nazi posters. Nonetheless, as of March 1939, the future Butcher of Lyons was a completely normal young man.

The following year, on 14 March 1940, his superiors and colleagues in the Gestapo turned the spotlight on him at Düsseldorf. He was judged to be predominantly Caucasian in type. As to his behaviour, it was deemed good and self-controlled: his conduct on and off duty was disciplined and he gave no cause for concern. His financial affairs were in order.

His superiors then went into some detail about his character and concluded that Klaus Barbie loved life, upheld truth, and had a fine sense of comradeship. He had a lively mind and a quick grasp of situations, together with 'pronounced' will-power and determination. His general level of culture and education was satisfactory. His view of life was sound and his judgement straightforward. Special characteristics: zealous and circumspect. Particular defects and weaknesses: nil.

The investigators noted additionally that Oberscharführer Barbie revealed firmness with regard to the Nazi ideology and that his practical and theoretical knowledge of the service, in matters of discipline and administration, was 'adequate'. The report ended with the confident conclusion: 'Warrant Officer Barbie is a comrade deserving of no reproach. His activity in the service is excellent. His behaviour as an SS officer, when on duty and otherwise, is irreproachable.'

For the couple awaiting marriage, all that remained was for them to make a declaration concerning their assets and their debts. Curiously, Barbie stated that he had 'not yet' obtained possession of his assets, and he also said he had no debts. His fiancée had no wealth and owed no money either.

Klaus Barbie also needed the authorization of his Divisional General, Baron von Schade, who had no hesitation in promoting Warrant Officer Barbie from his previous rank of staff sergeant. Baron von Schade wrote: 'Barbie has an honest character and is a qualified worker. From the standpoint of the SS, no criticism can be made. As regards duty, he can be considered one of the finest employees in the SD Western Section.'

At that juncture there was no question of asking the Church, either Catholic or Protestant, to bless a marriage or carry out a christening. The wedding ceremony followed the rites of the 'ancestral espousals' under the supervision and with the sponsorship of an SS chief who offered the couple bread and salt in accordance with some supposed tradition going back to Ancient Greece.

The couple needed two witnesses for the wedding: Karl Hönscheid and Willi Schmidtsiefen, both SS captains from Düsseldorf. They had to vouch for Klaus Barbie and also for his bride, Regina Willms. Hönscheid and Schmidtsiefen affirmed that the young lady was trustworthy, a good comrade, thrifty, loved home life, liked children (since she worked at a nursery), and that she was suitable to wed a member of the SS. However there was a snag and Schmidtsiefen pointed it out: the fiancée was indeed keen to defend the concept of National Socialism, but her family continued to display a strong attachment to Catholicism. This was no great problem, though, and on 30 March 1939 Dr Poppendick signed the authorization to wed.

Helmut Poppendick was a doctor specializing in hereditary ailments, and appointed by Himmler to oversee demographic policy and RuSHA. Not a single request to marry from an SS member and his fiancée failed to pass through his hands. Poppendick would examine each file with an eagle eye, so that any risk of a mistake was avoided. The race had to be pure and beautiful. In 1943, he was appointed Chief of Staff with the official doctor, Grawitz; so he must have been informed of experiments on prisoners in the concentration camps, experiments such as those performed by the loathsome 'Doctor' Joseph Mengele, who had a penchant for child vivisection.

Writing from Dortmund, Barbie informed RuSHA that his future wife was unable to attend the 'Fiancées' School' at Brüggen, where she had registered, because the establishment had been temporarily converted into a garrison. RuSHA said that Klaus and Regina could go ahead anyway, but that the young lady would have to complete her studies at the School for Mothers before the end of April 1942. She promised to do that and the wedding finally took place on 25 April 1940 at the City Hall, Düsseldorf North. Germany was attacking Norway at the time.

The Barbies found a place to live in Dortmund, Horst-Wesselstrasse 28. While he was away, Barbie's mail went through the military sorting offices, and was simply addressed to 15177 AA.

The records staff at the Gestapo made a meticulous note of the birth of the first Barbie child, a daughter, Ute

Regina, born at Trier on 30 June 1941. Their son, Klaus-Georg, was not born until after the war, in 1946. Himmler advised SS men to have four children, and in this regard Barbie did not do his job.

Obersturmführer Barbie wrote a letter from Lyons on 19 April 1944 in which he informed the authorities: 'Statement: I wish to explain why we have not had a second child so far. My daughter, Ute, was born on 30 June 1941. Subsequent to a very difficult birth, my wife had to rest for almost a year. During this period my wife, who formerly lived in Dortmund, went to stay with her mother, in Trier (address: Liebfrauenstrasse 5, near the Dome), because of the bombing. The circumstances were such that two other married daughters with husbands at the front were also living with their mother. One of these daughters also had a child. I sent a letter to the District President at Trier asking him to help my wife find a home, which is absolutely essential for the birth of a second child. So far it has not proved possible for me to settle my housing problems in an acceptable manner. It is my wife's wish that this should be taken into account. Furthermore, I should like to mention another reason; in 1942 and in 1943 I had leave on only one occasion, owing to the demands of the service in Lyons.'

Once the marriage formalities were over, there was nothing to keep Klaus Barbie in Germany, and he was ordered to leave with the Reich forces and make use of his skills elsewhere. He began in the Netherlands, where he went when his wedding leave was over. Before we see to what use he put those skills in Amsterdam let us briefly outline his career.

Barbie joined the SS on 1 October 1935. Proudly wearing his two bronze medals, the SA Sportabzeichen and the Reichsportabzeichen, he rose from staff sergeant (Scharführer) to warrant officer (Oberscharführer) on 20 April 1939, Hitler's fiftieth birthday. On the Führer's fifty-first birthday he was again promoted, to second lieutenant (Untersturmführer) at the SD in Dortmund.

Less than seven months later, on 9 November 1940, he became a first lieutenant. Then the decorations came: first the KVK, the War Merit Medal Second Class with Swords in 1941, also awarded on Hitler's birthday. Then on 1 September 1943, just after the torture of Jean Moulin, Head of the French Conseil National de la Résistance, he received the same medal, this time First Class.

On 24 January 1944, when his pay was increased due to his rank of B9b higher echelon, he was recommended for the rank of Hauptsturmführer (captain), and was granted the office on 9 November by General von Herft. Meanwhile Barbie collected two more distinctions: the black Wounded Insignia on 7 April, the day after the Izieu tragedy of which more later, and the Iron Cross Second Class on 12 June, exactly a week after the Allied landings on the Normandy coast.

2

I F THERE WAS ONE spot on the globe where the new recruit to the SD could use his talents against the enemies of the Reich – for example, those pariahs of society, the Jews – it was Amsterdam.

The Nazi machine rounded up no fewer than 80,000 Jews in Amsterdam; they amounted to one in ten of the population. In essence Klaus Barbie's business seems to have been Jew-hunting; there is no trace of his having fulfilled any other duty.

The horror Barbie left in his wake remains today solely in the memory of the human beings who lived through the period; with the exception of only one item – a single signature by Barbie – there is no archive material. The whole lot went up in flames: the lists of Jews singled out for deportation, the names of collaborators with the Gestapo, the addresses of the best whores, and the inventory of jewels and other valuables that went into the pockets of the master race. In order to learn about this time we have to listen to the survivors who witnessed it all, and scrabble around for a few lines penned by historians, now dead, who recorded their own recollections and those of others.

What we know of Barbie from these various sources has been corroborated by the contents of his personal file, found intact at the RuSHA offices in Berlin. It may count for something in terms of historical data, but not as far as justice is concerned – the Dutch judiciary has closed the file. In February 1984, the Dutch Queen's Prosecutor Paul Brillman, investigating the matter of crimes against humanity, formally concluded that it was not possible to bring Klaus Barbie to justice in the Netherlands on the grounds of insufficient evidence. At the end of 1983, accompanied by a conscientious elderly police officer, J. J.

Koppe, who had been investigating Barbie's record for years, the Prosecutor visited Lyons with a list of seventy questions; the French Chancellerie had consented to an interrogation of Barbie by the Dutch in his cell at Saint-Joseph Prison. (Their American counterparts, incidentally, had been refused this only a short time before.)

Judge Riss, the examining magistrate, and his clerk Mademoiselle Delamare attended, along with a couple of interpreters conversant in German and Dutch. The prison doctor stood by. Barbie merely glanced at one of his lawyers and declared: 'I am a Bolivian citizen. I have been extradited unlawfully. I will not reply to any questions.' The whole thing was over within five minutes.

Barbie reached Amsterdam on 29 May 1940, having only recently been promoted to the rank of Untersturmführer, second lieutenant. He was twenty-six and his job was to investigate the religious communities, Christian and Jewish, along with the Freemasons and other secret societies – those groups who, it was deemed, could put obstacles in the way of the German advance, even though their resources might be modest.

With the direct authority of the Sipo-SD* office of The Hague, he set up in the heart of Amsterdam his *Aussenstelle*, a type of regional headquarters. For the Dutch the name Barbie had an Italian ring, and was easy to remember, in contrast with Willy Lages, Aus der Fünten, Fischer, Dittges, Lauhus and others who were typical SS types, with their black uniforms and caps mounted with the death's-head. (This badge was intended as a warning to the enemies of the Reich and was a symbol of the SS man's total dedication to Hitler's service.) Barbie liked to wear a soft hat and a beige three-quarter-length coat, the typical James Bond outfit of those days. Lacking in physical

---

* Sipo: Sicherheitspolizei (security police), part of the Sicher-heitdienst (SD).

stature, he had to jerk up his chin and sway on his toes in order to meet the gaze of the 'terrorists', as he called them. It was a look of steel that met their eyes.

Barbie's Jew-hunting operation was to prove more significant than that of The Hague. His headquarters were located in some old buildings at 485 Herengracht, where the Canal des Seigneurs curves round. From the security angle, it was a good site, safe from bomb and other attacks. The canal was only a few paces away, giving assailants no room in which to 'fall back'.

Several witnesses assert that Klaus Barbie arrested the ageing General Hermanus van Tongeren, Grand Master of the Freemasons. His daughter Charlotte said a short time ago that Barbie maltreated members of her family. Barbie, she claimed, used to chuckle and put up the volume of the radio so that it blared out German songs when visitors tried to speak. General van Tongeren was deported to Sachsenhausen camp and died five months after he was arrested. Barbie delivered the death certificate personally to Charlotte. She will never forget him, she says. In September 1944, it was he who reportedly murdered the general's son in Haarlem.

In an interview obtained by the Brazilian journalist Ewaldo Dantas Ferreira in Bolivia in spring 1972, Barbie said: 'Around July 1940 I was incorporated into a group operating near The Hague in preparation for the invasion of England. The invasion did not take place and it was a fairly quiet period for me.' He added that he went to Germany for a training course at an espionage college.

The Koco tea-house was run by a couple of hard-working Jews called Ernst Cahn and A. Kohn. Located at 149 Van Woustraat, it was an easy target for the 'blacks' – the NSB Fascists in the Netherlands, equivalent to the German NSDAP, and a local National Socialist group. Time and again the Koco was wrecked by the black commandos on Jew-bashing expeditions – while the Dutch police looked on. Cahn and Kohn formed a self-defence group and rigged up an ingenious deterrent in the form of a push-button system that picked out the attackers with a searchlight and sprayed them with ammonia from a battery of containers at the entrance, which were normally used for keeping ice-cream cold. Around midnight on 19 February 1941, Ernst Cahn pushed the button, but the adversary on this occasion was not a bunch of Dutch Fascists – it was a patrol of the German SD.

Barbie was among them. We have an account from him that first appeared in the West German magazine *Stern* in 1983, although it was obtained by Gerd Heideman in 1979. Barbie said: 'I saw Cahn with his big bald head and managed to grab an ashtray and throw it at him. It tore open his skull down to his shoulder, and we arrested him. Later I was ordered to command the firing squad. I felt sick when I saw his brains.'

It is unclear whether this was deliberate provocation by the German SS or whether they just happened to be there. The Jews were cornered in the back of the premises and seized. Ernst Cahn was the first Dutch Jew officially put on trial by the Germans. He was executed on 3 March 1941 after the formal death sentence; his friend Kohn got ten years' jail but died after deportation.

The Koco incident, coupled with the killing a week earlier of the activist Koot, marked a turning-point. The top man in the German police, Reichsführer Heinrich Himmler, supposedly heard that 'the Jews have bitten to death a man from the WA armed division' and at once ordered the deportation of 425 Jews from the Netherlands. During the weekend of 22–3 February the SS seized a total of 389 Jews. A German soldier took photos, and the photographer who developed the film kept a second copy of the prints until the end of the war. The 389 Jews were sent to Schoorl camp on the North Sea, and then taken by truck to Alkmaar, where the Germans crammed them into a train that delivered them to Buchenwald and Mathausen. There were no survivors. It has been confirmed that 160 of the victims died in experimental gas chambers. This was the beginning of the wholesale deportation of Jews that reached its peak in the summer of 1942. In all, some 107,000 Jews were deported from the Netherlands, and only 5,200 survived.

As a result of these early deportations, the clandestine Communist party organized a strike, notably at factories in Hilversum. The Communists demanded the release of the Jews in a pamphlet that also called for a pay rise. The leading figures in the Council of Jews were summoned to SD headquarters and warned that, if such incidents continued, another 500 Jews would be eliminated.

The strike was the cue for the Germans to change tactics. Willy Lages arrived to supervise operations, and from now on trade union leaders were no longer merely kept under observation, they were arrested. Barbie's superiors Dittges and Lauhus were posted elsewhere and Barbie himself was promoted.

Barbie was also involved in the events at Wieringer-meer, a polder to the north of Amsterdam where German Jews had been gathering since 1934 with the idea of one day leaving for Palestine. They were farmers and market gardeners who were building up an ironworking and cabinet-making business. On 20 March 1941, a few weeks after the threat of the 500 reprisals, at a moment when anti-Jewish activity in Amsterdam seemed to have died down, the village siren wailed, telling the local people to gather. Seven blue buses from Amsterdam were lined up in the middle of the village.

Julius Reutlinger, who was twenty years old at the time, has described what happened: 'I still don't know why we all went to the main building rather than take flight. There were five or six Germans in civilian dress and just one in uniform. [This was Willy Lages, later given life imprisonment but let out for health reasons; he was then the oldest German prisoner in the Netherlands, and died a few years afterwards.] Among the civilians was Klaus Barbie, that has been confirmed. But don't ask me now whether I remember him clearly. I just know he was there, but I cannot recall exactly how I picked him out.'

The Germans gave no explanation but simply herded most of the Jews together, including all the young ones. They left a few adults to look after the livestock and the crops. Did they want merely to arrest the young Jews? Did they want to eliminate any threat from spies in this area? Was the idea to provide German farmers with fertile land? It is not clear.

Julius Reutlinger's account continues: 'Lages was yelling, telling us to leave the settlement, saying we had ten minutes to collect our things. Most of us were absolutely certain we were going straight to the concentration camps.'

In fact, when these Jews reached Amsterdam they were billeted on various families. No explanations were given. So far Barbie had played a minor role in this affair, but more was to come. For three months nothing happened. The Germans told the leading Dutch Jew, David Cohen, that it was in the interests of the Jewish community to cultivate 'good relations' with the SD, and the President of the Council of Jews therefore called on Barbie two or three times a week at the Canal des Seigneurs offices.

One day Barbie took the hand of the ageing David Cohen and bestowed a bland smile on him. He said, 'You say you need help at the Wieringermeer farm. We agree to let the young people go back. Give me a list of all their names and I'll arrange it.'* Barbie's idea was that, as a result of this gesture, young Jews would feel safe when they were sought out. David Cohen got in touch with the leaders at the Wieringermeer, who said they would be delighted to have the youngsters back. So on 11 June 1941, Cohen handed Barbie a list, though it was not a complete one. These names would prove immensely useful to the Germans for the second consignment of deportees. All that was needed was a pretext – an attack on the Wehrmacht

* This account is based on David Cohen's *Mémoires*, as quoted by the Dutch historian Jacob Presser.

telephone exchange provided the Nazis with the excuse they wanted.

Julius Reutlinger was working at Sloten, south-west of Amsterdam, when he got a message telling him to go back home at once. Later he said: 'I suspected something and did not go home. I had a kind of premonition, and I was right because I was the only one on the list who survived!'

Barbie and his Sipo-SD colleagues failed to net all the Jews they wanted; some of them got away, mingling with the population in and around Amsterdam. So the Germans took others at random to make up the quota of 300. They were sent directly to Mathausen, where it is understood some of them were used for experiments with the gas ovens.

According to an account Barbie gave *Stern* magazine in 1972, he was transferred to the Soviet front in April 1941, going via the port of Königsberg, now renamed Kaliningrad. Barbie said: 'We were afraid of nothing, except for the women, the battalions of women! When they caught any of us . . .' He also told of a column of troops being scalded by boiling water and tar when they went through a village: 'So we drove our tanks onto the pavements, crushing everything . . . Then we used incendiary weapons.'

Barbie did not say whether he returned to the Netherlands, but said he was posted to France around June 1942.

A young Dutch historian, David Barnouw, told me: 'Don't believe Barbie when he says that the orders he carried out in Lyons were the result of action by terrorists. You can see already in Holland he had committed crimes against humanity.' By February 1984, only one document signed by Klaus Barbie had been unearthed in the Netherlands – an item about a *'Vertrauensmann'* (a *V-Mann*)*, or confidence man. It was signed by Barbie on 4

* The *V-Leute*, as they were known in the plural, were of capital importance to the Gestapo throughout the occupied territories during the war. The SD (North-Western Section) in 1937 issued

December 1941 – so he was definitely in Amsterdam that day.

The document in question was a curriculum vitae of a *V-Mann*. The Obersturmführer added the comment: 'This *V-Mann* has in recent months shown a favourable attitude towards the New Europe. He has supplied me with accurate weekly reports.' The *V-Mann* was Guillaume Meertens, who sought refuge after the war in Spain, where he came across other Nazi sympathizers. Living outside Alicante, he became friends with Otto Skorzeny, the man who led a daring commando operation, code-named Cicero, to free Mussolini from detention at a hotel in the Abruzzi. Later, we shall see that Barbie had links with Skorzeny; and Guillaume Meertens visited South America several times when Barbie lived there. The Dutch judiciary initiated inquiries into financial trafficking; the names of a Saudi Arabian sheikh and Prince Bernhard of the Netherlands surfaced. For Klaus Barbie, co-operation with Meertens was to prove significant, for Barbie adopted the pseudonym 'Mertens' in an attempt to evade his pursuers. He appears to have been far from inventive with his false names. Altmann was doubtless taken from Adolph Altmann, Rabbi of Trier, who sought refuge in Amsterdam in 1938 and was deported in 1942.

---

an instruction reading: 'Each command chief will set out to obtain the assistance of one or more *V-Leute* in his region. Each of these agents will himself have informers who should under no circumstances realise that they are working for us. *V-Leute* should be recruited among people having a minimum of culture, common sense, objectivity and logic.' In researching into the SD, historian Heinz Hohne noted that it was in this way the SD built up its own ghost army whose tentacles reached into the smallest nooks and crannies of German society. The information gathered by the SD did not come solely from gossips and part-time spies but from magistrates, businessmen, merchants, artists, scientists and others of social standing. Prior to the war these key sources did a useful job in Germany; the same network was repeated wherever the Germans invaded or threatened to invade.

When Barbie left the Netherlands he had reason to feel pleased with himself. He had acquired the rank of Obersturmführer (first lieutenant) on 9 November 1940; on that occasion he is believed to have spent a few days at home in Saar – at any rate his first child, Ute, was born nine months later. If the traditions of the Race and Settlement organization were observed, baby Ute received a silver goblet and spoon as a present from the SS.

Diepgrond, a Dutch interpreter working for the Gestapo, recalls that Barbie's departure from Amsterdam had nothing to do with family matters: 'It was because he could not get on with the top man, Willy Lages, who reprimanded him for not being strict enough and for spending too much time with women.'

What about Belgium? Barbie's file mentions that he went there, but it is doubtful that he stayed long. Barbie certainly deported some Belgian Jews, including Marcel and Paule Mermelstein, aged seven and ten, who were at a children's home for Jews at Izieu in the Ain *département* of France, but there is very little evidence of his having been in Belgium, and historians agree he simply went to Brussels on his way to take up his new post at Amt VI (Intelligence) in Gex, France, in the spring of 1942.

Gex is also in the Ain *département*, hard by Geneva, which rivalled Lisbon as an espionage centre. Barbie has said that, on arrival, he conducted an investigation in Switzerland into a group of Soviet spies who had caused havoc in the German ranks by infiltrating the top echelons in Berlin. No mean task for a beginner! A certain Werther was sending vital data to the Soviets from Switzerland, but in 1972 Barbie was to admit that he turned up nothing on him; he said in 1972, that he had, however, left the Swiss police with enough material for them to dismantle the network in early 1944. Who was the mysterious Werther? My colleague Victor Alexandrov thinks Werther was a code name adopted by cavalry captain Wilhelm Scheidt, who was in Hitler's immediate circle, or perhaps

— 24 —

a certain Colonel Gehrts, who was Goering's military adviser.

Switzerland was of interest to Barbie for another reason. It is there that some of the French Resistance movements, particularly Combat, sought funding for their networks – not Swiss money, but American, made available by Allen Dulles, head of the US secret service in Europe. For de Gaulle in London was unable to get from the British as much as was needed (although he may have preferred to use his funds for other purposes).

Meanwhile, laying aside his SS flash and donning civilian garb, Barbie toured the 'free' southern zone of France, calling himself Karl Meyer*, or Mayer, or posing as a Flemish cloth salesman, which would explain his heavy accent.

It could be that Klaus Barbie was on the look-out for a certain Max, Rex, or Régis, head of the Resistance in France. The Gestapo was unaware of Jean Moulin's real name, but it knew that General de Gaulle had a supremo in France who appeared to be moving freely between the southern and northern zones. If Barbie had thought to visit Nice, and more particularly the Romanin art gallery, he would have found his man. For Jean Moulin was a painter, signing his pictures 'Romanin'. Using his real name, Jean Moulin opened the gallery on 9 February 1943, an event attended by the local prefect, who was able to admire works by Matisse and Bonnard under the lugubrious portrait of Marshal Pétain. The story goes that the Marshal's portrait fell off the wall during the ceremony, but that is not part of France's official history.

The German intelligence people might also have made inquiries about the prefect in Chartres, who cut his throat in the summer of 1940 to avoid yielding to the Germans. If

* He appeared as Meyer in an initial list of war criminals drawn up in Algiers by the special services of Colonel Paillole, although this data was not given to the Gaullists at the time.

they had, Barbie's subsequent itinerary would have been quite different. For in June 1940 the prefect of Eure-et-Loir was Jean Moulin.

When the German troops arrived, Moulin set about administering the lives of those who had not fled the invader. In a sense he was already resisting by ensuring the continuity of the French State in his region. On 15 June he wrote to his mother and sister Laure: 'My poor *département* is mutilated and bleeding profusely. Nothing has been spared the civilian population.' In a postscript to the letter he said: 'The Germans are capable of anything and if they try to make me say dishonourable things, you know already that they will be untrue.'

Two days later, the Germans entered Chartres to be received by Prefect Moulin in full regalia, 'since the fortunes of war have decreed that you should enter as victors', as he wrote in a report to the Vichy Government. The Germans came for him that evening, saying that he must meet their general. But they also demanded his signature to an affidavit stating that a detachment of Senegalese troops had massacred women and children at Saint-Georges-sur-Eure. Jean Moulin refused to sign and the Germans began beating him up. He still refused, and they took him to the hamlet of La Taye where the alleged crime took place.

The Germans led him to a farm. They approached a large barn, and one of his escorts heaved open the big double doors and said, 'How's that for evidence?'

In his book *Premier Combat*, Jean Moulin described the carnage: 'He waved his hand at nine bodies lying side by side, swollen, disfigured and shapeless, with torn and stained clothes. You could hardly distinguish their sex, and there were several children among them . . . The Nazi said: "That's what your charming niggers have done." I replied: "These unlucky people have been hit by shells . . ."'

They shoved Moulin towards a corner where the limbless trunk of a woman lay on a trestle table. A German gave Moulin another push towards the body, and the door was closed.

Moulin said: 'I was projected onto the human debris. It was cold and sticky, and my own bones turned to ice. In this dark corner, overcome by the nauseous odour from the bodies, I shivered feverishly.'

The Germans finally opened the door and came in with the affidavit. They then pretended to let him run away, and fired three shots. The prefect was unhurt, but he fell, and the Germans tied his wrists with a dog leash. They tortured him and took him back to Chartres, throwing him into a room where a Senegalese was already held. An officer quipped: 'Since you like niggers so much, we thought you would like his company.' Jean Moulin knew he could not hold out long against his tormentors. He wrote: 'I realise I am now at the limits of my endurance, and that if they start again tomorrow I shall end up by signing. It is a terrible choice, to sign or die. Flight is impossible, I can hear the guards pacing in the corridor and outside our only window. And yet I cannot sign, cannot be an accomplice to this monstrous conspiracy that could only have been conceived by crazed sadists. I cannot consent to this outrage against the French Army and bring dishonour on myself. Anything but that, anything, even death. Death? Like thousands of other French people, from the outbreak of war I have accepted the idea, and have now seen it at close quarters many times. I am not afraid of it . . . My duty is clear, the Boches will see that a Frenchman too is capable of scuttling himself.'

A few pieces of glass lay on the floor, and the prefect picked one up, paused a second and slashed his throat. It was about two or three in the morning. At dawn when a German unit came in, he was still alive.

His sister, Laure Moulin, was to write: 'He was extremely weak but he got to his feet somehow and tried to face them. The Germans shouted in alarm.'

Anyone else would have remained sprawled on the

ground, but he was the official representative of the French State. He could not know that within a matter of hours General de Gaulle would broadcast his celebrated call for resistance from the BBC in London.

Jean Moulin was rushed to hospital and his life was saved. The Vichy Government sacked him.

At twenty-seven, Moulin was the youngest prefect in France. And it was Moulin that General de Gaulle appointed as his sole permanent representative for the entire territory of (Metropolitan) France. His role was to forge a united Resistance from the political formations that responded to the 18 June call by de Gaulle, along with the various trade union movements – an immense task in view of the groups' dissensions, ambitions, jealousies and vanities. Jean Moulin was to set up the Conseil National de la Résistance (CNR). Barbie knew about the plan, but not Moulin's identity.

In retirement at Colombey-des-Deux-Églises, de Gaulle wrote: 'Moulin had excellent judgement, he saw things and people as they really were, and he progressed step by step along a road mined by adversaries and cluttered with obstacles set up by friends.'

'Max' (Moulin's code name) became the supreme head of the French Resistance, acting for de Gaulle, who was prolific with orders as well as suggestions. Squabbling among the different resistance movements was a constant feature of the war, since they were all behind de Gaulle's strategy as a military man, but were not in agreement about his political objectives.

Max was able calmly to consolidate resources, communications and finance when certain movements strove to maintain their independence. The three major movements which formed the Resistance were Combat (the first group to appear and the largest), Liberation and Franc-Tireur. Combat was set up by Henri Frenay ('Charvet' in the Resistance); the Libération movement by Emmanuel d'Astier de la Vigerie ('Bernard'); and Franc-Tireur by Jean-Pierre Lévy ('Gilles').

Sixteen people attended the first meeting of the CNR on 27 May 1943, at 48 rue du Four in Paris. Already Jean Moulin, who chaired the meeting, had achieved virtual unity, but took care to give a measure of weight to the Socialists and other political persuasions. His purpose was to create a unified force representing all those fighting in the shadows, from the working man to the aristocrat, from the Communists to those on the right of the political spectrum. He took care to rise above the parties, trying to smooth out differences while holding to his beliefs as a democrat, and he was criticised for doing so.

Jean Moulin was fully aware of the existence of concentration camps, as they were set up prior to the war. It is unclear whether he knew much of what was going on at those camps – the hard labour, the gas ovens, the summary executions. Historian Henri Michel found evidence that London informed Moulin of the fate in store for those who were deported, and Moulin is reported to have told Resistance worker Suzette Olivier: 'If I fall into their hands, I hope they shoot me before!'

Before what? Torture? Deportation? Tony de Graaf, who was Moulin's secretary in the southern zone, remembers hearing him use this same expression at the time of the arrest of Joseph Monjaret ('Hervé'), who was a liaison officer and for a while Moulin's radio operator. He thought that Moulin meant 'before he spoke to the Nazis'.

This would suggest that Jean Moulin, like everyone else, was afraid of giving in to torture, brave though he was. When Moulin was finally arrested, the Germans had in their power the man who knew everything, but he revealed nothing.

3

FOR KLAUS BARBIE, Lyons was at the heart of the war. There, he was to achieve fulfilment. In this dark drama, most Germans wore civilian clothes and spoke fluent French, and many French people rapped out 'Heil Hitler'. These French proved to be invaluable henchmen.

Lyons was Barbie's reward after his excellent work in the Netherlands and his distinguished intelligence work on the Swiss border. While the ageing Marshal Pétain had chosen Vichy as his base, Herr Barbie took up residence in Lyons, the city that would become the capital of untamed France. With backing from London, the French Resistance developed most strongly in and around Lyons. The Obersturmführer finally had something he could sink his teeth into – every French citizen faced the stark choice of either working with the occupying forces (in the Service de Travail Obligatoire – the STO) or joining the Resistance.

Barbie was not even twenty-nine, but the Reich evidently saw that as the ideal age. In Berlin the top brass wanted young, vigorous and blindly loyal men at the head of the SS, whose emblem, along with that of the SD, struck fear as well as respect in the hearts of the regular Wehrmacht forces.

The Gestapo secret police (Geheime Staatspolizei), which had been set up in 1934 by Heinrich Himmler and Reinhard Heydrich at the old Prussian Folk Museum at 8 Prinz Albrechtstrasse in Berlin, held supreme sway. We can get a clear sense of its importance from the way the Gestapo was structured in the Lyons region.

Riding in black cars, the Gestapo moved in at the end of September 1942, immediately before the invasion of the South of France and under cover of the Armistice Commission, with the task of preparing for the arrival of the armed forces on 11 November. Their top priority was to flush out the radio transmitters used to converse with the Bureau Control de Renseignements et d'Action (BCRA) headed by General de Gaulle in London. For this purpose they had completely new radio-detection devices. They called their mission Operation Donar – *Donar* signifying 'lightning' or 'thunderbolt' according to German mythology. But against Donar was pitted the French Arès, meaning 'Mars'. The mission of neutralizing the clandestine radios quickly turned into a radio hide-and-seek game, for when the Germans got hold of the French transmitters they continued talking with London, turning parachute drops of weapons, ammunition, documents and food to their own advantage. Frequently it was the Germans who provided the reception committee when secret agents wafted down from the skies.

Many years later, in Germany, I met Helmut Knochen, one of the Gestapo's top men in France, who told me that the presiding genius of the radio operation was Hans Kieffer, eventually tried and hanged by the British.

Research by the historian Jacques Delarue tells us that the Lyons Gestapo detachment seized four French radio stations and their operators at Caluire, Rochetaillée, Châtelguyon, and the centre of Lyons.

Operation Donar had another purpose, however: to help establish the celebrated Sipo-SD in the erstwhile Free Zone of France – Section IV of the Sipo-SD became known as the Gestapo. The Donar personnel searched buildings and neutralized last-ditch opponents of the Vichy regime. They also started compiling lists of local Jews, as an offering to Eichmann in Berlin and his delegate Dannecker in Paris. This large-scale operation warranted enormous funds. The Reich did not hold back. Under the authority of the Paris-backed Commander of the Sipo-SD, the radio-detectors installed themselves first of all in the casino at Charbonnières, to the west of Lyons, established a direct link with Vichy, and then, since nothing untoward had upset their progress, decided to move in quite openly with the Sipo-SD, whose offices were in the Hotel Terminus, a few yards from the railway station – near the trains, near the centre of Lyons, and half-way between the Rhône and the Saône.

When the Gestapo was finally forced to leave Lyons, they burned most of their records. Their base on the Avenue Berthelot was only one of those destroyed in May 1944. As a result, the story of the Gestapo's activities unfolds mainly through the accounts of German prisoners and the confessions of French traitors who spilled as much as they could with the hope of staying alive a little longer before going to the firing squads. Curiously, the very first post-war French police report (on the Gestapo in the Lyons area) that I found in the military court archives, number 3933/2 D3, unsigned and dated 15 February 1945, concerns a humorous German poem. This delicately penned document was written by some members of the Gestapo to be declaimed at a celebration in the Hotel Terminus to mark the twentieth anniversary of Adolf Hitler's first putsch on 9 November 1943. The poem caricatured fifty-one members of the SD. No one was spared, including the Obersturmbannführer, the cook, the accounts staff, the filing clerks, even the drivers. When the French police discovered the poem in 1945, they did not think it at all funny: their report begins by saying that the complete translation of the material was of little interest and that they preferred to relate only basic extracts. The report citing the poem tells us that under Dr Knab ('strict at first, he quickly improved when he got a private villa and chauffeur, valet and cook') was Klaus Barbie, 'head of Section IV, with an excessive liking for wine and women'. The poem notes that the Einsatz-Kommando (EK – special commando) programme was started immediately after he arrived in November 1942 at the Hotel Terminus, its aim being to counter Communists, Jews, Freemasons and terrorists, to crush the Resistance movements and to seize English agents dropped by parachute, along with combatants, Gaullists, Anglophiles and Giraudists.* Clearly, while quaffing schnapps from special deliveries, the SS never lost track of the duties expected of them under the Nazi ideology.

More importantly, Antoine Chardon, inspector with the criminal police, reconstituted in his report the Sipo-SD Lyons structure, and added appendices covering Savoy, the Loire, Drôme and Isère.

Colonel Fritz Hollert, succeeded by Lieutenant-Colonel Werner Knab, who had previously run the SD in Oslo and Kiev, was in charge of the Sipo-SD in Lyons, which comprised six sections: I – Administration; II – Legal Affairs; III – Surveillance of the French Economy; IV – Political Crimes and Offences; V – Common Law Crimes and Offences (chiefly black-marketeering); VI – Intelligence, including the listing of French agents.

Section VI, headed by SS officer Moritz, who was a harsh adversary of the Resistance, was bigger than the Abwehr intelligence service, and Sergeant Heinrich Sasse had 160 informers in Lyons. Even so, the leading Section was Section IV, otherwise known as the Gestapo, headed by Klaus Barbie.

Section IV had a number of sub-sections: IV or (A1) – anti-Communist activities; IV A (or A2) – counter-sabotage; IV B – Jewish affairs; IV C – detection of persons with false documents and workers who had fled Germany; IV E – counter-espionage (military, political, economic); IV F: record office for jail sentences and deportations.

Knab had a separate office at 23 Boulevard des Belges, where he had at his disposal a sergeant adjutant; a captain liaising with the Wehrmacht; a driver, Hildebrand; and two women typists, Beyer and Ross. Similarly, Obersturmführer Barbie also had a special staff, consisting of seven SS people: his secretary, Betersdorfer (shot by the Resistance in June 1944); Hans Becker, who

* Henri Giraud was the commander of French Africa from 1942.

arranged the sub-sections' work load and was posted in November 1943 to the SD at Annecy, to be replaced by Adjutant Klaempfert, then later by Adjutant Bleininfeld; Chief-Adjutant Alfred Lutgens, who had protruding eyes; ex-police officer Kusmierz, acting as secretary; Sergeant Bartel, who sometimes worked as a chauffeur; a former teacher, Henseler, whose special job was transferring prisoners; and Quartermaster-Sergeant Koth from Berlin, who handled transport before he was posted to Grenoble.

The military court report described Klaus Barbie as an SS captain, alias Barbier, alias Barby, alias Meyer . . . corpulent, pink complexion, thin lips, particularly cruel and brutal despite a jovial appearance. And we find details such as: 'on the left earlobe, wears a ring with blue stone'.

In the course of his work Barbie moved freely among the sub-sections, and also in Sections V and VI. He held the number two job in the entire organisation, until he dropped to third place with the advent of Knab, and Hollert's eviction. Barbie had keen aides around him, like Stengritt, who spoke fluent French and tried to pass as English when he was not in uniform. He had, in 1942, served in the Geheime Feldpolizei at Maisons-Lafitte, and later at Alençon with Lutgens. There was also Erich Bartelmus, a lantern-jawed Oberscharführer with a Bavarian accent, who rolled his r's and specialized in rounding up Jews; the 1943 document (the poem) said he was 'the Jews' friend, as he disinclined them to lying with the aid of Felix [doubtless a nickname for a cosh]'.

One particular detail is likely to come out at Barbie's trial: Barbie countersigned all the messages on the teleprinter which was set up in the Section IV office. Invariably, Klaus Barbie's signature was preceded by the letters I.V. or I.A., meaning 'In Vertretung' or 'Im Auftrag', meaning 'by order'.

Who were these messages sent to? Mainly Colonel Knochen at the Sipo-SD Headquarters in Paris, who received fortnightly reports from the provincial Gestapo offices. In 1968 my colleague Philippe Alexandre, political expert at the RTL radio station, met Helmut Knochen in a Munich beer-cellar, but the interview was never published. Knochen had been sentenced to death by a Paris military court, but his sentence was commuted and he spent eighteen years in prison in France.

Fifteen years later, I met Knochen in the suburbs of Frankfurt. He told me that from 1942 on, the German police switched from mere intelligence-gathering to fighting the Resistance. Its valued auxiliaries were the special brigades of the French police, who were after the Gaullists, the Communists and Jews. Knochen said he admired two close colleagues, Kieffer and Bömelburg. The former was 'an ace in Funkspiel [the radio-detection unit]', the latter, 'a model police officer', knew his job inside out and believed that 'the prime counter-spy weapon is psychology'. Bömelburg was well versed in the insurrectional tactics of the Communists, and had a keen flair for unearthing them.

Knochen went on to explain that after the Wehrmacht's setbacks – after Stalingrad – the Resistance gradually gained strength and spread like a cancer. He admitted that Allied agents and Resistance people managed to infiltrate his own services. On the other hand, the Germans had the *V-Leute*, the confidence men whom military courts were to dub traitors. These *V-Leute* kept the Gestapo supplied with information, not only for money but out of political conviction. They were dedicated *collaborateurs*.

Knochen said: 'In fact, we kept our distance from those who mainly did it for money. In Lyons Barbie did not need to ask for authorisation to use the *V-Mann* network; they were his responsibility.'

Discussing the general outlook of the Gestapo leaders, Helmut Knochen told me: 'Heydrich, the police supremo, believed collaboration would be more successful in France than elsewhere. That is what he told me. Soldiers returning from the Eastern front who were sent elsewhere were jealous of us. Paris meant food, cabarets, women, not war.'

He continued: 'About the interrogations, Kieffer said

that hitting a prisoner was the best way of stopping him from talking. [This was a defence argument used at Knochen's trial.] His view was that you only needed to imply that you knew, and then hand them a sheet of paper. The rest was easy. You gave them sweets, cigarettes, or whisky, or took them out drinking, all very friendly. Except the Communists; they never squealed. I cannot remember a single traitor among the Communists.' Then, as if he did not wish to forget a single detail, Helmut Knochen said he was told by Admiral Canaris, head of the Wehrmacht intelligence service: 'Hold no prejudices. Use Jews if need be.'

On 16 December 1942 Obersturmführer Barbie went in SS uniform to a prison in the Ain *département*, since his first task on arrival in Lyons was to inform the Tunisian nationalist militant Habib Bourguiba that the Führer had decided to free him. Bourguiba was surprised, having been a prisoner for two and a half years at Fort Saint-Nicolas in Marseilles, then in Montluc, and finally in Fort Vancia. Barbie told him: 'You will be better off in Tunisia defending your country. Get ready to leave.' The Tunisian combatant was quick to tell the French junior officer guarding him of Barbie's command, so that there would be no suspicion of connivance with the Nazis. Bourguiba quit the jail, but turned up in Rome instead of Tunis.

Actually, the Germans had sought to compromise the Neo-Destour leader by introducing him to Mussolini, in the hope that waverers in Tunisia would see their country as an extension of the Axis powers. Later, Barbie would boast to his Bolivian pals about this scheme, although he neglected to add that it flopped politically. Hardly had Bourguiba ended his Roman holiday than a pamphlet was going the rounds in Tunis, reading: 'There is no other case of a party leader being maltreated as I was by certain French people, yet staying loyal to France and refusing to play along with France's enemy, even though they had given him the thing a man prizes above all – freedom.'

Bourguiba never uttered a hostile word against France, the Allies, nor the Jews – not an easy stance at that point, when challenging Hitler and Mussolini meant returning to jail.

In Lyons the only thing not in short supply was martial law courts. Until 1949, you needed coupons to buy bread; cheese was rationed at 75 grams a week; cigarettes at two packets every ten days.

Yet here during the war the SS lived like lords in the Hotel Terminus. They went short of nothing – especially since French informers often handed over a gift with their news. A bar of chocolate accompanied an anonymous denunciation of an enemy of the Reich; a bank note or a cheque arrived along with the name and address of a Jew. Henri Amouroux might have been close to the truth when he said there were forty million Pétainists.

The SS requisitioned some sixty rooms at the Hotel Terminus. On the third floor was a score of rooms for interrogating prisoners, who were brought every day from Montluc jail. Perhaps the hotel contained no specially equipped place for torture, but that does not mean there was no questioning with the aid of coshes.

In due course the number of Resistance people and Jews arrested grew very large, and the hotel became too small to accommodate them. The staff needed room to breathe; bigger premises were required to match the size of the programme.

In early June 1943, the École de Santé Militaire, located at 14 Avenue Berthelot, was selected. One reason was that it was safer than the hotel from Resistance attacks. Another was the network of cellars and long passageways leading to thick-walled areas with arched ceilings that would muffle the screams.

Barbie was determined to quell the Resistance once and for all. So, too, were his buddies in the Abwehr, particularly Herr Moog, from the Dijon office; Barbie was supposed to co-operate with Moog, but he double-crossed him instead. The Sipo-SD HQ in Paris turned a blind eye to the methods adopted by both men as long as 'terrorists' were caught. Since the big shots in Berlin not only lacked imagination but also insisted on putting everything in writing (which proved useful at the Eichmann trial), the Sipo-SD outposts had standing orders. I found this directive in the Gestapo files from the Reichssicher-heitshauptamt (RSHA, or Security Ministry): 'In order to augment the effect of terror, the following points should be observed: in no case should the internee be notified of the duration of his internment. The only advice that should be given is: "Until further notice". Do not hesitate to increase terror in difficult cases, by skilful hearsay campaigns indicating that the prisoner's case is so serious that he may not be released for two or three years.' So-called 'reinforced interrogation' is suggested: 'This may be applied following a flogging. It may include a diet of bread and water, hard bedding, darkened cell, sleep deprivation, exhausting exercises. In the case of more than twenty strokes a doctor must be called.'

This was the theory. Survivors I met who recalled Barbie's questioning said that in practice the punishment was more refined.

On 12 June 1942 the security police chief in Berlin sent all heads of Sections IV a set of instructions that declared: 'Reinforced interrogations can be applied only against Communists, Marxists, Bible students, saboteurs, terrorists, Resistance members, parachute liaison agents, maladjusted persons, refractory workers, Polish and Russian vagabonds . . . In all other cases, in principle, my prior consent is necessary.'

What other cases, one wonders, who else was left? Maybe there were a few non-vagabond Polish folk about, but there is always a suitable regulation if you look hard enough. And how about those Polish nationals? The staff needed only to delve into their files where they would find this note from the Reichsführer, in which he equated the Poles with Jews and gypsies: 'The Poles and nationals of countries in the East are inferior races living on the territory of the Reich. This entails grave dangers for German public order.'

Directives like that caused no heart-searching for Herr Klaus Barbie, who found in them an incentive. The more so since in 1942 Hitler had stated: 'I shall make putrid the countries I occupy, I shall make people denounce one another and shall denounce people by designating them the denouncers of others . . . I shall spread mud.' Klaus Barbie was a diligent reader of such prose.

Since the Resistance people were not exactly standing on street corners waiting to be picked up, Barbie had a method that has proved effective throughout the world, wherever the Gestapo mentality prevails. He seized the families of the adversaries he failed to break. In this he was well served by his informers, who gave him names, addresses, hide-outs, details of wealth, lists of relations, friends, women acquaintances. His victims may not readily have yielded but they were highly sensitive under pressure to threats about loved ones. It was a technique worse than a thrashing on the genitals, worse than head-ducking, worse than tearing out fingernails. Resistance fighter Guillain de Bénouville described the process in his book *Sacrifice du Matin*. Not one of the Resistance survivors would fail to recognize the anguish he describes: 'The moment you think the sufferings you are threatened with, the pain you endure, could be applied to those you love – well, you weaken. You are vulnerable through others.'

Several witnesses' stories reveal that Barbie was not a great psychologist but that he used these methods simply because they were as old as torture itself. Barbie just liked to hit people. To hit and hit again, with anything that came to hand. With a table leg, his riding whip, his fists, his boots.

His reputation was such that he was quickly added to the Resistance hit list. Barbie was the second most wanted man on the list, after Francis André ('Crooked Jaw'), who founded the Mouvement National Anti-Terroriste (MNAT), a pro-Nazi French organization. André, an ex-boxer, known and initially loved in Lyons sporting circles, enjoyed torturing anyone who went against the collaborationist stream.

Mario Blardone, known in the Resistance as 'Maurice', had the specific job of getting Barbie. It was no easy task – not that Maurice was scared, quite the contrary, but he was afraid of messing it up. So he set about studying Barbie's habits and peculiarities. He had learned from an elderly hunter how to make explosives. He blew up pylons and electricity transformers. At the age of nineteen he was shooting at German troops.

Maurice Blardone had two photos in his breast-pocket: one of a collaborator named Max Payot; the other was of Barbie, although he did not know that was his name. The first picture was an identity photo; the second was an action picture – it has now been lost. The five others in his group, the Group d'Action Immédiate, also had photos. Between blasting operations, he continued working as a technician at Venissieux, a suburb of Lyons, while watching the movements of the Obersturmführer. It was known that Barbie had a woman friend who lived at 48 Cours Morand (now Cours Franklin Roosevelt), wife of a rich Jewish captain who had only one arm. She was from Savoy, and was older than Barbie, and reputedly an excellent cook. After Lyons was liberated, the woman was held for several months in Montluc jail and confessed all. In order to entertain Barbie, she would tell her husband to go into hiding with friends as she had heard the Gestapo were out searching. The husband, a captain in the First World War, would quit the premises until she called him back. By then Barbie would have finished taking his pleasures in the large bedroom with its wooden parquet floors bright with polish, and with pastel stucco mouldings of angels over the mirror, which are still there today.

Blardone knew of another mistress at Rue Laborde in

Bron. He watched the place, and told me recently: 'I saw Barbie arrive on his own in a black Opel. But I could not shoot him just then. I had to be sure he was not being followed, or covered from behind.* I saw him again in uniform, with several officers in the Moulin à Vent restaurant, in Place Bellecourt. There were too many of them. I would have needed a machine gun.'

Blardone was subsequently arrested, probably because someone gave him away, and he was jailed in Lyons in one of the cellars at the École de Santé Militaire.

The initial questioning was done by a Frenchman, the notorious Francis André. Then he was taken to the floor above, where Barbie was waiting.

Maurice told me: 'At first he interrogated me quietly, using the familiar 'tu', showing me wads of banknotes, saying we could work something out together. He urged me to co-operate. Once he handed me a pistol. I took it, but it was empty. I had no illusions; I was sure I would be executed. I wanted him to respect me as a soldier, as I was caught with weapons on me. No luck, because he dismissed me to the adjacent room. Other men hit me with riding sticks, with Barbie looking on, smartly dressed in civilian clothes. He just watched. Then they ducked me in a bathtub of water.

'Barbie had two dogs, one held close – a German sheepdog for biting – the other used solely to mate with women who refused to answer his questions. Before questioning, the women were undressed by subordinates, and then spreadeagled on a table. Barbie came in. They stuck me in a corner and forced me to watch. If the women refused to talk, he had the second dog brought in. He enjoyed seeing them mounted by the dog.'

* Barbie displayed a certain pride in moving about without escort on occasion. It was a challenge designed to show his colleagues and subordinates how ineffective the Resistance commandos were, and also to give the impression that he was leaving alone for ultra-secret meetings.

Blardone was indirectly rescued by the English. A bombing raid in May 1944 partially wrecked the École de Santé, and Fritz Hollert, Commander Knab's assistant, and some other SS men were killed. The prisoners were safe in the cellars, but when the raid was over the Gestapo had the inmates transferred to Montluc. Blardone had spent eighteen days in the cellars. On arrival at Montluc he claimed he had just been caught up in a search operation. Barbie was not around. Blardone was deported, one of the people who left Compiègne for Dachau in the 'death convoy' on 5 July.

Maurice still wakes up thinking he is in Block 9, delirious, and gabbling nonsense. But he made a promise to Edmond Michelet, one-time minister with General de Gaulle, never to tell what happened on that convoy. He has never broken that promise.

4

W HAT DID KLAUS BARBIE know about the gas ovens?
Did he or his superior Werner Knab or his colleagues in the Jewish sub-section know that Jews were
being eliminated by the Reich on a mass scale, at Auschwitz,
Mathausen and other sites?

We could ask Barbie himself: 'What happened to all
those Jews your section IV sent off in the trains for
Drancy, where their fate was decided?' But Barbie has
already replied. In 1944, he said: 'They were shot or
deported, there's no difference.'

When the Allies reached the camps, newsreel pictures
were shown throughout the world of the living skeletons
in their vertically striped tunics, either stumbling along,
piling naked corpses into vast pits, or pushing bodies into
the ovens. What was Barbie's reaction to the photographs
of children totally lacking in any muscle power, and of old
men aged thirty, their hands gripping the barbed wire?

It is too late today to ask whether his response was one
of astonishment, mere surprise, or detached curiosity or
foreknowledge. We will never know.

Herr Doktor Werner Knab is dead; his body was
identified after an air raid on a German highway.

The subordinates have stuck to their story: 'The Jews?
Not our job!'

Barbie has said: 'The Jews? That was not my affair.
Wenzel, Bartelmus and the others were in charge of
that.'

Dr Bartelmus was the last head of sub-section IVB in
Lyons. The Lyons military tribunal gave him eight years
hard labour in 1954, and then he went home quietly to the
suburbs of Berlin. He was found not guilty of hunting
down Jews, having thrown all responsibility onto his
superiors. The judges held that he was very much an

underling, and he was absolved from any crime against humanity. Who was to blame then? The boss, the number two, or the underling who merely extracted the truth with the aid of a truncheon?

This matter was considered by the German judicial authorities a long time before Klaus Barbie was officially discovered in his hiding-place across the Atlantic, for in February 1971, a new ruling came into effect which allowed Nazis already sentenced in France to be tried in Germany. The whole Barbie business probably would have been dealt with then and forgotten, were it not for the Nazi-hunter Beate Klarsfeld.

The stance of the German judiciary at the time was that the Sipo-SD staff in Lyons did not necessarily know about the so-called Final Solution for the Jews, which was a Reich state secret and subject to the highest secrecy safeguards.

The German investigators possessed details of the Nazi raids against the Jewish children's colony at Izieu and the Union Générale des Israélites de France (UGIF), which had been set up by Kurt Lischka of the SS to represent the Jewish population to the French authorities and the German occupiers and had incorporated the former Fédération des Sociétés Juives de France. They also possessed cables signed by Barbie telling Paris that the work had been carried out correctly. But the German authorities wanted definitive proof, and they still do.

There are scarcely any witnesses to these two incidents left alive.

The UGIF deportation was one of the first acts of genocide organised by the Lyons Gestapo. The raid took place on 9 Feburary 1943, at the offices of the Jewish Welfare Organisation at 12 rue Sainte-Catherine. Only one man managed to get away. There often seems to have been one person who escaped: here as at Sant-Genis-Laval, Bron, Izieu. In each case the person remembers it as if it were yesterday.

I met the man who got away from the UGIF raid, Michel

Kroskof Thomas. 'When I shut my eyes I can still see Barbie in civilian clothes behind the desk,' he said in December 1983 after he had flown to Lyons from New York to confront Barbie.

Michel Thomas was born in Poland, although he is very touchy about it and refuses to give his date of birth. He was arrested by the Vichy administration as a Resistance member, and in July 1942 was interned at the Les Milles camp for Jews. He broke out and rejoined the Secret Army in the Grenoble area. In February 1943 he was back in Lyons with a series of drawings that he was ostensibly trying to sell; his real mission, though, was to contact young Jews – whose only address was the UGIF – and get them to come out of hiding and join the combatants, to enter the Resistance.

He recalled: 'When I was going up the stairs to the offices on the second floor I had a premonition. You know how it is sometimes – you can't explain it, but something holds you back. Anyway, I carried on. As I got up there, the door was pulled open sharply and I was told "*Kommen Sie herein!*" It was the Gestapo. I pretended I didn't know German. I saw there were dozens of people in the next room, packed like sardines. "We must introduce you to the top man," said one of the Germans, giving me a shove towards Barbie, although it wasn't till later that I knew his name. He was the only Gestapo man in civilian clothes. Behind me I distinctly heard the Germans say: "Shall I fire in his ear or his neck?" They were trying to trap me, but I did not react and still pretended I didn't understand.'

Michel Thomas was using the name 'Sberro' at the time; he handed over his forged identity documents and ration cards. Barbie dismissed him and Thomas hurried downstairs.

He said: 'That was how I gave the alert to the cafés where I knew the Jews were.'

A total of 86 people were seized that day and only one returned from the concentration camps. It so happened that the woman in question was sent to Auschwitz, not to

Sobibor. And two other Jews managed to escape Fort Lamothe, where they were kept by the Wehrmacht because of lack of space at Montluc. Klaus Barbie sent a letter to Paris on 15 February 1943, saying there was no more room, doubtless to make sure the Gestapo did not get blamed. He gave the names of the escapees: Aron Luxenburg, aged fifty, and Siegried Driller, forty-seven.

None of the 84 Lyons Jews transferred to Drancy on 12 February survived. They were all gassed and perished the day they reached Sobibor camp. All, that is, except a fourteen-year-old lad called Paul Breslerman, who almost got away. He was recaptured by the German police and sent to Auschwitz, later to die. Paul used to employ the name Guérin. He was born in Leipzig, and despite his accent he successfully made out that he came from Marseilles. He was a Jew but French too, which at the time was supposed to spare him from deportation. He had been taken in charge of a furrier who originated in Bessarabia but was also French.

In train number 53, leaving Drancy on 25 March, the Germans sealed each vehicle so that not a single ray of light entered them. When the train stopped at Epernay, the prisoners heard shooting. The Germans said they had shot four Jews who were trying to get away. Terror swept through the cattle trucks at this news, especially when one man, Sylvain Kaufmann, attempted to saw through the floorboards that evening. When the train stopped at Metz everyone in Kaufmann's truck was singing 'La Marseillaise' at the top of his voice to hide the sawing noise. One man was so frightened that he had to be bound and gagged to stop him from spreading panic. Like many others, he had no idea that when he got to his destination he would not have long to live. The furrier managed to keep people calm, but it was no easy task in this coffin on rails. He spoke in a confident tone, not too loudly, and paid special attention to the more agitated of the prisoners.

Survivor Sylvain Kaufmann told me: 'I was just finishing the opening in the floorboards and he said I should look after Paul Guérin. "If I were twenty years younger, I'd do the same," he said.'

Young Gúerin, Sylvain Kaufmann and eleven others that night managed to get away. Their escape took place on German territory and was a unique event in the history of the deportations. There are three survivors today. Guérin was re-taken the next day and died in a camp. In his train were 1,000 Jews, of whom 985 were sent straight to the gas ovens; the other fifteen were designated workers.

Thomas later joined the US Seventh Army. He was in one of the units that liberated Dachau, and he interrogated the man in charge of the ovens. He stayed with the Americans and became one of the Counter-Intelligence Corps (CIC) agents. He produced a detailed report on the Gestapo and Barbie. Michel Thomas has a good memory. He even recalls that Barbie's right ear was lower than his left. Thomas was taken in to see Barbie at Saint-Joseph prison on 20 December 1983. He said: 'He's an old man trying to look innocent, but I recognized him for certain.' The lawyers acting for the former SS man deny his story.

One witness is not enough, of course, and Serge Klarsfeld has been delving into the archives. A wire signed by Barbie and dated 11 February 1943, informed Colonel Knochen two days after the raid:

'Subject: Comité pour le soutien des
émigrants et des juifs necessiteux
[Committee for Needy Jews and Emigrants]
Reference: local decision 7209,
10 February 1943.

The action against the above-named committee was carried out from here, the Jews naturally being placed under the guard of the German authorities. This concerns 86 persons who

were transferred today via Chalon-sur-Sâone
to the appropriate camp.
Head of EK – Lyons IV

Barbie, SS Obersturmführer'

In early 1943, the liaison between the Jews and the Nazis
was Kurt Schendel, a Jew who had been a lawyer in
Berlin. He operated in Paris and was subsidized by the
Commissariat in Vichy covering Jewish affairs. When he
was located in recent years by Beate Klarsfeld, he told her
he did not know Barbie personally but knew that he
ordered the arrest of Jews in Lyons 'with quite particular
zeal'. He said: 'It is certain that the head of section IV in
Lyons knew what happened to the deportees just as well
as Röthke or Brunner, the SS men handling the Jewish
question in Paris.'

He clearly recalled that during a southern zone UGIF
delegate meeting someone quoted Barbie as saying: 'Shot
or deported, there's no difference!' That person was
Maître Raymond Geissmann, who subsequently confirmed the remark.

Whether Barbie knew or pretends not to have known
about the Final Solution, he is sure to plead orders from
above. Of course, as a good SS member, he would carry
out instructions to the letter. There is, however, this
observation to be taken into account: 'The rules of war
contain no provision for a soldier who has committed
shameful crimes to escape punishment by claiming that he
simply obeyed orders from superiors, especially when
those orders are flagrantly contrary to all notions of
human morality and the customary international rules for
the conduct of war.'

Noble sentiments – from Goebbels! The same Joseph
Goebbels, Propaganda Minister, who was named by
Hitler as his successor, who killed his family and himself
in the Berlin Chancellery bunker on 29 April 1945. The
passage is from an article dated 29 May 1944, quoted a

decade later by Colonel Bourely, French Government Commissioner, in the indictment at the second trial against Barbie *in absentia*.

The judiciary in the mid 1980s has a tricky problem. There is an enormous difference between a Jew and a Jew who is also a Resistance fighter. The distinction has had immense implications in France since General de Gaulle persuaded Parliament to adopt the concept of crimes against humanity twenty years ago. Victims of Barbie who were Jews and only Jews could yet send him to prison for life. If the victims were Jews and Resistance fighters, Barbie has nothing to answer for, since war crimes are covered by the twenty-year law of limitation that came into effect in 1965.

Elie Nahmias, an apprentice cobbler, was seized in Lyons on 1 July 1944. He was in the entrance hall at *Le Progrès* newspaper, lining up to sign a register to the memory of Philippe Henriot, the Vichy Secretary of State for Propaganda, who was killed by the Resistance on 28 June, when a member of the Red Cross approached him and gave him a letter, asking Elie discreetly to take it to 33 rue Victor-Hugo on the other side of the Place Bellecour. He went there, climbed the stairs, but found nobody at the address he sought. On his way downstairs, he came face to face with Barbie.

Nahmias told me: 'He pushed me back like I was some piece of furniture. He snapped: "You're a Jew, aren't you," I told him I was a Moslem, and he told me to recite a verse of the Koran. I couldn't, so he took me up to the fourth-floor Gestapo offices.' (After the 26 May 1944 raid, the Gestapo moved to the Place Bellecour.)

He was thrown into Montluc prison, and told the other inmates how he was arrested. They identified Barbie for him. On 27 July Nahmias met up with Léon Pfeiffer (one of five people executed outside the Moulin à Vent bistro that same day). Pfeiffer was feeling pleased at having kept quiet during a beating from Barbie. A week later Elie Nahmias was in Auschwitz, and he remembers that there were 400 children in his train. When they got to Drancy, people tried to get the children out of the train going to Poland, but the French guards moved in with machine guns.

He said of the deportation: 'After it was over nobody would believe me when I said we lived with death constantly, that I was able to sit on bodies eating a potato I had stolen. Nobody could believe it. Of course it was the Liberation then, and everyone was celebrating, they had plenty to eat then, they weren't interested in what we had been through.'

In 1983, during one of his early encounters with plaintiffs, Klaus Barbie said in an indirect confession: 'Why would I have arrested you? You do not look like a Jew.' His lawyer signalled to him, but it was too late, the clerk had taken it down already.

A sense of the gulf that has developed between the Jews and the Resistance over the Barbie affair (as if there were no Jews in the Resistance) can be gathered from recent remarks by Dr Aron, President of the Comité de Co-ordination des Communautés Juives in Lyons: 'We should not forget that Barbie's victims were Jews on the one hand and Resistance fighters on the other. The Resistance were arrested for action in war, the Jews were taken because the universalism they represented went counter to the fierce nationalism of the Germans. We are trying to make sure that there is no merging of the two causes at the trial, and our friends from the Resistance agree with this.'

Beate Klarsfeld in her book *Partout où Ils Seront* has written: 'No attack, no act of sabotage, no rescue attempt occurred to stop the train's progress towards death, or the progress of all those trains that went before it. Halting ammunition trains and troop trains always had priority over trains loaded with Jews, even those carrying children.'

At the time of writing this book, several Resistance associations are in favour of linking up with Jewish organisations, with a view to preventing a fragmentation of the Barbie trial.

At 10.10 p.m. on the evening of Holy Thursday, 6 April 1944, a cable was sent to Gestapo headquarters in Paris reporting that the Jewish children's home in the Ain *département* had ceased to exist.

It read: 'This morning an end was brought to the activities of the Jewish children's home at Izieu, Ain. A total of 41 children aged three to thirteen were arrested. In addition the whole of the Jewish personnel, 10 persons including 5 women, were arrested. No money or other valuables were found. Transport to Drancy will take place on 7 April 1944.' The message was signed: 'Der KDR. der SIPO und des SD Lyon roem. 4 B 61/43. I.A. gez. Barbie SS-Ostuf'.

This means that Obersturmführer Barbie signed for the commander of the Sipo-SD section IVB. That much is clear. But the initials 'I.A.' (*Im Auftrag*) mean 'by order'. Klaus Barbie has since claimed that to sign by order is not to sign, and that the signature is a forgery.

His lawyer, Maître Vergès, affirms that the message itself is a forgery, since Barbie did not have to sign for a subordinate such as Wenzel or Bartelmus, who were more closely involved in handling Jewish matters. He claims that it is obviously a forgery also because two of the date-stamps used to record the message in Paris, on 6 and 7 April, were in French and said *Avril* rather than *April*. Maître Vergès says it is astonishing that the Germans had no stamp of their own (and moreover, the two stamps are not even the same). Besides, he says, the original has not been found – Judge Riss has only a photocopy. Barbie has lodged a formal complaint, a move that caused widespread surprise and indignation. Inquiries reveal that the original document is in fact missing; it had been in German archives discovered in Paris after the Liberation, either at the Reich's embassy in the Rue de Lille or at the Avenue Foch or the Rue

Saussaies offices used by the Gestapo.

However, the cable in question was used as evidence at the Nuremberg trials; it was produced by former French Premier Edgar Faure, deputy prosecutor at the time. It should have been in the archives of the Nuremberg evidence kept in the safe-deposits of the International Court at The Hague, but inspection of these archives reveals only a photocopy, certified as number RF 1235 and bearing the reference H. 4826, but the original is not there. The experts at The Hague say that, in view of the bulk of documents produced at Nuremberg, it was decided to make a selection; in order to prevent loss of the items sent by each country, many documents were photocopied, recorded as sufficient proof, and returned to the official who submitted them.

On 17 February 1984, Serge Klarsfeld at last discovered this telegram, which was incorrectly filed in the Centre de Documentation Juive Contemporaine dossier on Otto Abetz, German Ambassador to Paris during the war. It is an item difficult to challenge, because on the back is a map of Northern Scotland; the Germans were short of paper and used the backs of maps on which to print their telegram receipt forms. Barbie did not consider that this meant it was authentic; but if it were a forgery, it would have to have been made prior to 1946!

Barbie was questioned closely for the first time on the subject of the deported Jews in 1983. He told Judge Riss: 'I knew the Jews were sent to a concentration camp, but I never saw any camps with my own eyes. I never knew what went on in those camps. You realise that many people came back from them. After the war I simply saw photos reproduced of what might have happened . . . Everything to do with the Jewish question depended directly on two or three people sent by Eichmann himself to the regional commands. Personally I had nothing to do with the deporting of Jews to Germany. There were two or three people in the Lyons SD dealing with that matter. I remember one of them was called Wenzel.'

On the Izieu children, Klaus Barbie told Judge Riss: 'It was Wenzel who had orders from Eichmann to dissolve the centre. I did not myself take part in the operation and I saw no children in the École Militaire. It is possible I had knowledge of the outcome and that I informed my superiors, but I had no personal responsibility in this affair. It is part of the whole Jewish question in France. While that operation did not concern me personally, it is possible that Knab took charge of it.'

It is indeed possible. Since it is so hard to find out forty years afterwards, we need to go back to the investigations that took place in Lyons after the Liberation.

The story of the deported children seems not to have worried the population unduly. Yet none of the children returned. Only in September 1945 did a report appear concerning the kidnap of the Jewish children. It was drawn up by a health inspector who had been asked to list the missing persons; he carefully did so in a single long column. At the end of the list, which totalled 55 adults and children, he recorded a five-line statement by a witness, Eusèbe Perticoz: 'At about nine in the morning a Boche car arrived, followed by two trucks. Three civilians, including a Frenchman well known by the name of B . . .* from Brens and about ten Boche soldiers from Belley got out. They got all the people up in the trucks for an unknown destination and pillaged the building.'

The report said that the culprits could have been 'three militiamen and twelve Boches'. Since the trucks were owned and driven by local people, in due course the gendarmes conducted their own investigation. They learned only one thing of interest to the judiciary: the driver of one truck requisitioned by the Germans was called Godani. He is now dead.

I heard a version of the events from another witness, Julien Favet, who said: 'I was working in the vineyards,

* Author's note: his guilt has never been fully proven, and he is not therefore named here.

waiting for the boss's wife to bring me a bite to eat. As it was already nine o'clock in the morning, I went up to the little village of Lelinaz and I saw about fifteen Germans pushing the kids into trucks.'

These children had been kept in Izieu in a large twelve-room house, rented out by Madame Sabrina Zlatin to a family from Belley since May 1943. Most of their parents had been deported, and some children eventually found their mothers again at Drancy, the final sorting-point before the death camps. This was true of Marcel Mermelstein, aged seven, and his sister Paule, ten (already cited in chapter 2), whose father had joined the maquis. Others, the Gerensteins, for example, caught sight of their deported father; Monsieur Gerenstein, a professional musician, had to play the trumpet in the Auschwitz orchestra that heralded the new arrivals as they passed under the iron arch with the inscription '*Arbeit macht Frei*' (Work Brings Freedom).

Why was Izieu chosen as a site for a home? At that time it was less dangerous to set up a children's home in the zone occupied by the Italians than in the zone held by the Germans. The children appear to have been accepted by the villagers and were often invited to farms, although they tended to speak poor French, since they were refugees from Austria, Hungary, Bessarabia and elsewhere. But an informer among the Izieu inhabitants gave them away.

Monsieur Favet told me: 'The youngest ones cried, the violence scared them, and they had only just woken up. The others, who were thirteen or fourteen years old, knew just where they were going, because they had been in hiding so long . . . I saw them leave in the trucks. The children were singing an anti-German song about Alsace and Lorraine.'

Julien Favet said Klaus Barbie was there, running the operation. 'It was Barbie who was in charge. In fact, he saved my life. One of the SS officers thought I was the doctor and tried to get me up in a truck. Barbie told him to let me go. While it was all going on, he was leaning against the stone fountain in the middle of the courtyard. He was in civilian dress, gabardine and a soft hat. He gave orders mostly in German and sometimes in French.

'For three days, five SS men were left on duty in the village. They ate at our place with their machine guns on the table. One morning they fired at a pig the home had been fattening up. Then they spent hours firing at the animal's body. They found some wine in the cellar, and spent each afternoon dead drunk. I reckoned I could have killed them, but what was the use? The Germans would only have burned down the whole village as a reprisal. So we just kept going, thinking maybe the maquis in Vercors might hear about it soon enough to intervene.

'It was a month before I dared go and look inside the children's home. On the canteen table I found baskets of bread and 43 bowls full of coffee, which the children didn't have time to drink that morning.'

It seems surprising from this account that the Germans should confuse this farmer with Dr Reifmann, the doctor for the home. This is only one strange aspect of the files; doubtless Barbie sees this not as a simple anomaly or historical confusion, but as false evidence.

Many years later, the Klarsfelds traced the children's names in the Auschwitz train lists. Madame Benguigui was already in Auschwitz when her three small boys were taken off in the Izieu trucks. She had hoped that they would find a refuge from the Nazis in the hills of Ain. In the spring of 1944 she recognized a pullover belonging to her son Jacques. It was now worn by another child of the same age, whose mother was a woman doctor held in Block 10; she had won a reprieve for her son in return for 'medical experiments' on her by 'Dr' Mengele or one of his aides. Madame Benguigui was certain about the pullover, she had knitted it in Algiers, and had run out of wool, so she finished one sleeve much later in another colour. Jacques, aged thirteen, Richard, six, and Jean-Claude, five, were in a train that left Drancy on 13 April 1944. All three perished at Auschwitz.

On 30 June 1944, another convoy took Minna Halaunbrenner, nine years old, and her little sister Claudine, five, to their deaths. Thirty years later their mother went with Beate Klarsfeld to La Paz, Bolivia, and brandished a placard that read: *'Boliviano ayudame, pido solo justicia'* (Bolivian, help me, I demand only justice). She chained herself to a bench, hoping the authorities would realise the moral standing of the man they were protecting.

Two adults eluded the Nazis at Izieu. One was the manageress of the children's home, Madame Zlatin, who had left a few days earlier for the Montpellier area – ironically, to find a safer place. The other was Dr Léon Reifmann.

Madame Zlatin told me in Paris: 'After the Italians moved out and the Germans came, we were on our guard. We had already sent a few of the children away, most of them to Switzerland, and we planned to get the others off after Easter.'

In the final phase of the war, Easter was a time for reunion for many families. The colony's doctor, Suzanne Reifmann, had invited her father, Moise, and mother, Mova, to Izieu. Her brother Léon, who had to suspend his medical studies in 1940, came too, arriving on 6 April just before 9.00 a.m. – about five minutes ahead of the Germans.

Léon says: 'On the way there I picked up two school lads who were to spend the holidays at Izieu. There was no need to go through the village, as a concealed path led to the home. I got inside and went up to the first floor and saw my parents, just as the bell rang for breakfast. One of the kids ran up to meet me on the stairs, shouting, "You're wanted". I looked through a window and saw Germans all about with machine guns.' The young man jumped down from another window onto the terrace, and hid behind a wall in an overgrown garden. He stayed there until nightfall, hidden in the bushes. 'I saw nothing, but I heard the cries.'

When darkness fell, two neighbours, Madame Perticoz and Madame Audelain, helped him to leave the garden and accompanied him to another village called Chantemerle.

After the Liberation, for weeks he kept going to the Hotel Lutetia in Paris, which was the arrival point for most people returning from the concentration camps. At last he found Léa Feldblum, a supervisor from Izieu, who had come back from Auschwitz, the only survivor of those deported from Izieu. He plied her with questions about his mother, father, sister and ten-year-old nephew.

'All dead, all gassed,' she said.*

Finally, the affair of 'the last train' from Lyons concerns Barbie, too. The date was 11 August 1944. In this affair we have evidence of the Obersturmführer's responsibility from a woman Resistance member, Madame Alice Vansteenberghe-Joly. The fact that she was a fine Aryan specimen did not prevent Barbie from smashing five of her vertebrae during questioning, before throwing her into a ground-floor cell at Montluc with ten Jewish women. On 11 August she was looking through the spy-hole in the timber door when she caught sight of Barbie in the central alley of the prison. She got up onto a shelf that was built into the wall to look through a kind of skylight. She had to be careful, because the Germans would shoot any prisoners they caught at the windows, but she was able to observe Barbie and hear his voice. What she heard were orders for co-ordinating the transfer of no fewer than 650 deportees, who were to travel directly eastward without passing through Drancy. On that day she was alone in the cell, as the other ten women had already been deported.

By now she knew Barbie's features well, particularly his

* Léa, whose father died in deportation, went with the children of her own accord. She had an alias but gave her real name to the Germans. When she returned from the camps, she went to Israel and undertook child care. Her husband died in the 1948 War of Independence.

left ear, which was creased in a particular manner. She could recognize him easily later on. She recalls: 'You know, I had plenty of time to study Barbie during the torture sessions at the Gestapo in Place Bellecour. I was half dead but I concentrated on the facial details, promising myself: "I'll get you one day."'

Madame Vansteenberghe-Joly, now a retired doctor, confronted Barbie in May 1983, during questioning by Judge Riss. The ex-Nazi was being kept in a newly prepared cell at Saint-Joseph, but Judge Riss had him brought to Montluc under heavy escort. The magistrate wanted further evidence about the prisoner's features. At one point Barbie declared: 'On 11 August 1944 I was no longer in Lyons.' Madame Vansteenberghe tried to jog his memory by citing an incident involving a child he took away from its mother in the Gestapo cells. Barbie used to remove children from their parents; he had them kept under German control at the Antiquaille hospital, since he did not want children at Montluc. It was not out of kindness, though, because the families were reunited for deporting. She went on about the incident, saying he could not fail to remember it. Barbie shook his head. 'But you're completely gaga,' Madame Vansteenberghe shouted at him, hoping no doubt he would lose his calm. Some hope!

The Obersturmführer had a special dislike for priests in the Resistance. As a young lad he had studied some theology, even considered it as a vocation. Priests were quite common in the Resistance, although there were also priests who acted as informers. The category of Christian which particularly roused his ire were those of Jewish origin who had become Catholics. One of these was Abbé Glasberg, of Ukrainian origin, a massive, overweight figure of a man with thick glasses, who was an immense comfort in his voluminous black cassock to young and old alike, and Barbie hated him for that. Wherever someone suffered from Nazi persecution,

Abbé Glasberg sought to help, whether they were Jews, stateless persons, Spanish Republicans fleeing the Vichy camps, or British military personnel trying to get back to England.

I heard about the Abbé from Jean-Marie Soutou, former Secretary-General at the Quai d' Orsay (the French Foreign Office), who was France's first diplomat in independent Algeria, the President of the French Red Cross. He told me: 'Glasberg's base was the Amitié Chrétienne, a relief body for refugees and exiles that was under the patronage of Cardinal Gerlier and Pasteur Boegner. It ought to have been called Amitié Judéo-Chrétienne because its top people included representatives from Jewish organisations. Its premises enjoyed a kind of immunity because of the standing of the churchmen behind it, at least until Pierre Laval returned as head of the Vichy Government. [Laval was executed by a firing squad in 1945.] One day Abbé Glasberg decided to buy a magnificent fur coat for the wife of a senior official who headed the Service des Étrangers. His aim was to get her husband to record forged passports at the central archives. Just as he was leaving for the préfecture with the parcel under his arm, he did an about-turn and in a crestfallen way told us: 'This won't work. He'll refuse; the parcel is too well wrapped. Better to say that the coat was among the clothes collected for the needy,' he muttered. So the parcel was undone, and the coat re-packed in some old wrapping-paper with scruffy bits of string.'

Another aspect of his work related to a disused barracks at Venissieux, a Lyons suburb, where a camp was set up for Jews arrested in the southern zone of France. Abbé Glasberg and his colleagues offered their services as welfare workers at the camp, with Cardinal Gerlier's approval. They acted chiefly as interpreters, and Jean-Marie Soutou explained that they translated somewhat freely with a view to getting concessions for the detainees.

As one batch of Jews arrived, the churchmen managed to take a peek inside an official's briefcase and found an instruction reading: 'Children under sixteen years of age are not to be deported.' This was news to Glasberg's people, and they assumed the order was ignored so that the officials could make up the numbers required for the trains. However, once the document came to light, Abbé Glasberg grabbed it and got all the camp children together, demanding that the children be allowed to leave. Monsieur Soutou recalls: 'Then began a painful but necessary business, the separating of parents and children. It lasted all that night and much of the next day. Abbé Glasberg was everywhere, forcing people to make decisions, patting someone on the shoulder, saying a word or two in German dialect or in Slav, and then scurrying off to another family slumped on a bedstead. There were hundreds of families involved, but only one refused to be separated from their young lad.'

Abbé Glasberg arranged buses, and the 84 children were taken off to a disused convent owned by the Carmelites, an immense building that had escape routes via tunnels linking buildings in the Saint-Jean district and even further afield. So the next day, when Vichy officials ordered them to be rounded up again, the children had already made their escape.

Soon after that, Jean-Marie Soutou was arrested by Barbie.

'Where is Glasberg the Jew?' Barbie demanded.

'He's not Jewish, he is a priest. It was Glasberg who married my wife and me.'

Barbie tossed his head and looked at Soutou as if he were an imbecile: 'Huh, you don't know that you can be a priest having been a Jew?'

Glasberg found a hide-out at Leriboscq in Tarn-et-Garonne. He died in 1981.

Soutou was held by Klaus Barbie for three weeks: 'I heard cries from the adjacent room. Barbie tried to fool me that they were torturing my wife.'

He also recalls: 'In January 1943 the Germans all got Christmas parcels. I could see them opening them; they had been expecting them for days. They were sent yule logs (*Baumkuchen*) and pine branches. They laughed a lot and got quite excited. Klaus Barbie gave them a little speech to mark the new year. That day, they were happy.'

Of the trial forty years later, Soutou told me: 'If there is to be a trial, it should be the trial of totalitarianism, not of its stooges. Before trying Barbie, they should try those who grew rich building the Atlantic Wall . . .'*

* German fortifications on the French coast against a possible invasion from the sea.

5

FOR THOSE WHO KNEW the Occupation and belonged to the Resistance, what happened at Caluire on 21 June 1943, when the betrayal and arrest of Jean Moulin took place, has prompted as much speculation as that which followed the assassination of President Kennedy in Dallas, Texas. Just about everything has been said before. Every detail has already been subjected to the most painstaking scrutiny. Only Vergès, Barbie's defence counsel, has dared to question the legend while survivors of the drama are still alive. And were they not, their children have been entrusted with the story and will not tolerate any inaccuracy of fact or interpretation. I know they are the watch-dogs of their parents' memories, the guardians of history. But I have one advantage over those eye-witnesses and those authors who have dealt with the subject to date: I can examine those grim years with the eyes of a journalist who has no political bias. I am an outsider who has been lucky enough to dig through what seemed like tens of kilos of neglected files, through yellowing documents now fragile as old lace. If I could have punched the Caluire episode into a computer, transcribed those thousands of procedural pages into machine code, I would probably have found out that no one could escape censure. The key question remaining would be this: how was it that Jean Moulin and his friends could walk straight into the lion's den? Barbie licked his chops for decades after.

The crassest of torturers know that some adversaries are dynamite. If Barbie had refrained from torturing Jean Moulin as if he were smashing a new toy he could not understand, his Bolivian fortress would never have been discovered. For it was the death of Jean Moulin that brought notoriety to this grey-eyed Hauptsturmführer and gave him the reputation as 'the worst brute of all'. Without Moulin, Barbie would have been lost in history. No doubt the story of the helpless children deported from Izieu to the death camps, and the story of the suppression of the Lyons branch of the Union Genérale des Israélites de France would have been submerged in the general holocaust. Barbie would have simply been war criminal 239 who escaped to the *yungas* of South America. But Barbie's visiting card has Jean Moulin's name on it. Beate Klarsfeld added to Barbie's credentials the phrase 'a little Eichmann' when she revealed that a commonplace war criminal was also responsible for crimes against humanity. Thanks to the Nazis, Europe finally decided that these crimes were punishable at any subsequent date, and that only death or madness could spare the murderers. Whether in World War II, Indochina, Algeria, Afghanistan, Nicaragua or Lebanon, the criminal who acts against humanity can no longer hope that the passage of time will excuse him his crimes.

What would the political map of France be like today without Caluire, if Jean Moulin had survived? What role would he have played after the war, with or without de Gaulle? Henri Frenay, leader of Combat, saw Jean Moulin as close to the Communists; Frenay, not one of Moulin's best friends, has made it clear in the 1970s that, unbeknown to de Gaulle, the former prefect was playing into the French Communist party's hands and would surely have aided its return when Paris was freed. This is a serious accusation coming from Henri Frenay, acknowledged as one of the greatest of the Resistance leaders. Others of Moulin's companions believe that the loss of Moulin created a political vacuum and directly led to a return of party politics. Much later, in 1962, de Gaulle brought in a Constitution under which the French electorate was allowed to vote directly for the President of the Republic. It is fair to say that the political history of France would have been sharply different if de Gaulle had been able to establish this 'presidential Constitution' in 1945.

If we are to comprehend the Caluire episode, we have to clarify the game that set the Gestapo against the leaders of the Mouvements Unis de la Résistance (MUR) and more particularly the MUR Secret Army. The main players were:

* Jean Moulin, who was in the prime of life, celebrated his forty-fourth birthday the day before his arrest. Those present were not supposed to know his true identity. Nobody was supposed to recognize the former prefect of Chartres, the first state official to join de Gaulle. He had returned from London three months earlier and was known to the Resistance people as Max, a name probably selected in memory of his friend the author Max Jacob, who died the following year at the camp at Drancy. Previous alibi names were Regis and Rex. The Germans knew him as Jacques Martel, an artist.

* André Lassagne, thirty-two, teacher of Italian. Max appointed him Inspector for the southern zone.

* Raymond Aubrac, aged thirty-one, whose real name was Samuel, paramilitary operations chief in the Libération movement. That day he was using the name Claude Ermelin. He played about dangerously with names, giving the surname Vallet when arrested in March in Lyons. As he was known in the Free Zone, Jean Moulin asked him to head the movement in the north of France, the Occupied Zone.

* Colonel Exile Schwarzfeld, fifty-seven, engineer, Catholic, lieutenant-colonel in the Reserves and member of the France d'Abord movement. A possible successor to General Delestraint, the recently arrested chief of the Secret Army.

* Colonel Albert Lacaze, fifty-nine former head of the 99th regiment in Lyons. Delestraint had asked him to

head the Premier Bureau at his Command Headquarters. He had taught Lassagne at the Reserve Officers' College (EOR) before the war.

★ Henri Aubry, alias Thomas Avricourt, Chief of Staff of the Secret Army (a rather too responsible-sounding title for him). Henri Aubry's number two was 'André', whom he appointed national inspector of the Secret Army, no less, without knowing who he was or where he came from. He turned out to be a German Gestapo or Abwehr agent! Henri Noguères has written: 'One is amazed at such conduct, such lack of prudence, and ignorance over the most elementary rules of security.' Since Henri Frenay was away in London with Emmanuel d'Astier de la Vigerie, head of the Libération movement, Aubry represented at Caluire the biggest Resistance group, Combat.

★ René Hardy, thirty-two, alias Didot, representing Résistance-Fer (the railway section) in the movement led by Frenay. He alone had experience of preparing, directing and following through the sabotage of railway lines. He was said to be an engineer, and a friend of Aubry.

★ Bruno Larat, alias Xavier Parisot, Jean Moulin's secretary. He had responded unhesitatingly to General de Gaulle's call from London on 18 June. After training in Britain, where, like Moulin, he learned to parachute in his forties, he was dropped into France one night and spent two months in hiding at the home of a woman German teacher. Xavier was a liaison officer whose special assignment was to receive goods sent from London.

★ Frédéric Dugoujon, physician, who had been living since 1939 in a tall house at Caluire, an old Roman village overlooking Lyons (for which the Roman name was Lugdunum) that eventually became one of Lyons' suburbs. Dugoujon did not take up arms. It was later learned that his half-brother was in the rightist militia. This isn't surprising; families were sometimes split between Gaullists and Pétainists. The half-brother joined the rightists as late as July 1944 at the age of eighteen. Dugoujon was an acquaintance of André Lassagne and willingly lent his home for this Resistance meeting, although he thought it was a gathering of ex-prisoners.

For the sake of simplicity, I shall use the names these nine men were known by after the war: Moulin, Aubrac, Lassagne, Schwarzfeld, Lacaze, Aubry, Hardy, Larat and Dugoujon. At the time of this writing only Aubrac, Hardy and Dugoujon are still alive.

Dr Dugoujon was not directly involved, so the assembly consisted of the other eight. Why was there a meeting? Because there was very little phoning and writing, if at all, and also because Jean Moulin wanted an immediate decision about replacing General Charles Delestraint, known as 'Vidal', a crucial figure in the Resistance who had fallen into German hands. Moulin could have consulted the others individually and just made the decision, but he preferred to hear what they had to say, to give them a chance to discuss it openly before the decision was reached. Everyone was to participate: Combat, Libération and the colonels – Franc-Tireur alone was not represented.

Raymond Aubrac told me that Moulin's natural authority was uncontested. He said: 'Moulin never raised his voice. He was ten years older than us. He understood us.'

Jean Moulin nearly always arrived at meetings on foot. He would spend anything from ten minutes to two hours with colleagues, explaining that they were not gathering to protest but to build up the Resistance. He arrived on foot because the Gestapo was making headway. Delestraint was being held by Bömelburg in Paris, his friends Gastaldo and Théobald were at Fresnes on the outskirts of the capital, and the Germans were seizing goods parachuted over from Britain. De Gaulle sought political weight within France to show the Allies that he truly led Fighting France. Moulin set out to give him this influence in spite of the setbacks and dangers. He would provide a new head of the Secret Army until the release of Delestraint. He would mould a new unified structure, so that the political parties, trade unions and Resistance movements would all be united in the service of Gaullism.

The Caluire meeting was to have been one of many in the development of the Resistance. Moulin was back in Lyons to reorganise the Secret Army Command. The meeting was almost a formality. But Barbie saw it as the perfect moment to capture the top man, for the slightly built Obersturmführer knew that Max, his prey, was in the area. Barbie was unaware that Max was the ex-prefect from Chartres who had an art gallery in Nice under his own name, Jean Moulin, and he possessed no photos of the man, no accurate description. But what he did have was a mass of reports that meant the fellow was within his grasp.

These reports came from Amt IV, the special service manned by Wenzel, Stengritt and others, but they came more often from information given to the Gestapo by Resistance people who had changed sides.*

By the early weeks of 1943, the Gestapo had collected a

---

* Barbie's lawyer, Jacques Vergès, confirmed years later what was known at the time, that a few Resistance people went over to the Germans. For forty years knowledge of the defections was kept quiet, since the war was over and done with. Even so, many historians knew the case of Lunel, who was an out-and-out coward; all that was needed to turn him were a few threats and suggestions such as : 'After all, there is Marshal Pétain as an example to follow.' To men like him, the Germans cleverly hinted that they might become double agents, without actually saying so. There was no need to change their behaviour, but the extra money from the Germans would help.

great deal of data, and was familiar with the general Resistance set-up.

Jean Moulin knew he was actively sought. On 7 May he sent a report to General de Gaulle: 'I repeat what I have often said previously, that we must make our presence felt. This is an absolute necessity from the military angle, if we are to halt the present confusion which is such a help to the Giraudist organizations. Mars (General Delestraint's initial code name) must have, in the southern zone as well as the north, people from London that he can depend on, and who are acceptable to all Resistance movements. I believe it is vital that I have a double in each zone and a number of people in fixed posts.'

A few lines later he gave this warning, a red alert if ever there was one: 'I am now being sought by Vichy and the Gestapo who, as a result of practices adopted by certain elements in the Resistance movements, are fully aware of my identity and my activities. I am resolved to hold on as long as possible, but if I disappear, I shall not have time to notify my successors.'

If he disappeared!

What exactly did the Germans know? Three key documents were later found in the archives of the Reich. Not all of them date from before the Caluire business, but they give a fairly accurate picture of the data held by the Gestapo: a first report compiled by Dr Ernst Kaltenbrunner, chief of the Gestapo, dated 27 May 1943; Kaltenbrunner's second report of 29 June 1943; and the Flora report of 19 July 1943, drawn up after Caluire but containing details of what happened before the gathering.

For historians the first report is the one that really counts. In twenty-eight pages Ernst Kaltenbrunner, who took over the Berlin Sipo-SD after the killing in Czechoslovakia of Reinhard Heydrich, sent a summary of all he knew to Foreign Minister Ribbentrop.* This report

* Both men were hanged on 16 October 1946, after the Nuremberg trials.

—— 68 ——

contained full details of how the Secret Army was organized – its links, its personnel, its resources. It landed on Hitler's desk two weeks before the Caluire meeting. The contents, including graphs, were drawn from material acquired by all the Gestapo offices in France, and they show that the Germans had a complete run-down of the Secret Army, and in some considerable detail. Kaltenbrunner's conclusion was that, in the wake of the North African defeats and with an invasion by the British and Americans a distinct possibility, 'the French Secret Army is achieving increasing importance'. In consequence, Max became the prime target of Klaus Barbie and his killers.

Jean Multon, now Monsier Lunel, was thirty-five when he was transferred from Marseilles to Lyons, where he was less likely to fall victim to a settling of accounts, having already combined with Klaus Barbie in an attempt to bring off a major coup – almost succeeding in catching Henri Frenay, head of the largest of the Resistance movements. Late in May, Frenay's heroic assistant Berty Albrecht fell into the trap, but managed to give the alert. Multon was about to hand Barbie one of the most beautiful presents a Gestapo chief could dream of: a message found in the iron box René Hardy used to contact railway saboteurs. It was not in code but in plain language, none of the 'Duchemol awaits with his white mice' kind of secrecy, but a straightforward 'Didot [Hardy's false name], the general expects you at La Muette metro station 9.00 a.m. on 9 June'.

The Gestapo, newly and powerfully established at the École de Santé Militaire on the Avenue Berthelot, spread the net. It had all the men it needed – more than one hundred Germans and French collaborateurs; it had proven methods and technical resources. Its prey was a resistance movement made up of youngsters and men over forty; it is curious how few there were in their thirties. The Resistance members made a lot of mistakes; experts in clandestine warfare would certainly have faulted them on many counts.

The iron box containing the give-away message was in

fact the letter-box of a certain Madame Dumoulin at 14 rue Bouteille in Lyons. The message was collected by Multon, former liaison officer with Combat's Chevance-Bertin group, and it sent Barbie's men to meet Didot at La Muette. Who were these men? Multon, of course, as he was proving so adept as a collaborator and wanted to be in at the kill. Barbie was especially anxious to succeed with his snatch, as Abwehr agent K 30 was also in on the swoop. The real name of K 30 was Robert Moog, but he was also called 'Monsieur Pierre'; he was brought from Dijon for intelligence work. Moog was an army man; Barbie was secret police. Moog was prepared to take his time dismantling the network and unearthing the sabotage programme, while Barbie wanted the top man – quickly. Moog was the brain, Barbie the brute.

Moog and Multon boarded the night train to Paris on 7 June 1943, occupying couchettes 9 and 10 in coach number 3818. Couchette 8 in that same compartment was booked for none other than René Hardy. But Hardy travelled no farther than Chalon-sur-Saône.

He claimed at the time: 'When I saw the Gestapo I got off the train.' But he admitted four years later that he had been seized by the Germans and that Klaus Barbie, who collected him personally, had interrogated him at length. Hardy's explanation for lying was that, since General Delestraint had been arrested because of his accomplices, he had every reason to be suspicious, especially of his own colleagues.

René Hardy affirmed that he failed to collect the message because he knew the letter-box was 'hot'. In any case, the head of the Secret Army, General Charles Delestraint, was picked up at La Muette métro station precisely at 9.00 a.m. on 9 June, as he was keeping an eye open for Hardy, whom he did not know by sight. He was approached by a Frenchman, Gestapo agent K 4 named Saumande, while 'Monsieur Pierre' (Moog) sat in an adjacent car. In all innocence, General Delestraint, wearing a beret and with a Légion d' Honneur rosette in his lapel, was soon confiding that he planned to meet his lieutenants Gastaldo and Théobald that same morning at the next metro station along the line, La Pompe.

So it was that Delestraint, Gastaldo and Théobald were taken to Rue des Saussaies and the Resistance forces lost their leader at the height of their activities against the German occupier. From that instant, and right up until his death at Dachau concentration camp from three bullets in the back, on 19 April 1945, Delestraint maintained that he had been betrayed by Didot. Jean-Louis Théobald later wrote from Saigon, where he was posted as civil administrator: 'The general, who was a very circumspect man, told me he suspected Didot.' Théobald added that he was deported to Germany, escaped to Algiers and by chance ran into Hardy, whom he informed of the general's suspicions. Hardy said he had been arrested and tortured, but it was not he who denounced the general.*

On learning of Delestraint's capture, Jean Moulin believed the general should be replaced at once. The Resistance had to get over the shock quickly and reorganise. That was the reason for the Caluire meeting, which, according to André Lassagne, was decided for 6.00 p.m. on 19 June at Jean Moulin's request.

The next big question is how Obersturmführer Barbie knew about it. Klaus Barbie says that Hardy told him directly, that Hardy showed him a piece of paper summoning him to the meeting, though it gave neither the place nor the date.

Raymond Aubrac told me: 'It was Jean Moulin, and he alone, who decided to hold the meeting.'

* Hardy always denied any guilt and has been twice acquitted. We shall look at this again, endorsing the reservations of his own defending lawyer Maurice Garçon on the fallibility of a verdict: 'A judgement is a necessary legal fiction, and it amounts only to a presumption of truth within a solely judicial context.' (Hardy's second trial in 1950.)

'You knew Jean Moulin well?'

'He was Max to me, and I knew his real name later. I had met him five or six times. The first occasion was under the arcade at the Théâtre Municipal, where we exchanged passwords, after which he pulled out a microfilm from under the bottom of a matchbox. It was his credentials signed in London by General de Gaulle. I said to him: "That proves nothing to me, but you had better get rid of it."'

On 19 June, Moulin, Aubry, Aubrac and Lassagne met at 7 quai de Serbie, where Professor Lonjaret lived, to prepare for Caluire. It rained that morning, but later it grew hot and all except Jean Moulin had their shirt collars undone; he wanted to hide the scar on his neck – a result of his suicide attempt in 1940. They agreed to summon all the others on Monday 21 June. There was no question of René Hardy attending.

The Resistance chiefs assembled again on the banks of the Rhône. Henri Noguères wrote of them in his *Histoire de la Résistance en France*: 'They were devoid of imagination.' To trick the Gestapo, they merely changed the name of the quay or bridge for the meeting. On 20 June, Klaus Barbie, looking like any other Lyonnais, except for his shiny leather jacket, was ready to pounce.

'I joined up with Aubry on the Pont Morand,' Gaston Deferre, a Socialist in the Resistance, wrote in a letter to Henri Michel, ex-secretary-general of the Committee on the History of the Second World War. 'We started walking along the quayside of the Rhône on the left bank, and as we went through a square we caught sight of Hardy. Next to him was a man unknown to me reading a newspaper . . . I thought he looked suspicious.'

Henri Aubry takes up the story: 'Walking along with Deferre, I noticed Hardy waiting on a bench. I gave him a slight wave. By his side was a man, but I couldn't see his face; he was holding a newspaper open in front of him . . . I left Deferre and beckoned to Hardy.'

Aubry's secretary, Madeleine Raisin, joined them, with

200,000 francs, the monthly budget for the rail sabotage work, for Hardy. Hardy suggested they sit down, but she refused because there was a chap there reading the paper.

Why did they choose Dugoujon's place? André Lassagne, with his perfect familiarity with Lyons, decided the venue. The Resistance people were rather careless and no longer as afraid as before – they were in constant danger, anyway, which dulled their vigilance. Lassagne switched the address each time. On this occasion he phoned his friend Frédéric Dugoujon, inviting himself to lunch the next day and asking to borrow the first-floor bedroom. Dugoujon asked no questions. He explained to me: 'As early as March a meeting with General Delestraint was in the air.'

At that time Barbie still had no idea where Jean Moulin planned his High Command session. He had pushed aside all other investigations in his quest for the head of the CNR. Moulin was too big a fish to lose. He conferred with his SS colleagues and sent out scouts to trace suspect 'terrorists'. One of the Obersturmführer's valued aides was a double agent called Madame Delétraz, who reported to the Sipo-SD offices once a week. He could also use other French people who had switched sides: Multon, Moog, Saumande, Doussot, and Francis André with his crooked jaw, so twisted that people thought he was pretending. And Barbie claims he had Hardy in his service.

As every police officer knows, in an inquiry, the first twenty-four hours of a man's detention count most. It is therefore fair to assume that Barbie's first statement, recorded three years after the war ended, is likely to be the closest to the truth. That is why this book contains details of the famous interrogation conducted by Commissioner Bibes, recorded on 16 July 1948. I have studied this evidence as carefully as I have listened to Barbie's victims. The document may not be admissible to a lawyer; indeed, Maître Garçon has rejected the interrogation completely. But it is highly relevant if we seek to probe the Barbie dossier fully.

What Klaus Barbie said in 1948 was this: 'Hardy, alias Didot, informed me that a Resistance leaders' meeting was scheduled for 21 June 1943 in Lyons, but when he revealed this to me he still did not know where it would be and who would be taking part. Hardy gave me this information four or five days before the date . . . It was via a document arriving in his letter-box from Paris that Hardy found out the details already mentioned . . . Every evening before the meeting I saw Hardy, and each time he gave me further details, obtained from his liaison agent. In that way he told me that Max would be at the meeting. Hardy revealed to me the true identity of Max, and told me his name was Moulin.'

The allegation that Hardy revealed Moulin's identity was untrue; the inquiry showed that Hardy was unable to name Jean Moulin at Caluire, although in May 1972 he said he knew him, having seen him once for ten minutes, but only knew him as Max.

Barbie said: 'I went to the rendezvous at Pont Morand with Stengritt. I was the civilian sitting on the bench reading the newspaper. Stengritt was next to me but paid no attention to me. We watched as Hardy joined two men. When he came to see me that afternoon he said the taller of the two men was Aubry.' Klaus Barbie already knew that Aubry was to attend the Caluire event.

According to Stengritt, the Abwehr agent Moog was also on the scene at the time.

That evening Jean Moulin had dinner with Claude Serreulles, a second-in-command finally sent to him by London on 16 June. He resumed their chat early the next day, and while he was slowly walking towards Rue Paul-Bert, where he was to see Aubry, he encountered Gaston ('Elie') Deferre.

Writing to Henri Michel in 1963, Gaston Deferre said: 'He seemed anxious and nervy. He recounted to me the trouble he was having with the heads of some Resistance

— 74 —

movements he was to meet afterwards, late that morning and in the afternoon . . . Moulin was very hostile towards the political parties, even those that were re-formed in secret. He had Brossolette's view on this.'

On French television, Channel 1, in January 1984 Gaston Deferre told me: 'That morning, on 21 June in Place Jean-Macé, I had a lengthy talk with Max – I knew then he was Jean Moulin. He mentioned his rendezvous that afternoon. I earnestly advised him against going there, because it was my impression that someone had acted unwisely. Jean Moulin said he would go anyway, even though it seemed dangerous.'

'What was unwise – the choice of the venue, or do you think it was a question of betrayal?' I asked him.

'No, I did not have the impression he had been betrayed,' was his reply.

Henri Aubry gave his version of what happened to historian Henri Noguères, President of the League for the Rights of Man, for his *Histoire de la Résistance* : 'It was Jean Moulin who summoned the participants to the general meeting, which was to follow our own meeting that morning. But Bénouville* asked to see me and said he wanted me to bring Hardy for the forthcoming sessions. After jumping the train Hardy had contacted all his comrades and wanted to see me. He had left several messages for me, suggesting we meet.'

Hardy had not, of course, informed his comrades of his detainment by the Germans.

So de Gaulle's envoy met Henri Aubry as arranged. His view is much the same: 'Jean Moulin launched into the discussion, attacking me violently for having collected weapons that were dropped by parachute in the Brive area . . . Jean Moulin accused us of wanting to go it alone. He talked of a split. As to Delestraint's successor, he said

* Pierre Guillain de Bénouville represented the head of the Combat movement, who was in London.

— 75 —

nothing at the time, since we were to discuss the matter that afternoon.'

At 2.00 p.m. on 21 June, the cream of the Resistance was assembling in the Lyons suburbs. They were to arrive on foot, on their own, or in small groups.

Barbie said subsequently that he still did not know the venue for the meeting and that Untersturmführer Wenzel was ordered to tail Hardy. Wenzel positioned a number of vans and set up a series of relay points, while Barbie waited with two or three cars on the banks of the Rhône. French auxiliaries Moog, Saumande and Doussot were to do the tailing, and a woman was also employed. Barbie could not recall her name, but the woman herself came forward later. It was Madame Edmée Delétraz.

Madame Delétraz, a comely young woman in a red blouse, went to the military post in the Croix-Rousse district of Lyons before midday with the intention of seeing Captain Menat, an officer in the Organisation de Résistance de l'Armée (ORA). Naturally the SS did not know of her movements. Menat was away and Madame Delétraz told someone else that the Germans had introduced her to a certain 'Didot, called Hardy'. She said: 'This man Hardy is to attend a meeting of the Secret Army and the Gestapo has told me to trail him and tell them the place.'

Giving evidence in 1948, Madame Delétraz recognized a photo of Moog. She said he was the man who told her on the morning of 21 June: 'I am going to show you a Frenchman who knows what's what . . . At two o'clock today he will be attending a meeting of Resistance leaders. You will follow him and tell us which house he goes into. Here is a pass. Report at the École de Santé at 11.30.'

Madame Delétraz attempted to warn other people, but none of the Caluire participants could be reached in time. The head of the celebrated Gallia network was informed only the next day.

When she got to the Ecole de Santé, Madame Delétraz

met René Hardy. 'Didot said: "If I carry my hat in my hand it means I am going into a nearby street or a house. If I wear it, it means I'll take the funicular, and you will too." Didot and the others chatted, and then the phoney handcuffs were tried on him . . . It occurred to Didot that the meeting might take place in a building with several storeys. He said: "Give me a packet of cigarettes, I'll empty it and drop the packet on the floor where I go in." He seemed quite relaxed, and he didn't seem like a man who was being forced to do something he didn't want to.'

Moulin, Aubrac and Colonel Schwarzfeld planned to meet at Croix-Paquet. The colonel was late, and Moulin and Aubrac waited for him, although every Resistance fighter knew the rule about never waiting more than fifteen minutes, a golden rule in clandestine affairs.

André Lassagne had volunteered to lead the second group, and he was waiting for Aubry to arrive. Unexpectedly, Aubry turned up with Hardy in tow, but Lassagne thought nothing of it when he heard Hardy say: 'I just want a quick word with Max. I need to see him.'

At a hearing on 21 January 1946, André Lassagne said: 'I had no reason to be suspicious of Hardy or Aubry. All I said was that Max didn't know he was coming and he might get annoyed. That it was unwise that too many people should attend the same meeting. But Aubry said we should have a quick first meeting with Hardy before going on to more important subjects.'

Elsewhere Lassagne reported that Hardy told him, 'I fixed it up with Max's secretary [de Graaf].'

Lassagne boarded the funicular first, taking his bike with him. He asked the other two to come by the next car.

The third group consisted of one of Moulin's secretaries, Bruno Larat, who was handling parachute drops, and Colonel Lacaze, for whom this was the first major encounter with the Resistance chiefs. Lacaze seemed especially anxious.

Xavier (Bruno Larat) went to Lacaze's place to tell him of the meeting early on the 20th. He told the colonel, who was fifty-seven years of age with seven children, that the meeting was scheduled to take place in an isolated house in Caluire, Dr Dugoujon's place, and that there would be eight to ten people attending. Lacaze says his conversation with Xavier took place before noon, but at that time, according to Lassagne, Dugoujon had not been asked to lend his house.

The colonel said: 'I warned him that the German police were on to something in Lyons. I told him the meeting should not take place and ought to be cancelled. I asked him to phone me with the decision.' The code for a message would be 'No fishing tomorrow'.

How could Colonel Albert Lacaze have known that the Germans were alerted to something in Lyons? He said: 'On 17 June, the gendarmerie captain of the Suchet barracks informed me: "Be careful, at Vichy we know the German police are on to something in Lyons."'

As the phone call cancelling the fishing party did not materialise, the colonel sent his daughter to reconnoitre the surrounds of the house at Caluire and on Monday around 9.00 a.m. she delivered a letter to the house explaining that if her father did not show up later, it would be because he was ill and could not get out of bed.

The preparations were certainly very slapdash.

Marcel Rivière, a top man in the Combat movement, who became editor in chief of the newspaper *Progrès de Lyon*, said in 1972 in an interview given to Renaud Vincent: 'I knew a highly important meeting was scheduled in the Lyons suburbs. I said: "That's crazy, you must have guards." The idea was turned down.'

Lacaze arrived first, just ahead of time. He was not too happy about it, and roamed round the house a bit before deciding everything was all right. He entered at 2.00 p.m. His sole aim was 'to see the boss before the meeting and ask him to send us away at once'.

Tony de Graaf, alias Gramont, secretary to Jean Moulin, would have asked, had he been present, that the Groupes Francs arrange to guard the meeting. On 21 June he lunched with Moulin. He told me that he asked Moulin: '"Are you sure you've got the security buttoned up?" Max replied: "The Secret Army are handling it. It should be good."'

The doctor's villa offered two escape routes. One involved climbing over the roof outside a first-floor window; the other was simply through the backyard. But not everyone knew about them, and they should have had a look-out man.

To foil any Gestapo scouts, Lassagne parted company with Aubry and Hardy on the Croix-Rousse uplands, and went off on his bike. He reached Caluire before the others, who took a number 33 tram, and he stowed the bike under the outside staircase at the villa, in front of a cellar door.

Dr Dugoujon came out. 'Will there be many of you?' he asked. Lassagne snapped, 'No idea.'

Lassagne then went off again to fetch Aubry and his guest at Place des Frères. The three returned, entering the garden through a wooden gate with a wrought iron Jerusalem cross on it, which the Gestapo took for the Cross of Lorraine. The three knocked and the housekeeper, forewarned by the doctor an hour earlier, took them straight up to the bedroom on the left. Xavier Larat was next. The housekeeper, Marguerite Brossier, was worried about their number, and sent Larat into the doctor's waiting-room on the ground floor. When the doctor came in to summon the next patient, Larat got up, and said, 'I've come for a special consultation . . .' Dugoujon sent him up to where the other four were already waiting.

Aubry said: 'We chatted a bit about nothing much, but wondered what would happen after General Delestraint's arrest. We waited a long time, until past 3.00 p.m. I sat next to the window.'

Colonel Lacaze remarked: 'I believe you are being closely watched . . .'

Hardy flapped open his jacket to reveal a pistol: 'I know, and in any case I've already been convicted twice *in absentia.*'

Albert Lacaze says that somebody asked if it had a silencer and was told yes.

We may well ask where Hardy got the gun. Barbie claims he personally gave it to him in his office.

Barbie has also declared: 'Prompted by Wenzel, Hardy used yellow chalk to mark places he had passed by: the garden gate, the stairway and the door of the room where they met on the first floor at the Caluire villa.' René Hardy has consistently denied Barbie's assertion.

How was Madame Delétraz getting on? Having followed the first group, she then returned to the Gestapo. She says she was hoping her alert to the Resistance got through and that the Germans would arrive too late. About this point, Henri Noguères comments: 'One can only express surprise . . . that when she reached the villa, knowing she had left the Gestapo well behind, Madame Delétraz never thought to go inside and warn them.'

The attractive double agent got into an SS Citroën and directed the driver, Barthel. She pretended she was not too sure of the way. Barbie had a map spread out, showing the whole of the Lyons area. The car meandered through the Les Mercières district, and Le Vernay and Les Marroniers. Barbie got annoyed, and it was not until an hour after she saw Hardy go into the house that she managed to remember the way. That was just before 3.00 p.m. What she did not know was that Jean Moulin, Raymond Aubrac and the colonel were very late too.

Aubrac told me: 'We could not be sure exactly how much the Germans knew about our affairs after they grabbed Vidal [General Delestraint]. On 20 June Max summoned me to the Parc de la Tête-d'Or, where my wife kept watch by walking around with a child's pushchair. I spent nearly two hours with him. He asked me to accept responsibility for the northern zone, and I agreed.'

They arranged to meet the next day in Place Carnot, where they would join up with Colonel Schwarzfeld and take the twenty-minute journey to Caluire on a number 33 tram.

Aubrac said: 'I rang the bell, the maid opened the door,

took us into the waiting-room where there were six or seven patients. Nobody was smoking and I put my pipe on the mantelpiece. I even found it there after the war!'

Assuming they were all genuine patients, as none of them asked for Lassagne, the doctor's housekeeper Marguerite Brossier did not show them up. Meanwhile, time grew heavy on the first floor and Colonel Lacaze snoozed in an armchair.

Klaus Barbie recalls: 'I had the villa surrounded, which was easy because it stood on its own. I gave the order that people could be let in but that no one must leave.'

Aubry said: 'I heard the yard-gate squeak and glanced down from the window, to see a whole lot of people in leather jackets. I just had time to pull back and tell the others: "It's all up, lads, the Gestapo's here!"'

Dr Dugoujon saw shadows mounting the stairs. He was taking a woman and her daughter out of his consulting-room, and unwittingly opened a door to let the men go upstairs, assuming they were more of Max's friends.

He was told: 'German police! You are holding a meeting here.'

Barbie hussled Dugoujon into his office and leapt up the stairs four at a time, while another German entered the waiting-room. Moulin told the doctor: 'My name's Jacques Martel.' He then handed Aubrac some papers from his jacket lining and told him to swallow them; Aubrac gave him some from his own pocket and Moulin swallowed those. The interrogation upstairs went on for more than an hour behind closed shutters.

Henri Aubry remembers that Hardy pulled out a pistol before the SS burst in. 'We all told him to put it back. The bedroom door opened and a small man ordered in French, then in English: "Hands up, German police!" He rushed over to me and I was hit, my head bashed against the wall, and my hands forced behind my back. The man said: "Well now, Thomas, you don't look too good. You were more cheerful yesterday on the Pont Morand, I was reading my paper, but it was such nice weather I thought

I'd leave you another day, since I knew we would meet again today!" Then the questioning started. In turn we were each taken into the dining-room.'

Obersturmführer Barbie seized a leg that supported the leaf of a Henri II table, and snapped it off to use as a club. The prisoners and even the patients and doctor were all handcuffed with their hands behind their backs – all, that is, except Hardy, who had a 'twister', a knotted cord with a piece of wood on the end, wrapped round one wrist, and it was held by a policeman. René Hardy, whom Aubrac was astonished to see there, was taken down to the ground floor and led into one of the Citroën cars where two women were already seated, a patient and the housekeeper. During his interrogation by a French police officer sent by the Resistance in 1943, Hardy said he tripped the German, punched him with his free fist and slammed the door in his face so that the man let the twister go. Hardy said he ran off to Place Castellane.

In 1948 Barbie declared: 'His escape was planned with Stengritt [Barbie's intelligence chief]. When they got to the car, Stengritt released the cord, Hardy assaulted him and got away as planned.'

This is an extremely grave assertion, but is it credible, coming from a killer like Barbie? Maurice Garçon, Hardy's lawyer at the two trials at which his client was acquitted, discounts it completely.

Barbie claimed: 'All the Germans with me knew that Hardy was to escape. I had told them when we worked out the operation. As Hardy ran off, my men fired into the air as instructed. But something happened. My driver Barthel had forgotten the orders and ran after Hardy; he fired but missed. The other men put him right and he stopped chasing him. Hardy later told me he hid in a ditch, and wounded himself with the small pistol I had given him for protection a few days before.'

Even if certain lies and omissions in Barbie's story make us inclined to reject the entire account, it does lead one to wonder. The fact is that several witnesses have confirmed

Barbie's version, not least some Gestapo staff.

Under questioning in Germany in 1948, Staff Sergeant Harry Stengritt said: 'One or two of those arrested had already been taken to the cars and were to be driven off. I came behind with Hardy and held him by a jacket sleeve, which I screwed up a bit round his wrist, twisting it. We were about six feet from the car and I said quietly in German: "*Los!*" (Run!) Hardy snatched his arm away and fled as I pretended to trip.'

Stengritt's version is that neither handcuffs nor twister were used on Hardy. Let us hear two other versions before we look at Hardy's. Housekeeper Marguerite Brossier was waiting in the first Citroën, which had turned round and was preparing to take the prisoners to the Gestapo. She wore handcuffs and was surprised, to say the least, at the ease with which the gentleman 'managed to get away', and she says the Gestapo men took a while to react. 'I thought how lucky he was!'

Another testimony comes from Claude Rougis, an elderly council employee, who was in Place Castellane at the time of Hardy's escape.

'I was scraping out the gutter . . .' He said the escapee threw himself into a ditch full of nettles. 'The Gestapo didn't think to look in the ditch among the grass and such. Funny, that. Instead, a little policeman fired two shots from a revolver into the nearest garden.'

The Germans went back to their cars and Rougis approached the man in the ditch. 'Are you wounded?' he asked.

'No,' Hardy said.

Inside the villa the Resistance people heard the shots. 'Two or three, not more,' Raymond Aubrac notes, even though the Germans had machine guns.

Yet René Hardy was wounded in the arm. Even before hearing Barbie and Stengritt in 1948, the military court in 1946 learned from German witnesses that Hardy inflicted the wound himself. He stumbled down a bank and sought refuge at the home of Madame Damas, who says she saw him arrive in a car. He was to return there again after a second escape. Hardy's Prince of Wales plaid jacket was found after the war and examined by experts. Although the hole was carefully patched by Hardy's pretty mistress, Lydie Bastien, the experts studying the lining concluded that the bullet that went through his forearm was fired from a distance of less than 40 centimetres. But they were unable to identify the calibre. The Seine Court acquitted Hardy for the first time on 24 January 1947, but he was detained again two months later after the wagons-lit ticket inspector Alphonse Morice suddenly recalled the Chalon-sur-Saône incident. The ex-chief of the Service de Documentation Extérieure et de Contre-espionage (SDECE) Roger Wybot began fresh proceedings, and Hardy found himself in court a second time. At first his lawyer Maurice Garçon declined to attend, but then he changed his mind. This time the judges were from the military. The first time Hardy had been given the benefit of the doubt; this time he got off because the verdict was so close: the vote was four found him guilty, and three not guilty, including, no doubt, Fire Captain Curie, who declared that even if Hardy was guilty, five years was long enough in jail.

Laure Moulin, Max's sister, commented: 'These acquittals convinced neither myself nor the victims of the Caluire betrayal.' Only her connection with Jean Moulin prevented her from being cited for contempt of court.

As to the Caluire prisoners, in the confusion they were scarcely aware that one of their number, the man who had invited himself, had got away. And yet Raymond Aubrac was intrigued from the outset by the double anomaly – Hardy's attendance and escape. Those who remained, and were handcuffed with their hands behind their backs, were driven to the Ecole de Santé Militaire, where Barbie had just set up his operation. Moulin, Aubrac, Dugoujon and the Caluire baker from Alsace, Alfred Fischer, who unwisely witnessed the scene from behind a tree that was thinner than he was, were in the same jeep. On arrival they were put in the cellars to await questioning. Moulin, Aubrac and Schwarzfeld were allowed to sit down because they were held in less suspicion; the others had to stand facing the wall.

In spite of their good knowledge of the Resistance, the Germans still had not identified Jean Moulin. Barbie struck Lassagne several times, thinking he was Max. Lassagne was about the same age and of similar build to Moulin. The prisoners were interrogated by the Gestapo, and then taken back to their cells at night in Montluc jail about a mile away, where all the warders were German.

As they were brought in, each wrote his name and other details in the register:

* Dugoujon, Frédéric, bachelor, born 30 June 1913 at Champagne-au-Mont-d'Or, Catholic, doctor, French – Caluire, Place Castellane (cell 129)
* Lassagne, André-Louis, bachelor, born 23 April 1911 in Lyons, Catholic, lycée teacher, French – 302 Cours Lafayette (cell 117)
* Ermelin, Claude [Aubrac], bachelor, born 7 February 1912 in Lorient, Catholic, office worker, French – 25 rue Montesquieu, Lyons (cell 77)
* Lacaze, Albert, married, born 21 May 1884 at Latron-quiere, Protestant, artist, French – 34 rue du Professeur-Sisley, Lyons (cell 69)
* Aubry, Henri, married, born 3 March 191? at Longwy, Meurthe-et-Moselle, Catholic, French – Rully, Saône-et-Loire, former reserve officer (cell 75) [Later the German word 'Hosenträger' was added, meaning 'trouser braces'. This could signify that he was an agent, that the Germans held on to him with elastic.]
* Parisot, Laurent-Pierre [Bruno Larat], bachelor, born 2 April 1914 in Bordeaux, Catholic, assistant teacher, French – 20 rue Thomassin (cell 136)
* Martel, Jacques [Moulin], bachelor, born 22 August 1897 in Picquigny, Somme, Catholic, decorator, French – 17 rue Renan, Lyons (cell 130)
* Schwarzfeld, Exile-Lucas, married, born 5 December 1885 in Paris, engineer, Catholic, French – 4 Cours Vitton, Lyons (cell 65)

These pages from the Montluc register have now disappeared; someone tore them out.

One of the three survivors, Frédéric Dugoujon, told me: 'The cell seemed to pitch about, and the walls moved; there were thousands of bugs. Three days later I was twice my normal size.'

Yes, it was a good day's work for Klaus Barbie. He went back to the Hotel Bristol suite and relaxed. The rest could wait until tomorrow.

On 22 June the Gestapo arrested Aubry's secretary, Madame Madeleine Raisin, and they seized large quantities of money and documents. But Barbie was solely interested in Jean Moulin, though he still had to find out which one he was.

'Jacques Martel', still seemingly unhurt, walked around in the courtyard on the second day of his internment. He slid through two ranks of prisoners and approached Dr Dugoujon, who was looking down at his feet. He told him to lift up his head and added: 'I wish you *bon courage*.'

Harry Stengritt was to recall: 'The day of the arrests I had to go to Barbie's office for a signature. I did not raise the subject, but Barbie said he wasn't certain but the new prisoners probably included a highly important one, de Gaulle's representative in France. He added that he did not know which one.' He also said: 'As soon as we reached Rue Berthelot, Barbie started questioning the man he thought was this key figure, a primary interrogation I attended for about thirty minutes. I remember that the man, who was Moulin, did not reveal his true identity while I was there. I recollect, too, that he did a drawing of Barbie on a sheet of paper.'

Obersturmführer Barbie has not forgotten the drawing either. Since Jacques Martel claimed he was a decorator and artist, Barbie had given him paper and pencil.

Barbie said, 'Jean Moulin, alias Max, displayed magnificent bravery, attempting suicide several times by throwing himself down the cellar stairs and banging his head on the wall between interrogations. He persisted with his claim to be an artist and he even did a drawing of me and a sketch of the secretary.' (This was probably Miss Neumann.)

Klaus Barbie has stated that those drawings were lost in the May 1944 bomb attack on the Ecole de Santé Militaire.

When Bruno Larat spoke to Dr Dugoujon after being questioned the first time he said: 'They already know a great deal.'

Who had given this information? Very likely it was Aubry, who said as much later. Aubry yielded to torture, especially when the Germans staged his mock execution. He was stood up against a wall and the Germans fired two shots to his side.

Raymond Aubrac said: 'I saw Aubry in the Montluc yard bare to the waist and black from beating. He told me: "I've been beaten, I've talked."'

Jean Moulin revealed nothing, even when he was later confronted with Madame Raisin.

Stengritt said: 'Moulin's attitude was far braver. He admitted nothing, on the contrary, he tried every way he could to kill himself, and we had to protect him against himself.'

Barbie said: 'Moulin was interrogated by myself only in Lyons. He was subsequently transferred to Avenue Foch in Paris, in very bad shape medically, after his suicide attempts. Moulin admitted nothing to me, but he was never maltreated by our services in Lyons. After the transfer I lost track of him and never heard any more about him.'

Various witnesses have indicated that Jean Moulin was not identified until 23 June. This can be deduced from accounts by Raymond Aubrac and Dr Frédéric Dugoujon, whom I interviewed at length. Watching through the tiny peep-holes in their cells, both saw Jean Moulin horribly brutalised, in a semi-coma, being carried by German soldiers. At that date the doors on the Montluc cells had small holes through painted iron plates, with no glass or covering discs.

Aubrac said: 'I saw Max's face covered in blood, going off for more questioning. He was like a collapsed puppet.'

Henri Aubry also remembers the warders bringing back Moulin that evening around ten o'clock. Late in the afternoon Christian Pineau, alias Grimaux, head of the Libé-Nord movement, who was being kept on the first floor at Montluc, and who had been given the job of prison barber, was ordered to the north yard. A junior officer took him to a bench where a man was lying guarded by a soldier. 'Shave the gentleman!' Pineau leaned over, and recognized Max.

Pineau said later: 'Max was unconscious and his eyes were very sunken, as if they had been pushed into his head. He had a ghastly bluish wound on the temple, and his lips were all swollen. He made a soft rasping noise. There was no doubt about it, the Gestapo had tortured him.'

Pineau asked for some soap and water. The officer went for them. 'I was able to get really close to Max, touch his clothing, his freezing-cold hand, but he showed no reaction. When the soap and water came, I started, avoiding the tumefied parts. I wondered why they wanted to pretty-up a man condemned to die. Then suddenly Max opened his eyes and looked at me. I'm sure he recognized me, but how was he to understand what I was doing there? He said "Boire" – he was hardly audible. I said to the soldier: '*Ein wenig Wasser.*' He hesitated a moment but then took up the mug full of soapy water and rinsed it out and brought it back full of water. I bent over Max during that time and muttered a few words in an attempt to comfort him. I can't recall what. Max tried to say a few words in English, but I couldn't catch them because he could barely speak.'

Dr Dugoujon noticed the word '*allein*' (solitary) on Moulin's cell door, which indicated that they now knew. He also said that after the Germans tortured Moulin, they had a doctor called to his cell: 'That Thursday evening, 24 June, at twilight, they brought him back in a dreadful condition, two warders holding him up. They lay him on

Klaus Barbie. A photograph taken for Nazi files at the time of his engagement to Regina Willms. (BERLIN DOC. CENTRE)

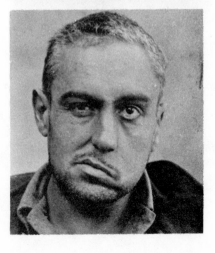

Opposite: The first round-up of Jews in Amsterdam, in February 1941. Negatives of these photographs, taken by a German soldier, were later found in the possession of the Dutch photographer who developed them. The man in a light coat (below, centre) could be Barbie. (R.I.O.D. AMSTERDAM)

Top left: Jean Multon alias Lunel, was turned by the Marseille Gestapo. (D.R.)

Top right: Robert Moog, Abwehr agent in Dijon. (D.R.)

Middle left: Henry Stengritt, head of Section IV in Lyons. (D.R.)

Middle right: Erich Bartelmus, specialist in hunting down Jews. (D.R.)

Right: Francis André, 'Crooked Jaw,' worked for the Gestapo in Lyons. (D.R.)

Left: The house in Caluire.
(DE HOYOS—SYGMA)

Below: Dr Frédéric Dugoujon (left) and Raymond Aubrac. (AUTHOR'S COLLECTION)

Opposite top left: André Lassagne. (KEYSTONE)

Top right: Colonel Albert Lacaze. (TALLANDIER)

Middle left: Bruno Larat alias Xavier. (TALLANDIER)

Middle right: Henry Aubry alias Thomas. He succumbed to torture by the Gestapo and betrayed the Resistance. (D.R.)

Below right: Raymond Aubrac alias Ermelin with his resourceful wife, Lucie, who saved him from execution. (D.R.)

Left: Jean Moulin. (MOBA PRESSE)

Below: René Hardy at the end of the first trial in 1947, which acquitted him of collaborating with the Germans. He is reaching out to embrace the man who successfully defended him, Maître Maurice Garçon. (KEYSTONE)

Above right: The summary execution that took place on the Place Bellecour. (CHEVALLIER)

Below right: The exact number of victims of the Saint-Genis-Laval massacre, 20 August 1944, has never been established. Having visited the scene shortly afterwards, Cardinal Gerlier told the Gestapo authorities: 'Those responsible are for ever disgraced in the eyes of humanity.' (D.R.)

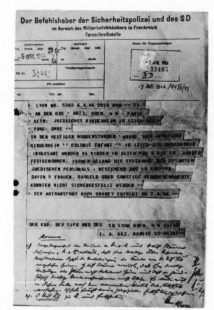

Left: The telegram signed by Barbie informing the Gestapo in Paris of the arrest and deportation of the children from Izieu. Barbie disputes the authenticity of the document and has pointed out the anomaly of the two French date-stamps (AVR for *avril*, not the German *April*). (AFP)

Below: On 6 April 1944 the Germans arrested 41 children at the Jewish children's home at Izieu. All the children died during deportation. (KLARSFELDCOLLECTION)

the straw mattress, leaving the door open, then watched over him all night in case he committed suicide. Next day they took him away. I never saw him again.'

What happened on 25 June is partially revealed by Gottlieb Fuchs, though the old Swiss man is no longer capable of saying much. It could be fatigue, emotion, loss of memory – he is eighty years old – or maybe a feeling of shame at his none too glorious past. He showed me his striped deportee's jacket, number 44110, at his apartment in Saint-Gall, with its inverted red triangle to show he was a political prisoner. He has a better recollection of the camps at Bergen Belsen, Buchenwald and Dora than of his time in Lyons, where Barbie used him as an 'interpreter'. Actually Barbie had no need of a translator, but he required someone to sort out the visitors calling at the École de Santé and show them the right offices where they could divulge their information, a task sometimes needing a linguist because not all the Germans were as fluent as Barbie.

We can put more faith perhaps in the veracity of a book Fuchs wrote after Barbie was unmasked in Bolivia, entitled *Le Renard*.

Gottlieb Fuchs was promoted to Generaldometscher (chief translator) and called himself Herr Doktor Edouard Rochard. Fuchs recalls some precise details, such as the way Barbie would gracefully run a hand through his hair, whistling the Hitler Youth song, and some photos of Ute munching Swiss chocolate before she was a year old, and a story about some pounds sterling he had stacked away in Bavaria somewhere. But he remembers little about the torture sessions.

Here is part of Fuchs' account taken from his book: 'It was 4.00 p.m. and I was on my own in the reception hall. There was a guard on the main steps next to the porch. I heard a clatter upstairs and someone was running down the stairs pulling a heavy object that bounced on the steps. I was facing the stairs directly and saw Barbie in shirt-sleeves, dragging a man by his feet. When he reached the hall, he took a breather but kept one foot on the man. Red-faced and with his hair flopping over his forehead, he lunged towards the cellar, dragging the man by a strap tied to his feet. The prisoner's face was badly bruised and his jacket was in shreds.

'When he came up again from the cellar, Barbie strode past with his head down, his fists clenched, talking wildly. I distinctly heard him bark: "If he doesn't peg out tonight, I'll finish him off tomorrow in Paris." Then he climbed the stairs, stamping his feet.

'I was on very good terms with the new guard, and I could rely on that soldier if I wanted to take a look round the cellar . . . I found the prisoner lying on his belly on the ground, half naked. His jacket had been taken off and thrown in a corner. His back was lacerated, his chest seemed caved in. I rolled him over on his side and folded up what was left of his jacket and put it under his head as a pillow. His eyes were shut, but he was still breathing. I wiped the blood off his eyebrows, and he seemed to be coming round. I was caught up in his silence, which was probably worth more than his life.

'The soldier stood next to me, shocked. I knew he supported my gesture; he kept shaking his head, saying: "All this is going to finish badly." I am certain he meant for the Germans.

'I found out that the man who had been dragged down like some filthy carcass was a prefect. Next day when I went on duty I discovered that this same man had been removed from the jail.'

In 1983 Gottlieb Fuchs told me: 'That is what I am prepared to declare on my honour in court.'

But what was Fuchs going to say when the court asked him what he, a Swiss citizen, was doing in Lyons? Will he recall that, after he was liberated from the camp with his jacket as evidence of helping the Resistance, he had to explain himself to the French and Swiss authorities? We shall never know, for he died a year later on 2 February 1984.

On Friday evening, 25 June, André Lassagne, Dr Dugoujon, Colonels Lacaze and Schwarzfeld, Henri Aubry with his secretary, were taken to Perrache station and put on a train for Paris. There they joined General Delestraint in Fresnes prison; by then he had been held for sixteen days.

Barbie recounts: 'The Sipo-SD HQ in Paris ordered the immediate transfer of Moulin to their offices, and I personally took Jean Moulin by car [probably on Friday, 25 June]. I handed him over to Sturmbannführer Bömelburg, and it was Section IV E, run by Kieffer, who took charge of him.'

Here is what was said by Commandant Flicoteaux, Government Commissioner at the Paris military court where Gestapo chiefs Oberg and Knochen were tried at a hearing on 14 September 1954: 'The maltreatment [by Barbie] was so bad that when Jean Moulin was taken by car from Lyons to Paris he had to be helped out by Misselwitz when he arrived.'

The doomed Moulin went to Avenue Foch but was taken almost at once to the villa for important prisoners at 40 Boulevard Victor-Hugo at Neuilly-sur-Seine, where Karl Bömelburg, who had been a central-heating installer in Paris before the war and was now the Gestapo's Section IV top man for the whole of France, would treat his 'guests' with a little more courtesy.

I tracked down his boss, Colonel Helmut Knochen, a few months ago in West Germany, an elderly but handsome figure of a man with blue eyes and a full head of blond hair, just back from some arthrosis treatment in Italy and sporting a suntan.

He confided to me: 'Bömelburg was furious, I remember, when he learned how Jean Moulin had been treated. One day Klaus Barbie cabled to Berlin that he had captured a key Resistance leader. Berlin told him to send him at once to be questioned there. Klaus Barbie, a short upstart of a fellow, realized he had brought off a first-class coup, and was annoyed at the idea that others would cash in on his triumph. He decided to start the interrogation himself, just to show Berlin what he was capable of doing. What a mistake!'

Helmut Knochen, still fluent in French after spending eighteen years in France as a prisoner, went on: 'Unless I am mistaken, Jean Moulin said right away that he was the representative of de Gaulle's government, but we had caught so many fellows who claimed to represent the General. We got our fingers burnt. When Jean Moulin was brought to Paris we notified Berlin and, as they were unaware of his condition, they told us to send him to Germany.'

Knochen's story ties in with Barbie's. Knochen said of Barbie, whom he met occasionally at meetings with Bömelburg: 'A fanatical Resistance hunter, very active, very keen. What he did after the war shows he was smart enough to look after himself.'

Late in June 1943 the whole group was held at Fresnes prison, except for the youthful Xavier (Larat) and Raymond Aubrac. Larat was not there because the Gestapo in Lyons was still grilling him about the parachute drops. Aubrac seems to have been overlooked; he was not classified with the others, who were treated under the so-called *Nacht und Nebel* (NN – 'night and fog') procedure, which called for total secrecy. Raymond Aubrac was not interrogated by Barbie until 28 June.

At Fresnes, Jean-Louis Théobald was quite near Jean Moulin's cell. He recalls: 'I could communicate with Moulin, who was on the first floor. He urged me to stick it out and not succumb, saying we had been betrayed.'

In February 1984, Monsieur Théobald revealed to me that at least two persons spoke of contact with Moulin in the Gestapo building. The first was Suzette Olivier, arrested shortly after he was. The other was General Delestraint (Vidal).

Théobald said: 'I met Vidal a dozen times at Fresnes prison. He told the Germans when he was taken that he was a general, and that he was de Gaulle's superior before

1940, so he had the right to an armchair and a mirror in his cell. Sometimes, on Wednesdays, mass was said there; there was no shortage of priests in the prison. I could chat to him then, or else in the anthropometry service, or in the vans that took us to Avenue Foch for interrogation. Delestraint spoke about his talks with Moulin . . . I don't remember exactly what Moulin said to him, but I remember that Delestraint and Moulin had the same suspicions.'

A few days later Aubry and Delestraint saw the CNR president again in the Gestapo offices. Barbie was there.

Aubry said: 'Jean Moulin was lying on a reclining chair, and did not move. He showed no sign of life, seemed to be in a coma . . . Barbie came in and clicked his heels very loudly in front of Bömelburg, who stood chain-smoking. Bömelburg told Barbie in German: "I hope they come through this."* They took away Jean Moulin on his sofa-cum-stretcher. Delestraint and the rest of us tried to comfort him.'

Then Aubry came out with this surprising remark: 'They knew that he was Jean Moulin, and he had swallowed a cyanide capsule. The SS man Misselwitz said so, and he said, "We'll save him!"'

How Aubry came to believe the story about the cyanide is of little importance; what counts is the phrase 'We'll save him.' It confirms that Berlin had given orders for the president of the CNR to be hospitalized in Germany in some distant locality where he would not be kidnapped – probably the police hospital in Berlin.

At Neuilly, General Delestraint and André Lassagne saw Moulin in his pitiful state. On return from deportation, André Lassagne described the scene, which he thought took place probably between 10 and 13 July. 'Max was lying on a divan with his head in bandages; his face

* Aubry knew German, but on another occasion he claims Bömelburg said: 'I hope he comes through this; you'll be lucky if he does.'

was yellow and he looked dreadful. He could hardly breathe and the only feature showing any sign of life was his eyes.'

Asked by the Germans to identify the man, Lassagne and General Delestraint detected a warning in Max's eyes, and the general said: 'I cannot recognize Max in this man.' This has been altered in the legend that has come down to us and Delestraint is quoted as saying: 'Monsieur, military honour forbids me to recognize Max in this pitiful shell of a man .'

Heinrich Meiners, the Gestapo interpreter, told at a hearing in Germany on 14 December 1946: 'The body was covered with cuts and bruises, and the chief organs showed internal bruising due to earlier blows, either from coshing or kicking.'

It was not until 19 October 1943 that the official announcement was made of Jean Moulin's death.

The Gestapo in Montpellier sent a courier to inform Jean Moulin's sister Laure of her brother's death. He told her: 'Death was due to cardiac failure.'

6

THE MOMENT LUCIE AUBRAC heard of the group's arrest, she sprang into action. When she described to me what she set out to do, as we sat together years later, I was amazed at her daring. Not that she made much of it, for this courageous woman was very modest.

At the time, Lucie Aubrac was a history teacher at the Lycée Edgar-Quinet (now called Edouard-Herriot). She knew at once what would impress the Germans. Madame Aubrac assumed the name of Mademoiselle Ghislaine de Barbentanne, daughter of a *'cadre noir'* at the renowned Saumur equestrian college. You could not get much higher than that and the SS would know it. She told me: 'At first I thought of telling them I was Max's fiancée, but the trouble was I didn't know under which name he had been arrested. So I decided to become Claude Ermelin's girlfriend, which meant I was my husband's bride-to-be! Well, it worked.'

Barbie scowled across at her from the desk in one corner of the large first-floor room next to a fireplace. The Obersturmführer wore a light-coloured suit and sported a pale green shirt.

He pulled open a drawer and threw a wallet onto the desk. Photos flew out, one of them showing Lucie and Raymond Aubrac on a beach playing with a child. Barbie did not ask who the child was.

'This guy comes from Saint-Paul,' growled Barbie. 'He was let out on bail.' Saint-Paul was one of the Lyons jails where Raymond Aubrac, using the name Vallet, was held in March.

Faced with the photo, Lucie feigned innocence and became confused. She said, 'Saint-Paul? Well, of course, we went to Saint-Paul-de-Vence a while back.'

Barbie was taken by surprise. The young 'fiancée'

began to sway, and almost fainted. She was pregnant. She started to weep, furious that she had weakened with Barbie. But suddenly she had an idea. 'I'd like to ask you a favour. Allow me to marry him. I am expecting a baby.'

Klaus Barbie perked up, pleased at being implored by the young lady; he liked people to appeal to his sense of honour. But on this occasion he was reluctant to make a decision.

Mademoiselle de Barbentanne left without discovering where Max and the others were being held. What she did learn, through friends, was that René Hardy had been arrested by the French police and transferred to the Antiquaille Hospital, run by the Germans, on 22 June. Lucie was convinced that Hardy had given away the Resistance men, and she decided to poison him by sending him a food parcel containing a jar of jam laced with cyanide – a small jar, so that he would keep it to himself and not share it with anyone else. Hardy did not eat it; the reason is unclear. He said later that he knew Madame Aubrac had tried to poison him.

On the following Tuesday, 29 June, her birthday, Lucie went back to Barbie, going straight past the guard without stopping. Within a minute she was softly opening Barbie's office door.

The Section IV chief snapped at her: 'Ermelin lied to you. They're all terrorists. What they need is a tot of rum and a dozen bullets in them!' Whereupon he slammed the door in her face.

Lucie Aubrac went off and told her wedding tale to another German, who grew accommodating with the aid of a little money, some cigarettes, champagne and silk. 'They took it all and it never occurred to them that they might be betraying Germany,' she sighed.

The upshot was that her story stuck; the Germans agreed to the wedding. Lucie and a friend, Maurice David, made a trip to Switzerland and came back with guns. Lucie was a member of Ravanel's movement, who made plans to kidnap her 'fiancé'. It could not be done at Montluc; the only chance was to bring about his transfer.

She suggested 21 September as the date for the wedding, the anniversary of their first meeting, and the Germans agreed. Looking appropriately nubile, Ghislaine de Barbentanne turned up in a hat with a veil, and Raymond could only blink.

He recounts: 'She drew close to me to kiss me and whispered in my ear: "You jump first." So I knew right away that an attack was planned. For the journey back to Montluc with the other prisoners I got myself chained to the youngest of them, a lad who would not be scared if things got hot. I was sure he would jump from the truck and we climbed up last.'

Ravanel's people were waiting on the Boulevard des Hirondelles; they had decided to use an umbrella for the rallying signal. Unfortunately the sky was completely cloudless, so the planned attack had to be abandoned. But at least they now knew the prison vans took that route.

Back in Montluc, Raymond Aubrac was expecting to be taken to the École de Santé again for interrogation. He told me: 'Barbie liked to hit people. I was handcuffed with my hands behind my back and he hit me: "Where's Bernard [d'Astier]?" "Where's Charvet [Henri Frenay]?" "Where's the money?"' Aubrac said in a hearing on 9 December 1948 that Barbie had precise information, in particular a 52-page document that was based on the interrogation of Aubry. 'I passed out a dozen times under questioning. During the grilling, Barbie would kick me back to life, and sometimes I would come round to see him with a woman on his lap, lipstick on his shirt. He loved to show off his power,' Aubrac said.

One day the Germans read out his death sentence to him, as handed down by some court or other. 'I wanted only one thing then, the firing squad. I didn't want to die like some of us, with a bullet in the neck in the cellars, like dogs. No, I wanted to face the bullets.'

A fellow prisoner, publisher Paul Lardanchet, released in August, took Aubrac's wedding ring to his wife. And then Aubrac simply waited for death.

But Lucie told the Germans the wedding had to be legal, that the spouses had to go before a notary. A month later on 21 October the same procedure as in September took place, but she wore no veil this time. The commando group was ready. It included Mario Blardone, who was trying to assassinate Barbie. Two trucks came into view and there was no telling which one contained Aubrac. The group selected the first vehicle, shooting the driver dead. The prisoners escaped, though some were later caught. As instructed, Raymond Aubrac jumped first. He was hit in the cheek. He told me: 'I shall never forget it. The attack took place just as the factory workers were going home. Right in the middle of the square, one factory worker running for cover was protecting himself from the bullets with his bike, of all things!'

Aubrac was operated on by Dr Joie – the bullet had only passed through the cheek – and he stayed in Les Presles clinic in Pollionay. The Aubracs' second child, Catherine, was born in London on 12 February 1944.

André Frossard wrote a book, *La Maison des Otages*, that admirably describes the Jews' hut, where he was held for nine months. He noted at the close of 1944: 'When you get to know Lucie Aubrac, you are closer to understanding Jeanne d'Arc.' The story of Aubrac's escape along with thirteen companions reached the prison, and everyone knew that from that time on prisoners would be heavily guarded in transit.

The German pressure on the Resistance eased up for a few weeks. In the eyes of the Gestapo, the Caluire swoop had been a numbing blow for the various movements. It seems that Barbie was away from Lyons between the end of August and early December 1943. Barbie ordered a search of Delestraint's house in Bourg-en-Bresse, without result.

During the 1948 interrogation, Barbie said: 'I stayed in the French capital until 5 December 1943, when I returned to my post in Lyons. In the course of this absence I went to

Germany and Northern Italy to work on the *Rote Kapelle* business.'*

Herr Barbie had cause to feel pleased with himself. Even though Jean Moulin had died, Himmler, the SS Reichsführer, had personally congratulated him for his 'outstanding achievements in the criminal police and his unstinting commitment in the fight against the Resistance organization in France' (letter dated 18 September 1943).

The period of the mass executions begins about this time. The first appears to have taken place on 4 November 1943. The French inquiry revealed no useful details; at that time the Lyons police were not particularly curious. One police report read: 'No. 3029. Death in violent circumstances of eight persons at the German police headquarters . . . The German officer [sic] showed us the bodies of eight persons laid out on the ground in a cellar at the end of the passage, some on their backs, others face down, in a pool of blood.' The names given by the Germans were then listed, eight men, aged thirty-one to forty-seven, four French and four Polish. Not one word on how they died.

On 10 January 1944, in these same cellars at the École de Santé, twenty-two hostages, arrested at random, were killed by machine-gun fire the day that two German soldiers were killed in the Saint-Clair district. To account for the bodies, the Germans said that the deceased had tried to escape. The French police noted this and took away the bodies. Commissaire Adrien Richard was told by an officer that the people were killed because they attacked. He said later: 'It was in the middle of the night when we went down to the basement. As we entered the passage we caught the pungent smell of warm blood. The cell door was opened by a junior officer, and a frightful sight it was: there were bodies stacked in one corner of the cell in a pool of blood. They were young men, and had

* The Red Orchestra European counter-espionage network headed in France by the Communist Léopold Trepper

been machine-gunned as they faced the door. While my superior officer was engaged in conversation, I saw about 180 or so machine-gun cartridge cases on a table. I counted them.'

This incident was recalled by Alexandre Angeli, sometime prefect of Rhône, during the trial of Gestapo chiefs Oberg and Knochen. He said: 'Knab was away, and we dealt with Lieutenant Barbie. All he said was that it occurred after a riot, when the young men threatened the warders, who had been forced to defend themselves.'

Under the west wing of the grey building there were three cellars specially prepared for inmates due to be taken to Montluc. They were packed like sardines for days. Inspector Chardon recalled: 'In room 6 on the ground floor, prisoners underwent their initial questioning before they went up to the fourth floor. On this floor there were several baths, and gas burners to heat up iron bars that were used on the inmates. The bath torture was common and many patriots underwent that ordeal several times. The torture methods varied. Apart from beatings, scaldings, and the bath-duckings, the men were tortured on the private parts. Electric wires were inserted in their penises or they were injected with tincture of iodine.'

In most of the post-war police reports used at the military hearings, Klaus Barbie was described in the following terms: 'He was the worst bastard of the bunch, and observed the torture of all prisoners.'*

Pol Chavet, arrested on 23 August 1943 because of an informer, says: 'Barbie seemed to get real pleasure from hitting people himself.' Chavet was forced to kneel on the cutting edge of a spade in the Gestapo headquarters.

A spade, a metal bath, dogs – they occur repeatedly in the dozens of accounts I have heard. They provide a fairly clear idea of the methods used to make prisoners speak. We can add hair pulled out, toenails extracted, mock

* Evidence of Armand Zuchner, formerly interpreter attached to the regional prefecture of Lyons

—— 100 ——

executions – the stuff of X-rated horror films.

Monsieur Jaubert-Jaunage saw Barbie coshing a young girl and breaking her legs. Monsieur Ducros had his nails torn out, his skin burned with acid and part of a chair was used to impale him. He recalls that the Gestapo's top man was named Klaus and that he oversaw all the interrogations and executions. Klaus broke a bottle of acid over Ducros's head and used a piece of the glass to slash the belly of another prisoner.

Then there is the account of Charles Perrin, who was 'executed' after being questioned day and night. They asked him: 'Do you know Thorez and Duclos?'* He remained silent.

In 1948 he said: 'I was taken into a torture chamber on the second floor. Barbie stayed. They took all my clothes off and clapped handcuffs on me. They put a wooden stick under my knees and tucked the ends under my armpits, then they dipped me in the bath. Barbier [sic] poured water in my mouth and eyes. I was transferred to Montluc. On 16 June I was taken to Saint-Didier-de-Formans where I was shot.'

He was indeed shot. But the Germans failed to kill every victim, and there were two survivors, Perrin and a man named Crespo, who escaped with wounds. Berlin would not have approved!

That was the kind of testimony sent to the Nazi-haven Bolivia thirty years later. The question of crimes against humanity had not arisen yet, only that of war crimes.

Among the episodes leading to Barbie's first death sentence pronounced *in absentia*, on 29 April 1952, was the Saint-Claude affair, which took place in April 1944. The FFI (Forces Françaises de l'Interieur – the Free French Forces), had inflicted heavy losses on a company of mountain troops from the Wehrmacht, and the Germans planned reprisals, using the customary 'police dogs' in the form of SD experts. The Lyons regional Gestapo chief was

* Leaders of the French Communist party

in the Oyonnax area, and we find that Barbie himself decided to lead his Lyons detachment on this operation.

Auguste Lathelier, the official investigator, said in his report of 20 July 1950: 'As head of this detachment and SD officer, Barbie had precedence over all other officers in the Wehrmacht, even those of senior rank to him.'

So it was that between 7 and 20 April 1944, immediately after the swoop in the Izieu Jewish children's home, Barbie wreaked vengeance in the Jura – killing, torturing, looting, raising fires, ordering deportations.

On 8 April a detachment of Germans under Barbie set up a command post in the school of Larrivoire. The teacher, Roseline Blonde, fled to the Maquis.

The first target was 74-year-old Joseph Perrin, beaten up because he supplied food to the Resistance. He was later shot at the hamlet of La Verrane. The next day Barbie was in the main square at Saint-Claude where the town crier declared on that Easter Sunday before high mass: 'By order of the German authorities, all men aged eighteen to forty-five will proceed to the Place au Pré this 9 April 1944 before ten o'clock. Any man found inside a house after ten o'clock will be shot at once without trial, including those who are ill.' The police inspectors from Dijon, who later heard witnesses by the dozen, said the manuscript order was not written by Barbie but 'was certainly instigated by him'.

With little idea of what was happening, the men gathered in the square holding their identity cards. Barbie organized the selection, the investigator said. As a result 307 men were crammed into buses and trucks and taken to the girls' high school, where they remained for some days before deportation to Germany. Only 152 came back from the camps in June 1945, in shocking condition.

One survivor was a pharmaceutical student, Pierre Vincent, who recounted: 'The journey was made in cattle trucks, which were sealed. There were 100 to 120 of us to a wagon when it could take only 40. It was so bad that several people died on the way, probably suffocated beause there were only two small barred apertures. We were in the trucks four days and three nights, and they were never opened. All we had to eat was a lump of bread when we started. Some of the men became raving mad, but they were not taken out, nor were the ones who died.'

Barbie may not have been responsible for the train journey itself, but he made the arrests and selected the men; the confessions of numerous French 'auxiliaries' tell us so. The investigators were told Barbie was 5 feet 4 inches to 5 feet 6 inches tall, fairly stocky, had a hard expression in his eyes, spoke French fluently and wore a white wrapper round his neck. Police officers at the trial showed witnesses a photo, and they identified him.

In his SS uniform, the reprisals supremo set up his headquarters at the Hôtel de France on the Avenue de Belfort (the retreat route). The hotel was anything but four-star but it had a good baker's shop opposite. Barbie had room 50; there is proof that he was there on that day, because his signature is on a pass issued on 9 April to Madame Claire Authier, aged sixty-eight, the only person allowed in the streets of Saint-Claude between 9.00 p.m. and 11.00 p.m. in her capacity as regional president of the Red Cross.

For trips outside Saint-Claude, Barbie used a machine-gun carrier, and he always took a Frenchman with him.

On 11 April he was at Villars-Saint-Sauveur looking for Resistance people. With his Frenchman, he entered a hotel, questioned the manager, Monsieur Joly, who said he had no one staying there. Barbie found a Tyrolean bag, climbing boots and a map.

'What about that?'

Monsieur Joly said nothing. Barbie shot him on the stairs.

The man he really wanted was Major 'Vallin', whose real name was Jean Duhail. To find out more, he arrested Jean Vincent, head of the local gendarmerie at Les Bouchoux. Vincent was taken off, tortured and killed. The Germans burned the body at Les Fournets, where four other bodies were later found. Worried about her husband, Marie-Augustine Vincent went to the Hôtel de France. Barbie, on his way out, said jauntily: 'Your husband, Madame? I lost him coming back from Les Bouchoux.' At that very moment his body and the four others were smouldering at Les Fournets. Several months afterwards, that was where Madame Vincent found his wedding ring, a stainless steel ring made by a relative.

April 12 was just as busy for the Obersturmführer, who embarked on a trip to Coyrière.

Madame Germaine Clément stated: 'Barbie questioned my husband, demanding to know if he had taken in and cared for some maquisards. My husband denied it, but Barbie started torturing him right away, hitting him with a cudgel. The thing broke, but he carried on with a cosh. Barbie got nothing out of him. He collected all the men in the village square and asked them about the maquisards going through.'

The SS grabbed six young men. One of them, Monneret, was so scared he agreed with everything Barbie said. That was all the pretext Barbie needed, and he started his executions. Monneret and Clément were among those whose bodies were burned at Les Fournets.

Then on 13 April Barbie was pretty sure he had got Major Vallin, but he wanted to make certain. He detained a businessman, Baptiste Baroni, and had him taken to a saw mill called Vers l'Eau. The group halted by the cadaver of Gaston Patel from Mollinges, who had just been shot.

'If you do not tell the truth, you will end up the same way.'

Barbie put his questions. Did he know Major Vallin? No. The rear door of a nearby truck was flung open and a young man named Potard, arrested three weeks earlier, was dragged out, his face swollen, bloated, and purple with beating.

'You know him?'

'No.'

'That's enough lies.'

Potard is supposed to have said: 'I know him, but he doesn't know me.' The Germans told him to run. Potard staggered a few yards, then plunged to the ground under a stream of machine-gun bullets.

Shortly after that Baroni was brought face to face with 'Vallin'. No reaction from Baroni.

On his return from Buchenwald, Baroni recalled: 'They got the Major up in a truck and made him lie on his stomach, hands tied behind his back. They told me to look in the direction of the clearing and said I had five minutes to come clean. Then they pretended to shoot me, but they fired in the air.'

Baroni was thrown down next to Vallin in the truck. He spotted a French auxiliary, Lucien Doussot, in German uniform.

The truck went to Viry, where everybody got out. The villagers were brought together and Barbie displayed Vallin on the top of his machine-gun carrier. Vallin knew the houses there would be set fire to, so he publicly claimed responsibility for the Maquis operations. Barbie had his man at last, and they took him to a wood.

On 21 June 1950, Baroni said: 'The two Germans who shot young Potard killed Major Vallin with a burst in the back, under orders from Barbie.'

Questioned later, the collaborator Lucien Doussot said he had nothing to do with Vallin's killing: 'It was Barbie who told me about it, and he said he was a first-class Frenchman who kept his dignity to the last.'

A few minutes before the Vallin slaying, a youngster, René Mermet, made the mistake of saying something to the Germans in their own language. They told him to run, and then they fired at him. He dodged about, found a ditch and according to eye-witnesses tried to get away along a path, but he was shot near his home. Meanwhile a woman teacher, Laurette Borsotti, was being interrogated by Barbie and two others. He wanted to know how she came to be in possession of three tons of rice. Barbie, still wearing his white scarf (made, it was said, from British parachute cloth), ordered the rice to be loaded on a truck. The hut where it had been kept was set on fire. At that moment René Mermet was running through the village. Laurette recalls: 'They fired from my window, too. Barbie grabbed a machine gun and started shooting. When he stopped, I heard him say: "He's not moving, he must be dead."'

Shortly afterwards the acting mayor of Saint-Claire, Eugène Delorme, went to Lyons to see the Obersturm-führer, whom he had seen on a balcony organizing the looting of the La Fraternelle co-operative building, from which 15,500,000 francs' worth of goods were stolen. Delorme was taken to office 81 at the École de Santé Militaire, where Barbie told him: 'The object of my visit was to check the Aryan quality of Joseph and Pierre Durandot and to obtain information about arrested persons.' The Butcher of Lyons also declared pithily: 'I hope it was a good lesson for Saint-Claude.' He went on to explain that the incident was due to slackness in responding to the STO (Service du Travail Obligatoire – compulsory labour in Germany). Monsieur Delorme added: 'Barbie told me he himself killed Monneret, the mayor of Villars-Saint-Sauveur, because he hid Captain Kemmler, supplies director and head of a Maquis group.'

Kemmler was a Resistance hero. German soldiers testified to his murder and recounted Barbie's brutal methods in such detail that in the 1980s West Germany again demanded Barbie's extradition from Bolivia.

Joseph Kemmler was an old-timer, fifty-five years old. He was a supplies official working for the Vichy Government, but also head of the Secret Army in Saint-Claude. Born in Lyons, the only son of a hairdresser from Alsace, he had an honourable military career behind him, with several medals and three bars to his Croix de Guerre. Kemmler was removed from the army reserves list in January 1943, and then joined the Resistance under cover of his supplies job, which was useful for making contacts. His alias was 'Jomarc'.

In April 1944 he was given away by the same man who pointed out Major Vallin to Barbie. Barbie had Kemmler brought to the Hôtel de France. On the interrogation that follows, we have the valuable testimony of the German corporal Alfons Glas, who was at the High Command of the 99th Regiment, First Battalion of Alpine troops garrisoned at Briançon from early October 1943, and who were sent to Saint-Claude to isolate the town. The account of Glas, twenty-four at the time, demonstrates how far apart were the Gestapo and the Wehrmacht.

He said: 'Klaus Barbie stood out because of his attitude, which was presumptuous and even arrogant. We soldiers were unpleasantly surprised to see that he felt no need to respect our officers with a salute. His belt was always hanging down crooked on one side where his pistol holder was attached. He carried a 9mm American pistol and he often had an American repeater pistol with him. He always wore gloves and he was a man without fear. He used to go around the town with no protection and he obviously had no fear of being shot by the partisans.'

Alfons Glas recalled the day the SS changed the hotel's first-floor dining-room into an interrogation centre: 'I was there. The prisoners had to stand leaning against the wall with their hands up . . . I was in the middle of the room, where they had several tables, and there was a piano, too. It was obvious that one of the prisoners was a local ranking member of the French Resistance. The rumour was that he was a section leader by the name of Kemmler, from Alsace. Kemmler was the oldest prisoner there . . . Barbie came into the dining-room only when the prisoners were all there. One of the SS men told the prisoners to turn round and I remember they were scared when they saw Barbie come in. Barbie asked some questions of the other civilians and quickly got to Kemmler. He questioned him in French, and Kemmler just kept saying "Never". After a while, Barbie, still wearing gloves, hit Kemmler in the face, repeated his questions, hit him again. After three or four times Kemmler started bleeding from the nose and the mouth. Barbie went across to the piano a few yards away and with his blood-stained gloves on, struck up with the song *"Parlez-moi d'amour"*.'

By nightfall Joseph Kemmler was the only prisoner still held at the hotel. Another German soldier, Alexander Bartl, stated that Kemmler was taken upstairs where the Gestapo dipped him alternately in cold and scalding water. The interrogation resumed the next day in another room separated from the dining-room by a glass partition. Alfons Glas was there again, watching. Before Barbie arrived, he watched two Frenchmen in SS uniforms take turns beating Kemmler. Barbie arrived. Glas saw everything but could not hear Barbie's questions.

Glas continued: 'The interrogation lasted an hour to an hour and a half, but by then Kemmler could not stand up, so the two Frenchmen dragged Kemmler to a chair, one with armrests so that he would not fall sideways. They stopped the questions and after about ten minutes Barbie and the two others left. Kemmler could see everything, though his head was slouched forward a little. He followed us with his eyes. After roughly half an hour, his eyelids trembled, he closed his eyes and his head slumped forward. Five minutes after that, a pool of urine formed under Kemmler's chair and I knew he was dead.'

Kemmler's death and that of the others meant Barbie had no reason to stay in Saint-Claude. On 22 April 1948 Lucien Doussot told a hearing: 'The night before the SD men and the officers left, they danced in the hotel. There were two or three girls. I don't know whether they were informers.'

These incidents were on Barbie's charge sheet on 29 April 1952, which meant the prescription came into effect on 29 April 1972 at midnight. There was hardly anyone in court that day; Barbie was already in South America and defence counsel was not provided, because, by law, accused persons cannot be defended *in absentia*. Barbie was found guilty at this first trial of 11 murders: Joly; Monneret,

Robert; Parrin, Joseph; Clément, Osias; Monneret, René [probably a mistake for Mermet]; Kemmler; Alphandari [stated to be a Jew]; Vincent; Patel, Gaston; Duhail, Jean, alias Vallin; and Potard. Barbie was also found guilty of complicity in looting, of complicity in arson and of deporting 300 French nationals. By law, any one of these crimes was enough for the death sentence, and the death sentence was handed down by the court after a meandering trial without the accused and without counsel.

Barbie's boss, Colonel Werner Knab, got hard labour for life for 'arbitrary imprisonment'. This did not worry Knab, who was dead, but Judge Vuillermoz did not know that.

The trial cost 5,900 francs. The clerk noted: 'The condemned persons have no known domicile or residence, and it was not possible to post the sentence at the town hall of such domiciles.'

The Obersturmführer continued his work until the United States Air Force bombed the École de Santé, among several targets, on 26 May 1944, killing a number of SS officers, including Wenzel, Hollert and Welti.

When confronted with witnesses in February 1948, one of the SD leaders in Chambéry, Ludwig Heinson, said: 'Barbie came from Lyons with a list . . . he had eight or ten men with him for the executions. Barbie represented the higher authority . . .'

Captain Poignet, the military judge, asked Ludwig Heinson: 'And the setting fire to 43 houses on 1 May 1944?'

Heinson: 'It was Barbie with his men, especially Crooked Jaw. I know he had a lot of houses set on fire [at École-en-Bauges], whereas the Wehrmacht officer wanted just the house where the weapons were found.'

'The twelve people shot, and the other fires?'

'That could only be Barbie!'

Several police officers and magistrates have questioned dozens of witnesses about a host of other crimes. Barbie always comes to the surface. Sometimes he is referred to as Lieutenant von Barbier, and it was not until 1951 that the Lyons court realised that Barbie and von Barbier were the same man.

Also sentenced to death was the French SD auxiliary Lucien Guesdon. Questioned at Montluc prison while awaiting execution, he said: 'I saw Barbie himself execute two people at Evosges, Brun and someone else whose name escapes me.'

The report by police officer René Blanc dated 30 April 1946 quoted Guesdon as saying: 'Von Barbier was regarded among SD men as a highly intelligent person but an unrivalled sadist. One day he had all the SD personnel in and, as they looked on, he himself hanged two SD men he had arrested the day before.'

Prior to the massacres of 1944, Klaus Barbie apparently went after just one kind of Resistance member – those in contact with London. And he was also interested in more important Resistance fighters. For example, he boasted to the French auxiliaries that he managed to win over a radio operator named Claude, doubtless a code name.

The previous autumn he had instructed his friend Harry Stengritt to get in touch with a young Frenchman he had seized, then later released when he agreed to work for the Reich. Stengritt stated at Tübingen on 13 December 1948: 'Claude was seized by Barbie while transmitting secretly for the Resistance. I was confronted with him by Barbie at Villeurbanne just outside Lyons. The man was ordered to contact his former leaders and keep us informed of any news. For this purpose I saw the man again twice a week at the above-mentioned place. After three weeks he told me he had contacted his leaders and that he had been selected to go to England . . . I notified Barbie, who went with me to the next meeting. He talked with Claude, advised him to obey the order and to report to the Funk-Kommando Werth (Werth radio section) so he could work out a code and communicate with him from England. A week later Claude was summoned by an unknown person to Perrache railway station. Barbie was told at once and followed him. Claude and the other person left by train. A week after that he came back and said the England trip was put back . . . I met up with Claude again early in October [1943] at the office of Section IV. He was injured from a shot by agent K30 [Moog, Barbie's rival from the Abwehr], with whom he had fixed a meeting and who took him for a Resistance man. I got him to hospital right away. A few days later he was able to walk, and around 10 October, he disappeared from the hospital. All searches were fruitless. His call sign as given by his chiefs and known to us was monitored subsequently by our Werth station. It was: "White mice have red eyes." That told us he got to England.'

In May 1948, during his first interrogation, Barbie said: 'While I was in Lyons I handled a transmitter-set business with the aid of a junior officer from the air force by the first name or surname of Claude, who lived near Bourg-en-Bresse and was placed by me inside a resistance network and later sent to London. Claude subsequently linked up with Limoges using the code "White rats have pink eyes." Claude never got back from London. About thirty transmitter stations were neutralised in this sector as a result of our efforts.'

So called terrorists, Jews and priests found themselves at Montluc in the company of people whose reason for being there was a mystery. Their anguish can be imagined. One example is the case of the manager of a restaurant in Lyons, Monsieur B . . . This thirty-year-old man was seized by the Gestapo and put in the Jews' hut, and fully expected to be shot within days. In fact he was moved to Compiègne on 19 June 1944. Feeling the hand of death on his shoulder, he gave a fellow inmate at Montluc his gold signet ring studded with a diamond, hidden in a bar of soap. 'It's for my wife,' he said.

By chance this inmate happened to be one of seven people in the Jews' hut who were freed just before the

Bron and Saint-Genis-Laval massacres at the end of July. He had been there for months and, as a Resistance man, strove to recall as much as he could of the executions, deportations, and torture – and the prisoners' courage. He also had his head crammed with messages for loved ones and others. It was the understood rule that anyone who got away should go and see the families. Soon after he walked out on 17 August 1944, he went with the signet ring to the restaurant and asked to see the man's wife. He was told to ask the cashier, who turned out to be Pierre B . . .'s sister. He handed her the ring and said, 'Where's Madame B . . .?'

'She went off with the Gestapo boss!' she told him.

This escapee, who wishes to remain anonymous for fear of creating antagonism among ex-Resistance members, learned that Barbie had locked up the restaurateur so that he could steal his wife with impunity. Sending him off for deportation with the terrorists was an excellent ploy. And a crime against humanity if ever there was one.

Whereas the Jews did not realise what awaited them when they were deported in the trains, the Resistance people knew only too well what to expect if they fell into the hands of the Gestapo or the French auxiliaries: torture and summary execution. They did not join the Resistance out of mere bravado but, despite evidence to the contrary, knew very precisely what the risks were.

Writer André Frossard says of Montluc: 'We bore the whole weight of others' sins and sometimes of their heroism, too! A chap would take a pot-shot at a Boche on a street corner for practice, some masonry might fall on a Wermacht colonel, or a fight break out in a bistro . . . Right away the Gestapo jumped in a car, went to Montluc, stuck pins in the little yellow cards in the index. "Shoot that lot, and double quick!" There was no deferment, no appeal, no pardon, no last will and testament. We were just there, available. Ready, counted and numbered for the massacre!' Frossard was one of the seven who survived the Jews' hut.

Executions behind closed doors were not the only kind. There were massacres carried out 'as an example to others', and there is little doubt that these killings impressed the population more profoundly than rumours of mass disappearances. The Tulle and Oradour massacres took place on 7 and 10 June 1944 respectively. Another unforgettable case was the execution staged by Klaus Barbie in Place Bellecour.

As Blardone has explained, Barbie and the other SS men from the Gestapo often used to drink coffee at the Moulin à Vent café in the Place Bellecour, a stone's throw from the new Gestapo offices. One night after closing time, there was an explosion that smashed windows and partition walls but injured nobody. Resistance fighters, believed to be from the Jura, had placed the bomb under some phone directories. The reaction from the Gestapo's Section IV was immediate. There would be reprisals. It was the Germans' favourite bistro and five hostages would pay for the outrage with their lives.

The next day, 27 July 1944, around noon, a jeep drew up in the crowd and a German officer got out slowly. He caught sight of a French policeman named Lucien Laurent and ordered him to clear the pavement. Troops began taking up positions outside the Moulin à Vent, rather as if they were expecting another bomb blast. The crowd waited to see what would happen, although people who guessed that a swoop of some kind was imminent sneaked into the side-streets.

From the direction of the Pont de la Guillotière came a grey jeep, halting outside the café with a squeal of brakes. The driver, in civilian clothes, a double-breasted navy-blue suit, got out of the car with a German who was in uniform and wearing a flat cap with a leather peak. The 'civilian' pulled a man out of the back of the jeep by his hair, the uniformed man helping. There was a hush as three others were also brought out.

The machine guns rattled and four bodies collapsed on

the pavement. A fifth detainee struggled inside the vehicle; eye-witnesses said he wore glasses. He was mown down like the others, his body left in the road, his head in the gutter. But then one of the men suddenly moved. A Red Cross nurse came up and tried to get to him. The SS men pushed her away.

The Germans vacated the scene, giving the order that nothing should be touched. They moved the crowd back, but not so far that they could not see the bodies.

A leading churchman, Cardinal Gerlier, rushed to Commander Knab's office and was told by Knab that Germans were getting killed too. The prelate then told Knab: 'Remove those bodies at once or I'll take them away myself in the back of my car!'

The bodies were left on display for three hours. The next day everyone bought papers to read the reports. All they saw in their local paper was a small fourteen-line item that had been approved by the censor. It was headed: 'Quick punishment for bomb attack'. The story read: 'Lyons, 27 July. A bomb exploded in a Lyons restaurant, Place Bellecour, during the night of 26–27 July 1944. This establishment was mainly used by German customers. A swift operation soon after led to the arrest of five persons from the terrorist group responsible for the attack. They were executed at the scene of their crime the day after the explosion.'

A totally false report, for the five hostages had no connection whatsoever with the attack. They were:

* René Bernard, twenty-nine, a driver, who was seized five days earlier at Macon
* Albert Chambonnet, forty, alias Didier, an air force captain, detained since 10 June. This was Blardone's superior who was never denounced by Madame Lesèvre (see chapter 1)
* Leon Pfeiffer, twenty-one, who was arrested a few days before while concealing machine-gun ammunition. In his book *Mémorial de l'Oppression* Professor P. Mazel

cites cellmate Jacques Silberman: 'Pfeiffer had been tortured with a cosh wrapped in iron wire. His back was swollen and bloody. His head was also badly bruised. During a third interrogation on 26 July he was attached at the neck with a leather belt and struck; each blow almost strangled him. Back in the hut [the Jews' hut] we asked for the doctor to treat him, but the sergeant told us: "It's not worth it; he won't need anything much longer." The next day he was called at 11.30. We did not see him again.'

* Gilbert Dru, twenty-four, a student of literature aiming to become a journalist, a Resistance member who had been arrested by the Gestapo on 17 July along with his friend Chirat
* Pierre Antoine Francis Chirat, twenty-seven, an office worker and member of the Catholic worker movement

The Germans handed the French police the list of names. But it proved impossible to identify the men individually. They were sent to the morgue for the usual check. On body number 362 the police doctor found two sheets of paper hidden in the clothing. The contents read:

'To the finder: Please send to Madame Chirat, 62 rue des Maisons Neuves, Villeurbanne, Rhone.

Fort Montluc. 22/7/44
Dear Mum, sister, brother,
I was arrested Monday, 17 July with godson Dru. We were at Delille's place in Rue Molière. We were taken to Place Bellecour to the German police department, where we were interrogated by French officials who included Roger [illegible].
I went through several interrogations. At the moment I am charged with: (1) contacting a representative of the Resistance (2) attending a meeting at Delille's premises where press policy was discussed.
So it's not serious. But I believe they send pretty well everyone to the camps in Germany.

— 115 —

It is very hot and there are bugs here.

This morning some trucks left for Germany.

I have seen Abbé Boursier. In good shape. "Fortunately there are priests in prison," he said to me.

Time drags in the cell (we are let out for ten minutes to wash and sometimes for a little fresh air in the yard). We offer every [illegible]. We pray for peace, for friends, for relatives. Still, I sometimes think I deserve just a little happiness, freedom, peace. So far I really haven't had any luck. Nothing has worked out well. Pray for me, that I have a little joy in this world all the same. In any case, that I always have strength to accept my sufferings . . .

I dare say I will be going to Germany. Do not worry, better to get things ready for my return. Stay young in heart and in good spirits. I want to see you again very cheerful, very affectionate . . .

Keep in close touch with our friends. Give them my news. Go and see them. Tell them to come often to the house to replace me. Try as well to see the young girl who came to the house for dinner 9 July. She is so nice.

Even if I can't write, I am very close to you, I will not leave you. The good times will return.

Let us remain hopeful.

A big hug for you all, especially you, mother dear. See you very soon. Keep in good health.

Francis.'

I discovered this letter in the military court archives. I cannot say for sure that the Chirat family ever received it.

Regarding Barbie's part in this affair, his colleagues assert that it was he who ordered the execution, but that he had it done by his killers: Bartelmus, Rudi Mischker, and Georg Frantz, along with the militia.

Now let us examine the Bron massacre, which directly concerns the Jews and was so horrific that it compares with Auschwitz and Treblinka.

Towards the end of the occupation in Lyons, on 15 August 1944, an air-raid attack destroyed part of Bron airfield. The Germans decided to repair the damage at once, and in particular to defuse the unexploded bombs. They detailed men – mostly Jews – to do the work. Whole truckloads were brought in, fetched from the prison huts at Montluc, where they were waiting to be deported. As evening came, around 6.30, the Germans allowed the requisitioned men to leave the airfield, but kept the Jews back. The next morning the same requisitioned men returned, but there were no Jews, just the tools they had left at the work sites. Time after time groups of Jews disappeared in this way. Several witnesses later said that they 'vaguely' understood what was happening, but said nothing. Only after the Liberation did the awful truth emerge.

Somebody thought he saw a head poking out of the ground. Nearby was a pair of legs sticking out from a bomb crater that had been filled in outside hangar 68. Ten days after the slaughter, the airfield sprang to life with rescue workers, policemen and all kinds of experts digging up the corpses. They found 18 bodies to start with, then moved on to other freshly filled bomb craters: another batch of 18 bodies, including 4 women. Close by another 25 victims were found, then 21 between hangars 75 and 80, then 26 more. In total, 109 corpses were dug out and, as the Germans passed through Strasbourg in retreat, the Lyons inquiry commenced.

It was not difficult to reconstruct the crime, thanks to the evidence of Vladimir Korwin-Pitrowsky, a Polish Catholic inmate in charge of the Jews' hut at Montluc. On his release he explained to the officials that on 17 August about fifty prisoners were picked out and taken off in trucks. They took no belongings; in 1944, that meant they would be extremely lucky to see 18 August. Indeed, on 18 August the Germans came for another 20. They were in a hurry to fill in the craters, covering the bodies with enough top soil to hide their work.

A former Legionnaire who had become a naturalised Frenchman, Huber Otto, was requisitioned by the Germans to act as interpreter. He asked a German adjutant what had happened to the Jews of the day before. The German answered: 'Don't you worry about that.' He added: 'They have been doing a good job, and there's nothing more to be said about it.' A n∍w group of Jews arrived (referred to as 'Israelites' by investigators at the time), including an injured man. The interpreter drew attention to his condition, but the camp commander bawled: 'Tonight he won't feel any more pain. Now do you understand what happened to yesterday's lot?'

Police inspector Jean Sarret took notes of everything he was told, even minor points: 'The injured man had to work just like the others until 6.15 p.m., resting a few minutes at midday, enough time to drink some clear soup.'

After working all day the prisoners were taken to other craters. The warders asked their superior: 'Will there be any music?' The answer was, 'Yes, come with me.' Whereupon the Germans set to work hitting the Jews with clubs and rifle butts, laughing as they did it, until the Jews screamed. The next morning the interpreter reminded the adjutant it was time to fetch the coffee for the labourers. The officer said it was more urgent to get a truckload of earth. Earth was loaded onto the top of the half-filled holes. Interpreter Huber Otto stated that the German in charge was named Brau and that he was from the infantry; he was a baker and pastry cook in civilian life.

On 21 August, a similar procedure took place. Various witnesses said they watched it all lying behind a bank. They saw prisoners thrown into the holes immediately after they got down from the trucks. They were fired on by the Germans, who used machine guns. Witnesses said there were French people killing as well as Germans.

One onlooker said: 'There were eight militia people, wearing blue clothing. They pulled the men by their hair, by their ties or jackets and threw them in the hole. The firing went on for half an hour.' This was the testimony of Joseph Bouellat, who was watching near hangar 69. He went on: 'At one moment a German guard posted there came up to me and spoke for several minutes. I said to him: "It's dreadful what they're doing over there, killing men like that." The German said; "It's nothing. They're only Jews, only good for making sausages for dogs."'

As with the Saint-Genis-Laval massacre the previous day, there was just one survivor of the Bron massacre. Jacques Silber was aged thirty-three at the time, and a knitting worker by trade. He was arrested by the Doriot squad of the Parti Populaire Français (PPF) and handed over to the Germans. As he was a Jew, the Germans kept him at Montluc pending transport to Drancy. Silber was in the first truck sent to Bron. On 17 August, when the victims were being assembled outside the Jews' hut, the Germans noticed that among the first 50 there were 2 Catholics. They were replaced at the last minute by Jews.

Silber told Professor Mazel, regional head of the War Crimes Investigation Service: 'At half past twelve, when it was time to eat, I slipped behind the warders and mingled with the civilians who were requisitioned. I jumped up into a truck and hoped it would move off soon . . . then I walked across some fields and reached Décines, seven kilometres away.'

The Germans did a count and found that one Jew was missing. A search proved unfruitful. The adjutant prepared to use this as a pretext for the execution, in case a subordinate judged the massacre unnecessary. The next day nobody got away. And the killings went on.

The 109 bodies were duly exhumed and identified. Among the Jews there were a few Polish Catholics, who could be distinguished by the medals they wore from the shrine at Lourdes.

The Bron mass murder was only one of many in the Lyons region. Even in 1984, officials are certain that some sites have yet to be discovered.

We have a description of Klaus Barbie at this time by

Francis 'Crooked Jaw' André, the head of the biggest group of French auxiliary killers, who was questioned at Montluc jail, where he was detained after fleeing to Germany. He said: 'Barbie was the real boss of the SD in Lyons, a very hard and bloodthirsty man. He led most of the expeditions into the country in Ain, Jura, and so on. In these parts he carried out a veritable massacre of farmers and rebellious elements [who would not co-operate with the Service du Travail Obligatoire (STO) in Germany, and who mostly ended up in the Maquis]. Barbie gave full backing to the Bartelmus's anti-Jewish activities. It is fairly certain he ordered the Moulin à Vent firing in Lyons. He covered those who did numerous killings involving Jews, Haron, etc. He certainly instigated or led the executions at Saint-Genis-Laval and a lot of others in the Lyons region.'

What happened at Saint-Genis-Laval is little known, compared with the horror of Oradour-sur-Glane and the concentration camp exterminations, but it is a symbol of Nazi brutality.

The slaughter took place on Sunday morning, 20 August 1944, when the American troops were only a few dozen kilometres away. It began with the arrival from Lyons of six light cars and two coaches, a yellow Citröen, and another marked 'Gendarmerie Nationale'. They stopped in Saint-Genis-Lavel to ask the way to the disused fort of Côte Lorette, then turned right and disappeared. The cars contained civilians, some wearing a yellow armband bearing black letters – probably SD – as worn by the Gestapo's French auxiliaries, although witnesses were unable to say for sure. Subsequently a third coach arrived with some fifteen militiamen in uniform with machine guns. With their full contingent at the fort, the Germans sent away a few bystanders, mainly farm workers.

Monsieur Roure, who had a house there and had climbed a tree in his garden to watch, told Professor Pierre Mazel, the war crimes investigator: 'I saw some of them take off their jackets. One wore shorts. They were whistling and singing. They brought the coaches through the iron gateway.'

Another witness was Gendarme Senior Sergeant Elie Clavel: 'Through the windows of the first coach we saw a lot of people standing up; we just saw their heads. They were packed tight. The second coach carried men of all ages, but there was a woman too. These people sat on cross-benches, each row of them attached by their hands to a chain going from one side of the coach to the other. The coaches were overloaded and could hardly reach the fort.'

German troops ringed the old fort, and at ten o'clock, long after the vehicles arrived, shots were heard in intermittent salvos. The firing went on for about forty-five minutes.

Elie Clavel and the Mayor of Saint-Genis strode towards the fort and were told: 'Raus!' Later reports said: 'The German authorities indicated to us that we should withdraw.'

The gendarme and the mayor were able to note that the German soldiers positioned explosives at the four corners of the fort-warder's house, which was already on fire. They withdrew one hundred yards and a huge blast occurred. From his treetop, Monsieur Roure saw three men jump out through the ground-floor window. The Germans and civilians fired. A tall blond man escaped across a field, but the other two were cut down, then thrown into the house, which was now engulfed in flames.

At 10.45 a.m. the coaches left with a few soldiers, followed by the cars loaded with civilians. Witnesses said they looked pleased with themselves.

While the firing was in progress, another German column had halted in Saint-Genis-Laval because of an air-raid alert. As luck would have it, some stray bullets from the fort whistled around them. The men assumed they were being attacked and started throwing grenades. They also searched some houses and arrested three people. When the alert was over, the three were released and the Germans set out again for Lyons, unaware of the massacre under way nearby.

At the fort the gendarme and the mayor were able to question a soldier: 'How many victims?'

'Bad work, not good,' the soldier replied.

'How many? Fifty?'

'More.'

'A hundred?'

'More, more.' The man added: 'Me Austrian, no German.'

Blasts continued until 2.00 p.m. and it was not until about 4.00 p.m. that the remaining guards left the site. Immediately the Red Cross moved in, but there was not a single survivor. Professor Mazel said in his report that the warder's house was simply a pile of blackened beams, stones and masonry among which were shapeless half-burned bodies. The odour of burnt flesh was overwhelming. Rescue workers fought to get at one body, but it was too hot to touch. Three champagne bottles lay nearby, recently emptied. A few bodies were retrieved in one piece; they all had their hands tied behind their backs.

A friar named Marie-Benoît, who identified and buried 29 victims, later declared: 'Some of the bodies were so reduced in size that we put three on a stretcher. So charred were they that we were really collecting glowing ashes. We placed them in round containers where they continued burning until the next morning.'

Evidence of possible torture was found on some bodies: certain corpses had nails in the throat, the chin or feet. These nails may have come from collapsed beams, but this kind of torture was indeed practised. Police commissioner Guépratte, who had been arrested on 31 May 1944, said that during twelve hours of torture, he had his nails pulled off and 'my feet had nails driven through them'.

On 22 August Cardinal Gerlier visited Saint-Genis-Laval, and was stricken by the horror of the massacre. He remarked that, as the remains could not be identified, some families would never know whether their children or parents were killed there.

At the archbishop's house, he sat down and wrote a letter to the head of the Gestapo, which he delivered personally. It read: 'I am sixty-four years of age,

Commander. I went through the 1914–18 war and saw some dreadful sights. But none of them revolted me as much as the one I contemplated a short while ago. Even supposing it were possible to say that all the unfortunate people executed the day before yesterday were offenders – and nobody would dare to claim that – I would still maintain that it was unworthy of a Christian civilisation, or indeed a human one, to put them to death in that manner . . . I do not hesitate to assert that those responsible are for ever dishonoured in the eyes of humanity. May God deign to forgive them!'

Cardinal Gerlier's protest received the customary response from Dr Knab: Germans too were killed.

Two witnesses said that a man got away. When the Germans finally left he was sought, but he evidently preferred to keep his mouth shut about the circumstances leading to the slaughter. After the Liberation appeals were issued, to no avail.

Then on 6 September a man called René Werlhen turned up. He was shown some bodies at the Saint-Genis-Laval cemetery, and then he decided to speak. 'They came for me in my cell, number 156. There were five of us. I went down to the first courtyard where about fifty or sixty prisoners were waiting. There were others in the second yard, tied up.'

The Germans tied them in pairs and got them into the coaches. At the fort they waited about fifteen minutes. Werlhen said he heard a guard say: 'We've got to do it quickly.' The Germans ordered: 'First six outside!' The first six were taken into the warder's house. Shots rang out, and everyone knew how it would finish.

Werlhen was roped to a man called Pellet. Werlhen said Pellet was told by an officer that he would stay alive. Pellet challenged an NCO: 'So are they going to shoot me too?' The officer cut the rope and kept Pellet back.

The survivor went on: 'So it was my turn, and I went inside the house. There was a front room, and another one. A small staircase and a tiny cubby-hole. The door opened and a man faced me, on his own, as he had slipped his bonds. He went through the room and I followed him. Two women heard us and came in too; two young Jewish girls, about eighteen and twenty-two. One asked me: 'Still tied up?' I said yes and she undid the rope round my wrists. Once free, I stood against a wall. Blood was dripping from the ceiling.'

When the carnage was over, said Werlhen, he saw a German come in with a can of petrol. A young civilian came next with a machine gun, which was probably empty, since he did not fire. The prisoner decided to make a break for it. One of the Jewish girls came forward with him, knelt down and cried: 'Don't shoot, don't shoot!' But Werlhen was already through the window, followed by two others.

He continued: 'I scrambled down a small bank, and they fired. I got into a yard through one gate and went out through another one. I climbed up on a roof and stayed there lying low until it was dark.'

He said he then got as far as the home of a Monsieur Neolier at Saint-Genis, who gave him something to eat and a cigarette and let him sleep in a barn. The following morning he shaved, borrowed twenty francs, travelled to Lyons and rejoined the Maquis.

Monsieur Neolier confirmed the story, but the military authorities smelt a rat and made inquiries. It turned out that Werlhen, formerly a waiter in Paris, was a pimp. He deserted in Lyons in 1944 and made contact with the Resistance. But he was then arrested by the Gestapo; under threat of execution, he yielded information. After he told his story he was back in jail.

Questioning of the Gestapo's auxiliaries produced other versions. It appears that on that Sunday a total of 120 prisoners were assembled in the Montluc prison yard and then crammed into the buses.

Max Payot, a huge fellow of twenty-three, who specialised in the bath torture at the École de Santé said: 'At the fort, the prisoners were executed on the first floor.

Two machine-gun rounds in the back of the neck was the rule. I was in the kitchen. The prisoners had to climb up over the other bodies, and blood started leaking through the ceiling. A woman went past one of the senior Germans. She was about sixty. She told him: "I'm dying for France but you, you brute, you'll die later." Sometimes the Germans had to walk over the corpses to kill off some prisoners who were still moaning. The corpses were sprinkled with petrol and set alight. The Wehrmacht men brought in phosphor bricks to ignite them – explosives, too.'

Further details emerged but unfortunately none that would make it possible to identify the victims. Only 16 bodies were identified with certainty, and the precise number of dead will never be known. The final estimate was at least 110.

Several French turncoats pointed to Barbie, saying he organised the carnage.

We have some evidence from Lucien Guesdon, who was condemned to death but was given a stay of execution 'to assist with further inquiries'. Questioned shortly after Christmas 1947, he said he saw a convoy of prisoners leave Montluc to be eliminated, and swore that Barbie went with them, along with Chief Warrant Officer Holler and a man called Boby Volker. 'It was the SD who conducted the executions,' Guesdon asserted. Volker burned his hands and arms at Saint-Genis, trying to set fire to a can of petrol.

On 18 June 1945, the head of the Lyons criminal police department received a report on the incident. It stated: '1. This execution was premeditated and ordered as a reprisal operation by Commander Knab . . . and his deputy Barbie, assisted by Lieutenant Schmidt of the SS. 2. It was organised and directed by Lieutenant Fritz Holler, assisted by SS Lieutenant Schmidt.' The report went on to give the names of eight French people and seven German officers and junior officers of the SS, who were participants in the massacre. Mention is made of German troops from the 19th Police Regiment.

Friar Marie-Benoît, who accompanied Cardinal Gerlier

to Knab's office, remembered seeing Barbie there. He said: 'Barbie had lost none of his grim attitude, but was also worried because he kept going over to the window overlooking Place Bellecour. It was true the Allied forces were only a few kilometres off . . .'

Jean Baptiste Seta eluded the massacre, a Montluc inmate who got away intending to continue the fight against the Germans. He was later executed. He recalled that the prisoners had been assembled in the yard on the day before the execution. The first roll call included a priest named Abbé Boursier. The operation was mounted by Barbie with the ever-present Bartelmus, together with Heinrich Schmidt and Krull. The Reich troops were to withdraw a few days later; the Gestapo were the last to quit, melting into the mass of the retreating forces, having destroyed their archives. But Barbie came back early in September with a group of men including some French collaborators. Jean-Baptiste Seta said Barbie was injured in one foot and on the jaw, and had hospital treatment at Nancy.

The search for Barbie lay ahead. It was to go on for 39 years, and many times the Butcher of Lyons was within an inch of being caught. He got away with it for so long by exercising his guile, by fooling the United States secret service, who claim today not to have realised who Klaus Barbie was.

It is unfortunate that the Americans did not possess a list of the Sipo-SD's activities in Lyons and its environs:

—countless cases of theft
—14,311 detentions, including 9,378 at Montluc
—290 rapes
—approximately 7,000 deportations
—4,342 murders.

Friar Benoît, who worked with the Red Cross on identifying and listing missing persons, was able to find no trace of about 1,200 people who had been through Montluc.

7

THE MOMENT LYONS WAS LIBERATED, the Allied intelligence staff got to work. They were particularly keen to find the top man, Werner Knab, but they also wanted Barbie and the others. In many cases data on them was vague; some Gestapo men were better known by nick-names, such as Willy and Boby. Patiently, the search sheets were filled in and updated.

An unsigned, undated file, referenced as 52/1239 ES, seems to have been one of the first reports compiled after the purging of the Lyons police. In it, Klaus Barbie is described as coming from Cologne; in fact, as we know, he came from Bad Godesberg close by. It is recorded that before the war he worked in a coal company that supplied German fuel to France.

The unknown official noted: 'There is no doubt that he belonged at that time to the German SR and it must be said he did not return home to resume his former activities.' Did the official suppose that Barbie one day would be unearthed as a spy, or was he trying to be funny?

The file mentions 61 people, ranging from the Commander to a typist, along with informers and the names of the prostitutes the Germans went with at the Escargot d'Or cabaret. Klaus Barbie is referred to as the person in control of the Germans' departure from Lyons, operating from a headquarters at the fort at Saint-Irénée or else the fort at Saint-Foy, where the Abwehr was stationed. The report contains certain errors, for example, that he had brown eyes. It repeats what appears in most reports on Barbie: 'He conveys a fairly confident attitude at first sight.'

Police services were advised that Barbie 'left Lyons only on Friday, 1 September, was probably unable to reach the

German border and might possibly be found between Lyons and Belfort'. Later Barbie declared he was wounded on 28 August 1944 near Bourgoin 'while fighting against American troops who took me prisoner'. During his flight he was stated to be wearing 'a lightweight beige coat and a grey suit', though of course there were hundreds who vanished, similarly attired, in civilian garb. The testimony of colleagues of Barbie, either SD Germans or French collaborators, gives us a good idea of how the Butcher of Lyons left. Harry Stengritt said the SD quit Lyons at the end of August 1944 for temporary quarters in Epinal, following a four-day stop-over at Dijon.

Stengritt declared at a hearing on 13 December 1948: 'While we were at Dijon there was a rumour that a French general had set up in Lyons [General Henri Giraud, co-president with de Gaulle of the Comité de Libération Nationale]. Barbie decided to return with a commando group, but on the way the Maquis attacked them and half of them were wounded, including Barbie. In February 1947 I saw Barbie again at Memmingen. As far as I remember, he was working for the Americans then.'

Some twenty-four years after Stengritt's statement, Barbie said he was given orders when the Normandy landings began on 6 June 1944 to merge his SS commando with the Wehrmacht troops and do battle on the Atlantic Front. 'The worst fighting was at Caen. We had to fall back to Falaise.'

Later, in La Paz (where the film *The Longest Day* played for weeks and weeks), this Normandy story that Barbie dreamed up enabled him to skip over the Bron massacre, Saint-Genis-Laval, and other less pleasant episodes.

The SD as a whole left Lyons in convoy during the afternoon and night of August 23–4. Barbie later said: 'For us, it was important to take Giraud, not only for military reasons, but for political considerations . . . He had the confidence of the Americans and was opposed to de Gaulle.' So Barbie was already working for the United States.

Barbie said of his injury: 'Around midday on 28 August we were getting close to Lyons and were caught in a guerrilla ambush [in another statement he said they were American troops].' He said he was hit in the face and more seriously in the left foot and leg. He says he made a tourniquet with his belt and, as he could not speak, gave orders in writing to carry on to Lyons. Several died in the ambush.

The SD was in fragments. From Epinal, Saint-Dié, Sélestat, some went to Germany (Werner Knab, for example), others to Italy (Stengritt). Barbie claims he was looked after for ten days in Lyons, then taken to a hospital in Baden-Baden, and finally to Halberstadt hospital (now in East Germany). This tale is partially confirmed by 'Crooked Jaw' Francis André, who said on 17 October 1945: 'Barbie returned to Lyons on 26 or 27 August 1944 with an injury to his right foot (not the left, as Barbie says), and he was evacuated to Baden-Baden and then to Prague.' Francis André was in the know, for he accompanied the Sipo-SD in their retreat to Germany, where he was arrested.

We also have the recollections of Georges Steffan, an Alsace station master in November 1944. In return for sending two suitcases to Germany for a gendarmerie lieutenant, he received a fine present, a small 6.35mm pistol with a holder that was as good as new, which would come in handy when he did his rounds at night. One day he was given away and sent for trial at a court in Wissemburg on the Lower Rhine. He said the prosecutor was Klaus Barbie and that it was well known he had just got back from the Lyons Gestapo.

Georges Steffan told me: 'I recognized him on television. I was brought into court after a fellow called Zimmerman, who was given the death sentence and executed. It was Barbie all right. He told me: "We are going to check this yarn about the pistol. If you are lying and it was not a gendarme who gave it to you, you will be shot twice: first for the pistol and then for the lie!"'

Steffan wrote to Judge Christian Riss in 1983, but has never received a reply.

With the Lyons police purged of its more pro-Pétain elements, war crimes investigator Professor Mazel probed Barbie's role in the area. At that stage there was no talk of crimes against humanity. World War II was still in progress and the atom bomb was yet to explode over Hiroshima.

Professor Mazel wrote to his headquarters in Paris: 'Barbie, Klaus, is personally responsible for a large number of arrests, tortures and crimes committed by the services under his orders . . . He is particularly cruel and brutal, under a jovial exterior . . .'

His letter said that Barbie's true name was von Barbier, an indication of how his successes in the hunt for the Jura Maquis fighters had gone to his head. He was promoted to the rank of captain on 9 November 1943, after the Caluire business; all he needed was an aristocratic title, so he gave himself one.

Military investigators were highly active in and around Lyons, against a confused background of hurried vengeance killings following the liberation.

In *Lyon Capitale 1940–44*, historian Henri Amoretti described the first days of the Lyons Liberation: 'At the city hall the guilty, eminent and insignificant arrived fifty or more by the hour, a parade of shaven women and men in rags. They were loaded onto trucks for Montluc prison and the FFI provost questioned them. Shy innocents were detained for short or long periods; killers escaped. The young women were the first to start talking . . . Some groups held at the city hall contained the occasional person suspected for no other reason than personal animosity, but there was also the mistress of the torturer Barbie, and her sister, both with shaven heads. She was called Yvonne.'

René Hardy was acquitted in 1947; Barbie was not available to testify. The Communist newspaper *l'Humanité* made no bones about it; it carried the headline: 'The traitor Hardy is acquitted'.

Laure Moulin, who was not satisfied with this acquittal, wrote from Montpellier on 20 April 1947 to the military magistrate, urging him to find out the full details of her brother's arrest and death. She suggested various avenues that could be explored and gave the names of people who could be questioned. She expressed surprise that Guillain de Bénouville backed his associate René Hardy after revealing everything in veiled terms in *Le Sacrifice du Matin*. She cited what she saw as a key passage: 'Judas was among us, but before the betrayal he was no different from the rest of us.' Laure Moulin asked for a stay of execution in the case of Dunker, and ended her letter: 'In Lyons it was thought he [Barbie] was killed at the Liberation . . . If it is true he is still alive, he should be questioned at once, so that the full facts can be brought to light, because this man knows everything.'

Where was Barbie? In Germany? I found the first official trace of his post-war existence in a pile of yellowing documents headed with the name of the *Service de Recherche des Crimes de Guerre Ennemis*, part of the Justice Ministry. This report, dated 3 May 1948 and referenced CB/52/784 No. 4599, was submitted to the Lyons magistrate and refers to the search for twelve participants or partners in the Saint-Genis-Laval carnage: 'Barbie, Klaus: this person's address has been found and searches are in progress.' That was all on the Butcher of Lyons. The same report says: 'Knab, Werner, is believed to be held by the Norwegian authorities.'

It was a Frenchman who found Barbie: Commissioner Louis G. Bibes, who had established excellent relations with the counter-espionage services, though far from the main field of battle. Before becoming a commissioner of police, Bibes had been an inspector-in-chief in Morocco. Born in Mont de Marsan, in south-western France, he hardly knew his own country, as initially he had served in Syria. While his fellow countrymen were fighting the Nazis, in February 1944 he arrested a man named Balafrej, head of the Istiqlal Moroccan independence movement.

Immediately after the Americans landed, Bibes was put in jail for two days by order of the Americans. He was then placed under the custody of General Giraud, and finally joined the Gaullists.

At the time of the Liberation, so much of the Paris police was suspect that experts from Morocco and Tunisia were sent to the capital, to do such jobs as searching through the Gestapo papers and noting the grafitti in the cellars at Avenue Foch; at least such aides were regarded as trustworthy. Louis Bibes was one of these men, and it was thus that he began tracking down various collaborators and German war criminals, first at Karlsruhe, then in Wildbade and finally in Gernsbach. Naturally, the search sheets relating to these wanted men were circulated among the Allied authorities, and the Central Registry of War Criminals and Security Suspects (CROWCASS) totalled some 70,000 names as early as July 1945. The master list was kept in London; Barbie was in 239th place.

Commissioner Bibes was anything but fluent in German and had to use interpreters. Two people he questioned were Oberg and Hagen, leading Gestapo officers in Paris, who were seized by the British. Bibes knew nothing of Barbie, although he had read Bénouville's book *Sacrifice du Matin* and was roughly familiar with the Caluire background. He held some prisoners for a year, including the head of the German army intelligence corps, who agreed to co-operate.

He bumped into John Dollar one day, an old acquaintance from Rabat. Dollar came from the Baltic, was a tennis coach, spoke six or seven languages and did espionage work for the French as he moved within high society in Morocco. But during the war he went over to the Germans, possibly because he came from Northern Europe and felt a certain affinity with them. Bibes found his name on a confidential list, and learned that he was shacked up with a mistress in Munich.

'I had plenty of arguments to persuade Dollar to work with us,' Bibes later revealed, when I interviewed him near Stuttgart in the summer of 1983. 'In the autumn of 1947 Dollar came to me and said: "I've found a guy who knows Lyons like the back of his hand. The Americans have got him and he is selling tip-offs at the Munich spy mart [the intelligence 'market' that had developed in Munich around Möhlstrasse and Mauerkirchnerstrasse]." And do you know he gave Dollar the Caluire story blow by blow? One thing he said was that he raised his hat to Jean Moulin. I gave him a bottle of brandy for his trouble and took the lead to my superiors, knowing I was onto something really big. Dollar was no saint but he was honest, and his parting shot was that the man called himself Altmann.'

René Hardy had just been detained a second time because he had failed to disclose that he was interrogated by Barbie in June 1943, immediately prior to Caluire. The Paris archives office sent the DGER (Direction Générale des Études et Recherches – a counter-espionage agency) office in Germany a signal saying the Hardy case was being re-opened on new evidence.

Bibes told me: 'I was dead certain that Dollar's guy was Barbie. As he was working for the Americans I asked our liaison officer, John Whiteway, to fix up a meeting. We called him Jack. He sold refrigerators in Paris before the war broke out. Whiteway was born in Canada, but had French nationality and was once a Legionnaire. He could fix up just anything; he was a natural diplomat.'

Bibes came face to face with Barbie at 9.00 a.m. on 14 May 1948 in the I. G. Farben building in Frankfurt, which housed the French liaison service. Bibes and his assistant Charles Lehrmann, also from Morocco, left their weapons at the door as ordered by the Americans. The US personnel also said they could only talk about one subject: Caluire, nothing else.

Barbie smiled as he sat with two American officials, one of whom spoke perfect French. So did Barbie, but to make sure there was no misunderstanding the questions were translated into English, the replies were in German, and the record was translated into French.

Bibes obtained enough material for five pages, but after an hour's to-ing and fro-ing the Americans suddenly cut the interview short. Barbie signed the five pages, his hand quivering. John Whiteway tried to insist that the meeting be continued later. 'We'll see', was the reply. What emerged was that Jean Moulin had been 'magnificently brave' and had tried to kill himself.

Four days later Lieutenant Whiteway arranged a second encounter. Still cautious, the Americans told Bibes to go to Munich, then took him to Augsburg thirty miles away, where Klaus Barbie was at the Counter Intelligence Corps (CIC) offices (the forerunner of today's CIA). The party returned to Munich.

Commissioner Bibes told me as he went over the notes he had prepared for Hardy's trial: 'It was in a requisitioned villa that we interrogated Barbie again. This time he proved rather more co-operative.' One of the American agents was a Dick Lavoy, whom Bibes had known in Morocco, when he was already working for the Casablanca CIC; he was fluent in French. Lavoy seemed to be prompting Barbie, and with good reason: it was believed that, under the name R. J. Lavoie, he had led a team that tried to seize Barbie more than a year earlier at Marburg (unless CIC agent Lavoy and CIC agent Lavoi were two different people). The operation had failed.

Bibes therefore found himself on familiar ground, and he obtained more co-operation than emerged at the trial. Moreover, he well recalls the details of the questioning, and even the restaurant in Munich afterwards where 'Lavoy really did us proud!'

This time the interrogation lasted two hours. Bibes sent in a report to the SDECE, the French counter-spy service, but it was still not sufficient, and nobody came out of it very satisfied, for Barbie continued to hold back material. The military judge, who knew the case by heart, sought to put certain specific questions – rather too specific, it was later suggested; they were leading questions. The Americans were getting impatient; they believed their

French colleagues had been infiltrated by Stalinists and were loath to admit they were using Barbie to combat Communism. But John Whiteway stuck at it. Without his determination, and without the complicity among agents in the same business, a third interview would never have proved possible.

The third session took place in the same Munich villa on 16 July 1948. Bibes produced a third report in small fine handwriting.

This time Barbie gave his answers outright in French. The list of queries compiled by Commandant Gonnot, Magistrate of the Paris Military Court, comprised no fewer than 49 questions – all about the Caluire case, which had become the Hardy case. The meeting started at 10.00 a.m. and finished in the middle of the night at 3.00 a.m. (see the transcript of Bibes' report in the appendix).

'The Americans were definitely protecting Barbie. There was no question of finding out where he lived, what he did. Following him was out of the question.'

'Did you manage to photograph him?'

'No chance.'

'Even unofficially?'

'Oh, I had a Minox that Dollar gave me, but no film.'

When I went through the relevant SDECE archives, I had the distinct impression that Bibes was preempted by other secret services. For example, on 13 July 1948, three days before the final interrogation in Munich, the SDECE sent front-facing and profile photos of Barbie to Commandant Gonnot. The inscriptions beneath the photos were blacked out with dark ink. In turn, the examining magistrate sent the pictures to Lyons.

I asked Bibes about the close protection Barbie was enjoying.

He answered: 'Three reasons. First, the Americans were naturally suspicious as regards espionage work. Secondly, they realised Barbie was a hot potato because a service from another country had managed to locate him. Thirdly, they were afraid their plans would be scuppered – they

— 135 —

gave me to understand that Barbie was highly useful in their research concerning the East European countries.'

Bibes told me: 'In spite of that, he did not give us the impression he was still working for them.'

I asked: 'Who suggested to Barbie that he should give evidence at the Hardy trial?'

'It wasn't me. I had handed the case to the DST.'

I discovered that the French applied to the Americans for Barbie's presence at René Hardy's second trial. The Americans said: 'We are willing to lend you Barbie, but make sure he is protected and send him back to us.' This proposition was rejected by the judiciary, and Barbie did not appear. Bibes did, however, and the court wiped the floor with him! He was asked why, as an officer (he used the name Captain Bernard Legarde when questioning prisoners), he had failed to arrest one of the leading war criminals. Had he compromised with the enemy? Why had Barbie not even been eliminated?

Humiliated in the extreme, and lambasted by a journalist as 'France's dumbest policeman', Louis Bibes slammed the door in the face of the French administration on 1 July 1950, resigning his post and vowing never to set foot in France again. He was one of the first French nationals to obtain a work permit in Germany. Roughly the same age as Barbie, he is still there.

Lieutenant John Whiteway was a kind-hearted Legionnaire who had served well in Algiers, acting as a contact with the Americans and the British, through the efforts of Colonel Paul Paillole, ex-head of the French Special Services.

Colonel Paillole was glad to run over old ground when I called on him in retirement just west of Paris.

De Gaulle, he said, was against a centralised counter-espionage outfit after the Liberation. The General ordered counter-espionage, along with the SR, to be split into three divisions: External Research (de Gaulle personally headed that); Military Security; and Interior Territorial Surveillance. As for hunting down war criminals, Paillole said he argued in favour of a single body, the BICE (Bureau Inter-Allié de Contre-Espionnage). His opinion was that this would have helped Barbie's capture, because it would have meant a unified effort in their search for criminals. De Gaulle, however, had an aversion to Yankee spies.

Paillole told me: 'The split-up would have been an excellent thing in time of peace, but we were still at war. So we did what we could relying on our own resources. Germany was divided into four, each bit handled by a separate secret service firm. In the French zone I got hold of Gérar-Dubot because he knew more about German affairs than anyone. Without Gérar-Dubot's personal contacts, Barbie could never have been interrogated. It was due to him that the Americans had Klaus Barbie brought from Italy, where he worked in intelligence against the Communists. You know, sometimes a few drinks could heal wounds caused by political or diplomatic rifts.' Colonel Gérar-Dubot had been honorary correspondent to the SDECE counter-spy outfit and editor of the *Journal*. Precise and meticulous in his approach, he had secretly organised a Military Security Bureau in Paris during the Occupation. Evidently secret service men can keep going as others cannot; I met him recently after his ninety-sixth birthday, and he vividly recalled the whole war period in detail.

Paillole remembers that Gérar-Dubot went straight to the Americans and told them: 'Lend us Barbie, we'll give him back.' They refused because they needed him; they were using him, Colonel Paillole said. The United States was convinced that the French police had been infiltrated by the Communists. 'That's what they thought, but in fact they were wrong.'

The Direction Générale des Services Spéciaux was dismantled, and the result was chaos, plus a great deal of bitter rivalry, and information deliberately withheld.

But thanks to Paillole, the Allies received an amazing secret master file from the Special Services in Algiers: a list of German and French war criminals, a total of some 3,800 names, not counting mere suspects, bound up into a single volume and issued in 1944 right after the Liberation of Paris. On page 13 were listed: Banzhaf, Barbie, Barck . . . The existence of this document shows that the more competent authorities already knew plenty about the Nazis' crimes and those of their collaborators. There was no need for the Allies to look further. These pages contained errors, no doubt, but they had been compiled while Barbie was still in Lyons!

Here's what was said about Barbie:

'Barbie, real name Mayer, SS O'Stuf [Obersturm-führer], original Bradenburg [over 300 miles out] 5 feet 6 inches, well built, pink face, thin lips, grey eyes, glasses, very brutal. In 1939 district police chief in the Rhineland. In 1943–4 head of section IV and deputy to Commander of Sipo-SD Lyons sector. Left Lyons temporarily end 1943 for mission in the Netherlands, replaced then by O'Stuf Floreck. Returned to sector summer 1944.'

As to the importance of Amt IV, which was the model for the section led by Barbie, there were plenty of details. Even today the document would strike terror into the heart of certain French families, if names contained in it were divulged. The contents were gathered over several years, and section IV is all there. Sub-section IVB is described as consisting of four parts: political Catholicism was the responsibility of IVB1; sects and political Protestantism of IVB2; other persuasions and Free-masonry were down to IVB3; Jews, evacuations, confiscation of goods from enemies of the people, etc., IVB4.

Evacuations, for pity's sake! Was Algiers feigning ignorance of what was happening in the camps?

The volume of duplicated sheets was supplied to the Allies just before the Normandy landings. Also included was the name Werner Knab, listed as an Oberregier-ungsrat, or highly placed government adviser, and other SS men of standing. In Lyons, Colonel Paillole's agents had successfully infiltrated the Gestapo, but they encountered big trouble, for about ten of them were arrested in March and April of 1943, including Major Lombard and Captain Missoffe. At all events, in Algiers they knew plenty about the Germans at the École de Santé.

I asked: 'Why didn't you go for Barbie, then?'

'Oh,' said Paillole, 'there were other priorities, starting with the French traitors . . .'

He proved especially discreet on the Caluire affair. He knew someone had betrayed the meeting, but from what he knew from German files, there was more than one squealer. In this matter Paul Paillole corroborates Maître Vergès's assertions that 'Jean Moulin was handed over to the Germans by other Resistance people acting for personal reasons and political reasons of power and self-interest, who have themselves been protected, and for the same reasons, by their comrades in combat.'

Indirectly Paillole conveyed to me that he knew enough to be able to state with total conviction: 'I am certain that Jean Moulin tried to kill himself.'

In due course Paillole was obliged to resign. Some subordinates wanted to quit with him. He told them: 'I advise you not to. The enemy's special services are still alive. They still remain to be destroyed. Twenty thousand shameful French nationals went with the Wehrmacht, and they are prepared to do anything in defence of a lost cause.'

That was in November 1944, and Berlin was yet to burn.

On the other hand, the Americans had no objection at all to handing over Harry Stengritt. Commissaire Bibes questioned him two weeks later in Stuttgart, where Stengritt willingly confirmed that he headed Section VI, Intelligence, at Lyons, and was highly forthcoming about Barbie, whom he regarded as his chief (see the extracts in the appendix). He played down his duties, made no mention of taking part in any massacres, but was not worried about talking of the Caluire affair, which he planned. Stengritt spoke freely; he knew the French investigators had not troubled Barbie. He was taken to Paris on the understanding that his evidence was the only thing that interested the French, after which he would be left in peace. But he was sentenced to death. He was reprieved and served a fifteen-year prison term. One of Bibes' assistants, Amédée Chapuis, who brought Stengritt to Paris by car, asked me last summer: 'You want to interview him? He won't talk, he's had enough.' Stengritt has paid twice over, for Barbie as well as himself, it seems.

Meanwhile Barbie was sitting pretty. The cops could come to see him, but he was safe with the backing of the Americans. After the three sessions with Louis Bibes, he had a call from the Sûreté Nationale. One of its detectives, Aimé Ferrier, was interested in quite another subject than Caluire: he was on to the French collaborators and wanted to know where a certain Doussot fitted in, a friend of Hauptsturmführer Barbie. The simplest way was to ask Barbie himself, and where better than at Barbie's place?

The report said: 'December 8, 1948. Summoned Barbie Klaus, aged thirty-five, businessman in Augsburg, Bavaria, domiciled in Kempten, 38 Schillerstrasse . . . who took the oath to tell the whole truth, and nothing but the truth . . .'

The detectives questioned him about his friend Doussot, the Gestapo collaborator, but Barbie remained tight-lipped.

Thereafter the French continued calling for his extradition. Invariably the Americans replied that they did not know his address. Of course the French might have considered whipping him from under the US noses, as had occurred with other wanted men. Barbie was a pretty easy target since he was always happy to talk. For a financial consideration, he was quite willing to chat away, as he did with the newspaper *Samedi Soir*, which published an interview with him on 4 December 1948.

It read: 'Obersturmführer Barbier of the SS [the 'r' on the end corresponds to the German pronunciation of Barbie] will accept 2.5 Marks, the price of a drink in a Munich or Augsburg bar, in return for Paris's second military court's most jealously guarded secret: the revelations that last October convicted René Hardy of collaborating with the enemy . . . "Hardy is certainly a traitor. He got in touch with us of his own free will . . . I had him arrested on the Paris train so that he would give his friends away. Promising him his life was enough. I swear on the heads of my two children that not a fingernail of his was touched."'

The author of the article, which was unfortunately unsigned, described Barbie as follows:

'Flat stomach, bony face, hollow cheeks and feverish eyes. He too has seen prison since the war. At Cassel initially, for taking part in a Nazi resistance movement that demanded ransom from old women living alone. Later the British locked him up in a Hamburg bunker. He escaped, reached Marburg in the American zone, where he started an office supplying false identity documents. One night the military police picked him up. As they were crossing a bridge, he jumped out of the jeep and plunged into the river, with machine-gun bullets sputtering around him. "That's the end of him," the MPs said.

'Six months later the dead man was running a cabaret in Memmingen. He was secretly placed in the war criminals' camp at Oberürsel for 200 days. Skorzeny was in the same camp.

'Barbier has used the names Becker, Spiers, Klaus, and others during his escapades. He resumed the name Barbier when he set up an agency for cabaret artists with its main office in Munich and a branch in Augsburg. The first client was Frau Barbier, an acrobatic dancer [doubtless his wife, Regina]. The profits were not enough for the boss, for his debts in

— 141 —

numerous bars meant he was not allowed credit. To get back in the black he was counting on selling an article on the Hardy case. He asked for 2,000 Swiss francs from the Associated Press news agency. Their reply read: "Allegations [on Hardy] uncheckable; five of the witnesses are dead and the sixth has disappeared to Russia".'

So that was Barbie in 1948, former head of Section IV, hitting the bottle, a womaniser and already selling his memoirs. At any rate, it shows that he saw no reason to fear French justice.

The French magistrates summoned the managing editor of the newspaper, hoping to find the author of the article and to obtain more details. But the managing editor of *Samedi Soir* sought refuge behind professional discretion and did not react to the judge's summons.

That was how things worked in those days.

Meanwhile the Resistance people were active. In spring 1949, 5 April, the newspaper *L'Agent de Liaison* ran the text of a letter the Lyons Resistance people sent simultaneously to the Garde des Sceaux (Justice Minister), the Foreign Ministry and the US Ambassador in Paris. It read: '[We are] informed that Barbie Klaus . . . is now in the American free zone and is running a business in Munich, in spite of the many crimes he committed in the Lyons region during the Occupation . . . [we] protest deeply over such impunity.'

The letter followed up with a list of crimes attributed to Barbie: the rounding up of Jews, the Jura and Nantua operations, the massacres at Saint-Genis-Laval, Bron, La Doua, etc.

It is curious that French diplomatic services in Germany had not yet raised a finger. They knew nothing of what was going on. The first request for an inquiry was not made until 7 June.

It was very polite.

'1. It would be highly appreciated if searches could be

undertaken to locate a certain Barbie, Klaus, in Munich, required by the French authorities to face charges as a war criminal.

2. In the event that the person is located, kindly inform us of the terms under which Barbie Klaus can be handed over to the French authorities . . .'

The document was signed by Pierre Giacobbi, Vice-Consul at the French Consulate in Munich. The search was agreed to.

An imbroglio of extradition requests and vague replies followed. Since diplomacy moves at a snail's pace, the military's judiciary employed its private contacts. For example, there was a telegram sent from Munich late on 13 June to Herr Zaguin, head of the judicial services at Baden-Baden: *'Durand nicht gefunden'* (Durand has not been found). The telegram was signed Leb.

Durand was Barbie's code name, and Leb was probably a man called Hirsch who searched in the Bogenhausen district of Munich. It is a pity Leb did not go to Commissaire Bibes, John Whiteway, or those who met the Lyons policeman Aimé Ferrier.

An idea of the gulf separating the official services may be imagined from the fact that Barbie's front and profile photos dating from 1946 had been with the examining magistrate for nearly a year. In formal parlance, Klaus Barbie had been 'the subject of six investigation orders', which means he was being traced in connection with six different inquiries, associating him with alleged homicides, arson, unlawful arrests, torture, theft, association with criminals, and so on. But, the tighter the net seemed to close around him in Germany, the less effective the search seemed to become – that at least is what emerges from scrutiny of the judicial and diplomatic dossier. And yet plenty of signals were flashing.

For example, the military governor of Lyons, General de Hesdin, wrote to the Defence Ministry: 'The crimes committed by the ex-Gestapo of Lyons are of such enormity that they doubtless amount to the biggest war crimes case to be tried in France. However, one of the chief accused, Barbie, Klaus, is in the hands of the American occupying forces, who have so far refused to hand him over . . . If sentence is passed in these circumstances [without Barbie's attending], the lawyers of Barbie accomplices now in detention will surely highlight our Allies' refusal to co-operate. The press will seize upon the affair and the public will be highly and justifiably indignant.'

At the end of his letter the general said: 'I ask you to oblige by intervening with the American authorities, drawing attention to the unfortunate effect that non-delivery of Barbie will have on the public.'

On 28 July 1949, Robert Schmelck, who later presided over the Appeals Court, wrote: 'From semi-official sources I have just learned that Barbie is currently living at Kempten [Bavaria, the US Zone] at 38, Schillerstrasse 7.' But he also noted that difficulties would doubtless arise if a formal extradition order were to be filed, because a certificate of residence would be necessary for inclusion in the dossier. The only body able to provide this was the US Public Safety Officer. A month later the Americans replied to Attaché Giacobbi, saying that Barbie's domicile could not be located. And yet, as Robert Schmelck said to me: 'On the whole, things worked smoothly between ourselves and the American and British zones.'

On the Soviet side, a tip-off indicated that a Barby (sic) might be living at Brunby in the Soviet zone, but this man later proved to be a different person.

Did the French authorities really want to lay their hands on Barbie as the second trial of René Hardy drew near? Were they not perhaps protesting too loudly so that at the same time it was made clear to the Americans that they would rather he was kept out of harm's way – and denied the opportunity to cast doubt and suspicion on the reputation of the Resistance and make some unwelcome exposures?

8

In 1945, Hitler's Germany rolled back and the Allied forces entered the concentration camps.

Hitler, leader of what was to have been the greatest civilization ever known to mankind, killed himself, while Berlin, surrounded by the Red Army, went up in flames.

Already the victorious powers had done the groundwork for the trial of Nazis. The Nuremberg courtroom was to show the world a new kind of criminal.

Gemany was divided into the American, British, French and Soviet zones. Berlin was also split into four sectors, but the entire area round Berlin was Soviet-controlled.

What interests us especially is the American zone, which extended from Kassel to Munich. The US forces moved into Munich some highly special services, which operated in twelve regions under control of the 970th Counter Intelligence Corps (CIC). The CIC was the counter-spy thrust of the occupying troops, which had the immense disadvantage that most of its members were very inexperienced, as compared with the OSS boys who went home for a well-earned rest after the fatigue of the war years. Naturally, the top echelons of the CIC contained a few first-class operators, but the subordinates lacked know-how and there was a sad need of informers.

This was the era of 'de-Nazification', when thousands of Germans and their foreign collaborators found themselves in the camps, being grilled by Allied experts who wanted to know the details of each and every Nazi. Lists like those drawn up by Colonel Paillole were circulating among the Western powers. There was much checking and cross-checking, there were lists of the wanted and the mere suspects, Germans and non-Germans. As the investigations went ahead, some names were crossed off, others were added.

But as far as the Americans were concerned, their adversary changed guise. The enemy was no longer Nazism but Communism. This was a godsend for an SS man like Klaus Barbie, who had learned to loathe the Communists even more than the Jews. Barbie was quite prepared to forget the past when it came to the Jews; that was how it had to be when you were fraternizing with the Americans. The Communist threat was a totally different matter – the common menace. The Americans were ready to turn a blind eye to the record of certain ex-Nazis whose anti-Communism could be relied on, once it was verified that they had not gone over to the Eastern bloc.

Klaus Barbie saw the likelihood of working for Uncle Sam as an informer, and the US counter-espionage services used him for three years, perhaps more, though Washington was not to admit it for another thirty-five years. Several reasons have been advanced to explain the silence of the United States, but one only is sufficient to elucidate this embarrassing decision. Immediately after World War II, the US used Barbie to spy on the French secret services and Barbie had another go at the French.

It is now virtually certain that, after he went into hospital at Baden-Baden, Klaus Barbie was taken care of at Halberstadt hospital until February 1945. His mother, with her natural skill at bending the truth, said she saw her son for the last time in March 1945 at Halberstadt hospital. She was questioned in 1950 by Inspector Lucien Ollier of France, who was trying to track down Barbie. The interrogation report dated 13 December 1950 referred to Alberstadt hospital in Berlin; as the French do not sound their Hs, it must mean Halberstadt, southwest of Magdeburg, now in East Germany.

Frau Barbie told the Inspector: 'He was being treated for a leg injury. I never heard anything more about him, I think he must be dead. . . He was the last family I had.' She had little more to say; in fact she refused to sign her statement.

Two days later Ollier wrote to his superior: 'To confuse the investigators, she has turned her name into Barbi. It should be noted that she showed bad faith during the course of questioning. . . Barbie, Klaus, whom we have been looking for without success in Triers, is rumoured to be in Berlin, where he is believed working for an American service.'

Well, some of that was correct. When he emerged from convalescence, Barbie was active in the Kassell area under the name Becker and later Holzer; he was trying to set up a kind of secret club for former SS people. Very likely, his underlying aim was to prepare a key position for himself in Germany's new society. This meant he had to form a fraternity of like-minded people who would be reborn with forged documents, such as identity cards and food tickets. His aim was to escape detection pending the advent of a Fourth Reich.

As Barbie has said: 'The Russians accused the Americans of tolerating a revenge-seeking Nazi organization within Germany. That was not true. All we wanted was to survive.'

Early in 1946 the Counter Intelligence Corps learned that a group of SS officers had indeed come together secretly, just as the Freikorps did after the 1914–18 war. (See chapter 1 in which Barbie explains the role played by his father in the Schlageter groups.) The objective of the ex-Nazis in particular was to acquire control of the German administrative machinery, according to a secret US report, revealed by the Ryan Commission in 1983. (At the request of the US Attorney General, the lawyer Allan A. Ryan and a team of experts investigated the links between the Americans and Barbie from 1945 to 1983; he submitted his report in August 1983 after seven months' research.)

So, for Barbie and his friends it was already a case of Germany for the Germans, a legitimate aspiration but hardly acceptable in the eyes of the victors, less than a year after the close of the war. Thousands of Germans were listed as suspect. The conquerors of the Reich were willing to restore responsibility to the Germans . . . but not to the Nazis.

An American spy who had studied in Switzerland and spoke 'Schwizer' like a native of Zurich managed to infiltrate the ex-Nazis' organisation. He stayed in it for six months and was accepted as a Nazi loyalist with a yen for the lost Reich. During that period he compiled a detailed dossier. In his report he noted that among the leading members was Herr Barbie, now known as Becker.

When he was not attending meetings, Barbie alias Becker found a neat way of making money, as learned by Beate Klarsfeld when she delved into German criminal records. Barbie, it transpires, recruited a distant cousin named Kurt Barkhausen and another man named Wolfgang Gustmann, both former SS members. On 19 April 1946, the three men, disguised as police officers, rang the bell at the home of a leading citizen of Kassel, Baron Forstner, living at 43 Parkstrasse. Frau von Forstner answered the door. Barbie said: 'Kriminalpolizei! You are hiding Kolbenheyer who is being sought by the police!' Barbie, respectfully addressed as Herr Kommissar by his assistants, entered the domicile and carried out a search. They confiscated a small case containing some jewellery and asked the good lady to accompany them to the Polizeipräsidium where a formal report would be drawn up. The baron's wife agreed, but forgot her identity card and had to go back for it. Barbie and his inspectors were off like a shot, one to the railway station, the other to friends with the case. Barkhausen and Gustmann were arrested in due course, and they declared that their boss Barbie had gone off with the loot.

Strangely, it was not until the spring of 1949 that the German police issued his description: 'Klaus Barbie, 5 feet 7 inches, dark blond hair (looks very Jewish), speaks literary German [Hochdeutsch], courteous behaviour.'

Serge Klarsfeld has noted that the case came up on 3 April 1950, though Barbie was absent, and that the arrest warrant was issued only two months afterwards, when the jewels had already been restored to the Stuttgart police.

The official report dated 16 April 1951, when Barbie had reached Argentina using the name Altmann, read: 'An American authority indicated where the jewels could be found. It can safely be supposed that the jewels were returned by the CIC. Already during the inquiries at Kassel it was suspected that Barbie was working for the American secret service. This suspicion is now further backed up. A written request was sent to the CIC, but has met with no reply. Subsequent approaches in this direction will doubtless prove fruitless.'

By now this part of Germany had won its sovereignty anew under the name of the German Federal Republic, separate from the German Democratic Republic, allied with the USSR. The criminal police department had yet to achieve full separation from US tutelage.

Barbie's activities in 1945 and 1946 are not clear. According to Barbie, he left hospital in February 1945 and went off to fight the Russians at the Branoff Bridge, even though his leg wound had only just healed. He got there too late and beat a retreat as far as the Berlin bunker, a stone's throw from Adolf Hitler. He then found himself in the 12th Reich Army, or what was left of it, fighting somewhere near Wuppertal, this time against the Americans. He claims that on 18 April he buried his weapons in this region in a wood by the side of the road.

The SS captain thereupon did a quick-change act, acquiring civilian garb. Like hosts of others, he tried to pass himself off as an ordinary soldier, one of the defeated, poor bloody infantrymen whom the victors would overlook. He used the name Becker.

He also said that, at this point, he had the idea of chancing his luck with the Americans as a Frenchman who had been in the STO, the Reich compulsory labour service. In this capacity he encountered an American soldier, who was completely at a loss as to who this gabbling fellow was and let Barbie carry on towards Kassel, struggling on a bike with his leg injury.

How did he survive? In 1972 he said he got work as a farm labourer near Kassel, where he met a chap called Schneider. He also obtained entry to the law school in Marburg-Lahn University. Barbie, now using the name Mertens, teamed up with Schneider to produce forged documents in the university. Schneider also used the name Merk or Merck, and the name Schneider-Merck was to reappear in Peru in 1971 (see chapter 9).

'We must have forged about 300 documents,' he boasted while in Bolivia. The foregoing itinerary tallies fairly well with an account he gave to the Americans. The US secret reports say, however, that Barbie – alias Becker, Behrends, Mertens, Spier and Holzer – was transferred on 11 March 1945 from Berlin to Düsseldorf, returning to his original Section VI (intelligence) job in the SD. But in the chaos of defeat, the office had moved to Essen for a few days. The Americans took Barbie's travel details at face value.

The ex-Hauptsturmführer did less well with the British. He was given away by someone and detained in November 1946 in the British sector. He related subsequently that the Field Secret Service planned to keep him in a 'concentration camp' at Neumünster reserved for SS men and top officials of the Nazi party. They got him as far as Hamburg, where he was locked in a cell.

But not for long. Barbie said: 'We got away on a public holiday, when there was only one man guarding the place, playing a flute. My two fellow inmates found an iron hook on one of the ceiling beams and managed to force the doors. They let me out as well. We thought of attacking the guard, but he was too busy with his recital.'

Barbie also says that he later met up with a former NSDAP official, who challenged him with the words: 'Hands up! Are you a good German or a bad one?' This man took him into his home and sent his wife to Marburg to move the forgery equipment.

Meanwhile Regina Barbie, whom he has never said much about, was pregnant for the second time. Klaus sought a discreet clinic in Kassel, helped by his chum Schneider, who explained that the lady's husband had disappeared during the war, while Barbie passed himself off as Regina's brother-in-law. Barbie realised he was on thin ice because there is nothing more obvious than to seek out criminals within their own family. He cleared off to spend a while with his mother, keeping very much to himself. The baby, Klaus-Georg, was born in December 1946.

It may be that his brief stay with the British kindled his desire to work for the erstwhile adversary – on the grounds that if you can't beat them, you should join them – or he may simply have been driven on by his hatred of Communism. Whatever the motive, we do know that a friend of his wanted to take him on as an informer, but Barbie hesitated. The friend was a German, Dr Emil Hoffmann, working as a spy for His Majesty's Government. Hoffmann said in evidence in July 1964 that Barbie successfully got a Dr Zarp, a Danish economist who had helped the SS, into the US secret service at Memmingen. This is said to have been in 1946, which, added to remarks by Stengritt and others, means Barbie entered the American service a year earlier than officially stated by Washington.

Barbie claims that he was arrested once more and got away a few minutes later. A woman had betrayed him; she and Barbie were being taken in a jeep to the American headquarters when Barbie escaped his captors. An American, probably Dick Lavoy, fired a shot, the jeep hit a tree, the woman broke her leg, and Barbie got away with only a finger scratched by a passing bullet!

There is a great mystery about Barbie's German–American period. Why did the known lists of suspects fail to reveal to the Americans the facts about the SS captain? The Americans do not seem to have been very inquisitive – or perhaps they were blinded by the use they could make of a Nazi like Barbie. One after the other, the Americans were to say that they were interested solely in Barbie's 1945–6 period. But there is plenty in CROWCASS, the Central Registry of War Criminals and Security Suspects, used by the Allies and containing 70,000 names in July 1945, which showed that Barbie was sought by France for 'murdering civilians and torturing military personnel'. The August 1946 edition of CROWCASS said a certain Barbi (without an e) was being sought by the Dutch for 'murders and deportation'. The March 1947 edition listed Heinz Barth, a killer I saw in court in East Berlin in 1983, for his part in the Oradour-sur-Glane massacre; on the same page were four Barbies!

They were listed as follows:

* Barbi . . . wanted by the Dutch [who remembered the Italian sounding name]
* Barbie, see Barbier
* Barbier, Klaus, or Barbie, Barby, Mayer, Klein or Kreitz. Hauptsturmführer, head of Section IV at Lyons in 43–4, sought for murder by France. [The lists did not mention Jean Moulin or the slaying of Jews, which is understandable since CROWCASS gave no specific details]
* Barby, see Barbier

I suppose anyone can mislay his reading glasses or forget that Barbie had already been detained twice. An American officer has recently suggested that the list was unreliable in that it was useful for repatriating political adversaries under the cover of their being war criminals.

Michael Thomas, who escaped the raid on the UGIF in Lyons in February 1943, has expressed his indignation over the Ryan report. He said it was inexcusable to have employed Barbie as a CIC informer. He told me: 'I was one of the counter-espionage officials in the town of Ulm. I myself wrote a full report on the Gestapo and Barbie was naturally mentioned in it.'

Michael Thomas joined the US forces when Lyons was liberated. Posted to the 7th Army, he followed the Germans as far as Dachau, and was one of the first people to discover the horrors of the Nazi concentration camps. Then he took a job as regional official with the CIC, staying there until April 1947.

Thomas said: 'Barbie was not yet working for our services [a debatable point]. When we came back, we were replaced by fellows who had no idea what to do. They didn't even speak German.

'By using Barbie, I consider they betrayed the 200,000 Americans who died fighting to stamp out Nazism. At the CIC our replacements could not have been unaware of who Barbie was. It was their duty, I tell you, to arrest that guy. He could have been had on three counts: as a member of the Gestapo, the SD and the SS. At Nuremberg the Allies condemned these three organisations as criminal. There was a moral obligation to bring them to justice. It is a disgrace to the United States to have saved that guy. Barbie has been condemned to death twice by France, and he is still alive, thanks to the Americans!'

Michael Thomas was speaking thirty-five years afterwards and was not satisfied with the expression of regret that the United States offered France, even if the apology was backed by a statement from President Reagan.

Curiously, the US secret services had begun chasing Barbie in the wake of the affair of the SS friendship club. The CIC were after eight persons in the Marburg region, and the police swooped at 2.00 a.m. on 23 February 1947, with no fewer than seven teams of men. They had fitted snow chains to the jeeps. These eight people were selected from a list of fifty-seven names; the CIC men were hoping to break up a whole network and perhaps arrest Barbie. Some of the teams included Frenchmen such as Xavier Vasseur and Joseph Birneaux, who were CIC auxiliaries. The mission included seizing documents, codes, letters, literature, pamphlets, identity cards, membership lists, photos, diaries, weapons, ammunition, tools, radio transmitters, clothing, money and so on. The order was signed R. J. Lavoie, who was later to attend the questioning with Commissaire Bibes.

Klaus Barbie was lucky or smart, for he had just left Marburg. But the Americans were to try again in April, according to a report signed by Lavoie and another CIC special agent, V. J. Kolombatovic. That evening around dinner time the CIC men rushed to the third floor at 35 Barfusserstrasse in Marburg to find Dora, Else and Margarete Schmidt, Marthe Ludwig and Heinz Schmuelling, who were questioned separately. It was learned only that Claus (*sic*) Becker, alias Barbie, alias Behrens, had been their lodger up until August 1946 before moving to Düsseldorf; there he stayed in a small room in the Reitallee where his mother already lived. As he was not fussy he would sometimes return with a small suitcase, spend the night and leave again via Himmelsberg, where a farmer would supply him with food. And the witnesses added that the farmer was 'a war colleague of Herr Becker'.

The Ryan Commission report states that Klaus Barbie did not join the Counter Intelligence Corps until 1947, sponsored by his friend Kurt Merk, a former Abwehr agent in Dijon, who had been in the employ of the Americans for some time. It is especially curious that while Region 1 (Stuttgart) and Region 3 (Frankfurt) of the CIC were looking for Barbie, he was employed in Region 4 (Munich), where he was in charge of the Memmingen sector. On the frontiers of Bavaria, Barbie was investigating the activities of Communists and other Germans, the movements of Soviet agents (and anti-Soviet agents, says one commentator) inside the American zone, and also the operations conducted by the French secret services.

Allan Ryan's report fails to reveal the exact nature of Barbie's information. It says nothing in detail about the espionage work he did, whom he gave away, what special contacts he had in the French zone. The Americans remained secretive about all that, although it must be said the Attorney General had not asked for such data. The inquiry was intended to reveal the links between Barbie and the Americans, not to discover the actual results of his work. Moreover, in the 600-page appendices to the report, the name of any person or place compromising the role of the US special services was blanked out by the censor, and remains Top Secret to this day.

For example, we have this extract from a report by John H. Dermer, special agent, in 1947, concerning Operation Flowerbox: 'Taking account of his background and experience with the GIS [German Intelligence Services], it is very possible that Barbie might be useful in penetrating the supposed Russian network in [censored]. He has indicated to X-3-I Sp Sqd that Barbie would not be unwilling to collaborate with X-3-I in such a venture.'

At that time Barbie met up with a certain Wenzel, of the same name as his colleague Wenzel of the anti-Jewish sub-section in the Lyons SD and supposedly killed in the bombing in May 1944. Wenzel was already working for the CIC in Stuttgart, specializing in Soviet matters. Dermer noted at the end of his report: 'It is recommended that Barbie not be interned as yet, but that he be used in an attempt to penetrate the supposed pro-Russian group at [censored].' He mentioned that Barbie should be watched, even so, and should be detained if necessary.

This went on for two months until an officer in the service who was looking for Barbie found, on 22 May 1947, that he was on the CIC lists as an informer. It was discovered that he was working with someone called Merk, the Dijon spy in an outfit bearing the name Büro Petersen. One hand didn't know what the other was doing. But having tracked him down surely the CIC command would arrest him – but no, he was left alone on the grounds that he was more valuable inside the CIC than in a prison camp for Nazis. So Barbie stayed in Region 4, his identity concealed from his colleagues.

But people change jobs, and promotions occur, and a certain Earl Browning eventually issued an arrest warrant. Barbie was detained on 10 or 11 December and taken to a special interrogation centre at Oberursel. His sheet mentioned that he had a scar on his right cheek.

This was the third time Klaus Barbie has been arrested, but he got away again, emerging with a clean record and available for work in May 1948. He was asked virtually no questions about periods other than 1945–6. Barbie gladly affirmed that during that period he had patiently waited for a chance to work for the United States against the Russians. Barbie was helped by his friend Merk who, as soon as he found him, recommended Barbie to the American supremo Robert Taylor. Released and re-recruited, Barbie became agent X-3054. Barbie had never wanted to hide his real identity from the secret services, and could not have done so anyway. Agent X-3054 thus acquired US protection, Virginia cigarettes and ration tickets.

The lid came off all this in 1983 and General Robert Taylor had to take the blame. Not that he cared: he was dead. Nobody else was pursued on the matter: they are all in retirement and prescription applies.

And yet, as a result of questioning, some former US agents have disclosed a few items kept secret since the war. One of the officers, Ehrard Dabringhaus, who became a German history lecturer at Detroit university, gave several interviews and has written a book, but he prefers to release his information sparingly.

He told *Figaro* magazine: 'Barbie lived in Kempten with Kurt Merck and his mistress, a twenty-five-year-old Frenchwoman, a young Frenchman and a man Barbie introduced as a lecturer in anthropology from the Ost Institut.'

Ehrard Dabringhaus had the job of contacting Barbie, setting him up in a comfortable villa and providing him with a secretary. He said that Barbie got $1,700 a month for his information, in US not local currency. (Allan Ryan believes the sum was nearer to half that figure.)

'In your opinion, why did he do this work?' I asked.

'For the money. He was prepared to do anything. One day I caught him copying an article from a Czechoslovak newspaper. He wanted to sell it to us as information!'

Dabringhaus was not alone in observing that Barbie often tried to sell the same tip-offs to various services. Colonel Earl Browning has said that some informers such as Barbie moved from city to city collecting several payments for the same information. Using more than one alias helped.

Dabringhaus told *Le Monde*: 'Barbie used to bluff, and he gave us practically nothing of any value. He claimed he had a hundred agents working for him throughout Germany, and said he needed money to pay them. The fact was he just pocketed the dollars.'

He was paid in kind, too. In the archives of the US secret services is an expense sheet drawn up by Dabringhaus on 1 October 1948 in connection with Barbie's associate Merk:

1 September 15: 10 packets of cigarettes [for information on] the Bavarian Trade Union Bureau
2 September 18: 20 Deutsche Marks and 1 food card
3 September 22: 100 DM
4 September 22: 10 packets of cigarettes
9 September 30: 1 food card . . . for data on 'troop movements in Soviet zone'
A total of 500 DM, 40 packets of cigarettes (possibly cartons of 20 packs) and 5 food cards.

On the matter of Barbie's meeting with Bibes and his assistant, Dabringhaus told Michel Faure of *Libération*: 'The French agents were too kind, too polite. They came in the office and asked me if I knew Barbie, whether I knew where he was. I said I did not and five minutes later they left. It was over. They didn't push me against the wall. If they had said this is what Barbie did, we have found the graves and we want him, I'm sure I would not have bothered about my superiors, I would have said yes, I know where he is, let's go get him. But they did not do that. They made my job very easy.'

Maurice Olivari, head of the Télévision Française Channel 1 office in New York, questioned Dabringhaus: 'So you didn't know who Barbie was?'

'Not exactly. I knew he had been an SD member . . . that was worse than the SS. We should have jailed him right away, but unfortunately the CIC wanted to use him. . . He did not look like a criminal. He was a businessman. But he always rolled his eyes to right and left . . . Merk told me he had tortured and killed prisoners.'

Barbie saw things differently. In spring 1972, he said: 'I was interrogated separately by the Americans, the French, the British, the Russians . . . An American official was present at all times and, at the start of questioning, he issued a reminder of my status as a US prisoner, saying I had the right not to answer.'

Another secret CIC report for Colonel Erskine, written on 3 May 1950, while the Hardy trial was in progress, stated: 'On 21 January 1949, Lieutenant Whiteway and Monsieur ['Lagarde' inserted in handwriting] interrogated Barbie sufficiently closely to satisfy their needs, without questioning Barbie on the network that had been established in the French zone or on Barbie's activities with the CIC in general.' The report also said that an officer speaking fluent French was present, to make sure that Barbie was not drawn on either of these issues.

Legarde could be Commissaire Bibes; he admits he used this name, but it might have been someone else. I have traced a French policeman who was authorised by the Americans to question the Butcher of Lyons, a Criminal Police officer who shared an office with Jacques Delarue, who later became a historian. His name was Jean Pouzol and he ended his career as divisional commissioner of the French Renseignements Généraux at Versailles. I found, however, no written record of his contact with

Barbie, apart from the authorisation. What was the purpose of this further interrogation? Did it concern Hardy, or the mystery of Jean Moulin's death? Jean Pouzol died in 1976, and he kept no such records at his home.

From the report submitted to Colonel Erskine we also learn that sometime in 1949 the French Sûreté had made several attempts to get information. The Americans saw this as the run-up to a kidnapping, and said the plot was doubtless fomented by 'Communist elements'. Paragraph 18 of the report stated that it was only on 13 May 1949 that the CIC first had knowledge that Barbie was a war criminal. They learned this from a newspaper report that Barbie used to burn his suspects with an acetylene lamp during the Occupation.

Eugene Kolb, Operations Officer in Region 7, declared that the torture allegations did not mean the end of Barbie's usefulness. Asked about the article, Barbie hinted that he had at one time resorted to intensive questioning techniques but that actual torture was not involved. So as far as the Americans were concerned, Klaus Barbie was a small-time bully at worst.

When the Butcher returned to Montluc in February 1983 another US counter-intelligence officer, John Willms, said from California that Barbie was arrogant and scornful, and that he had to protect him from the French, who wanted his guts. Willms, who was in a group that escorted Barbie for interrogation by the Allies, said he remained standing and armed in case the French tore Barbie to pieces. He further recalled that Lieutenant John Whiteway urged him more than once to turn a blind eye and let them 'look after' Barbie; they could always explain away anything untoward that might happen to him. Willms added that the French agents never forgave him for protecting Barbie at that time.

Yet another US agent, Gene Bramel, ex-CIC in Augsburg, told the *Daily News*, of Dayton, Ohio, on 27 March 1983, that the Americans and French were so much at loggerheads that 'we trusted the French just about as much as we did the Russians'. It was seriously thought that the Americans might simply bump off Barbie so that they did not have to deliver him to the French: 'If worst came to worst, whoever drew the short straw would drive him up the Autobahn at night, pull off in to a car park, shoot him, push him out and come back.'

We also have the evidence of CIC man John MacLoy, who told Margaret Jay of the BBC that his people set up obstacles in the path of the authorities asking for data, so that time could be wasted until the trials were over.

It would seem he was referring to René Hardy's second trial and the proceedings that the French were preparing against Klaus Barbie; his deceased superior, Colonel Werner Knab; his Gestapo subordinates; and the French auxiliaries. In this TV programme, produced by Tom Bower, John MacLoy added that the basic reason why Barbie was protected was the fear that the French secret service would question the SS man on American operations. The more so as MacLoy believed the French police had been infiltrated by Communists. In that sense, they would have been handing over US intelligence to Moscow, he explained. It was a view shared by many in the US Army.

All these shenanigans were ploys adopted by the secret services and diplomats to counter France's numerous demands for extradition. The hide-and-seek game they played resulted in a voluminous exchange of letters over a period of more than three years. There is no point in detailing the process whereby the judiciary and diplomats made a formal application for extradition. All that really counts is the date of 4 May 1950, when the CIC decided that Barbie should not be handed over to the French. This irrevocable decision came four days before René Hardy's second acquittal. It was a close shave. For a few weeks before the trial started, the Americans, responding to a suggestion from John Whiteway, indicated that they were prepared to 'lend' Barbie to the French. But there were several provisos that were almost calculated to be unacceptable to the French: Barbie's protection was to be officially guaranteed, his stay in France was to be of limited duration, and he had to be returned to his employers after giving evidence in Paris.

The French Defence Ministry replied to this on 14 March 1950 in a letter to the military prosecutor: 'I have the honour to inform you that, in view of the nature of the witness's war crimes . . . I consider it is impossible and certainly inadvisable to agree in his case to the undertakings requested by the Présidence du Conseil [the premier's office].' This referred to the undertakings required of the SDECE, which was responsible to the premier's office. The author of the letter, Monsieur Turpault, added: 'In the event that Barbie simply rejects the summons you have made and which I had brought to his attention last February 11 through diplomatic channels, his evidence will have to be dispensed with for the Hardy trial.'

The US decision of 4 May not to give up Barbie coincided with Commissaire Bibes' humiliation for failing to produce Barbie at the military court, despite the fact that he had got on to Barbie's trail two years earlier.

Referring to the stalemate over Barbie, President Meiss observed: 'We know the unacceptable conditions laid down by the Americans for Barbie to come to France, because they say he is "useful for the national defence of the United States". I regret having to mention such evidence. Nevertheless, the court will evaluate it.'

Louis G. Bibes did not help his own case. He turned up in court grinning and chewing gum. He also said that he had failed to put on the pressure while questioning Barbie. Asked what he meant by pressure, he replied: 'er . . . moral pressure', the kind of pressure he usually had at his disposal when questioning. The defence team, particularly the brilliant Maître Maurice Garçon, seized on this and described 'Commissionaire' Bibes as a mere inspector. There was no follow-up; Hardy was acquitted.

The Americans continued to lie low. Immediately after the verdict, Lebègue, head of the judiciary in Baden-Baden, told the Americans in so many words that they could hardly claim to have no knowledge of Barbie's whereabouts and seek details from the French, when the man had been interrogated in their zone and under their protection. The reply came from Jonathan B. Rintels on 31 May three weeks after the Paris trial: 'We are pursuing our efforts to locate Barbie.'

From the fall of Berlin until November 1947, the Americans handed over 1,292 criminals to France. But they stopped the exodus from that date. It was the start of the Cold War. They would no longer agree to any extradition sought by the Soviet Union and its allies in the Communist bloc: Bulgaria, Czechoslovakia, Hungary, etc. The Russians had asked for five Nazi generals: Guderian, von Leuttwitz, Rheinefarth, Rode and von Vorman. The answer was no. These men had not even appeared before the Nuremberg international court, and they were too valuable to US defence interests. Simon Wiesenthal has recently pointed out that the East Germans continue to employ Nazis.

The French Embassy in Washington kept up its pressure, but to no avail, yet the Americans sensed that the impunity accorded Barbie could worsen relations. For example, a gala evening was arranged on 6 June 1950 at the Eden Cinema in Villefranche-sur-Saône to commemorate the Allied landings. On this occasion the US consul was tackled directly on the Barbie affair. The local newsmen made no reference to it, but the consul drew up a report immediately after the event.

Frequently, on the insistence of local officials at Saint-Claude and elsewhere, the French authorities sent off thick files containing evidence from witnesses, and other proof of Barbie's crimes. But nothing came of it: they could not touch agent X-3054. Some of the Americans wanted to clear up the whole business, but they always held back for fear that Barbie would reveal how he operated, the tricks he had got up to. He might have disclosed the names of other people working for the US secret services, even though they might be small fry.

When Allan A. Ryan drew up his report to the American government, he provided a further explanation of why Barbie was not handed over. He said the Americans could not lose the confidence of their other agents, and in the fight for democracy they could not abandon those who remained loyal to the United States. That was why Barbie was neither surrendered nor eliminated. Instead, arrangements were made for him to take a trip on the liner *Corrientes*.

Missing from the Barbie dossier are 13 documents relating to the period from December 1950 to March 1951. These are included in the microfilm catalogues, but there is otherwise no trace of them. They would have told us something of the decision to allow the Butcher of Lyons to get away via the notorious Rat Line, which enabled other such undesirable characters to cross through Austria and Northern Italy and finally board a ship bound for Egypt or South America.

What is clear is that Barbie was released from duty on 19 January 1951. The Americans fixed up a last meeting with the Hauptsturmführer's mother, Frau Anna Barbie, somewhere near Augsburg, where they said their goodbyes.

Then the Barbie family, Klaus, his wife, Regina, and his two children, Ute and Klaus-Georg, left in a jeep for Salzburg, where they were taken in hand by Austrian CIC men. The Barbies had been ordered to keep away from the consulates. The secret service people provided them with forged identity documents in the name Altmann, and they also had visas, which were genuine.

It is doubtful whether the 'Altmanns' had much to say to one another during the train journey through Linz, Bolzano, Verona and Milan to Genoa. It was safer to keep quiet as they set off on their rather special vacation six years after the war.

The head of their escort from Augsburg to Salzburg drove back and gave his report to Major Riggin, who wrote in the informers' list: 'Barbie Klaus, released with full protection'.

9

ON THAT MORNING IN 1951, the palm trees of South America beckoned to Klaus Barbie. Early on 16 March he walked out of his room at 6 Via Lomellini in Genoa to complete the final formalities that were to take him to safety.

He had finally given up any idea of trying to lose himself in the new Germany that had emerged after the war, a land divided between four occupying powers and still the best haven for some Nazi criminals. But Barbie was running scared, afraid he would eventually be handed over to the French or that he would suddenly come face to face with a survivor on some street corner. Others from the SS had come to grief in exactly that way. René Hardy had just been acquitted by the French courts for the second time, and he might well travel to Munich. A French Resistance newspaper in Dijon had published Klaus Barbie's address: 38 Schillerstrasse, Kempten, close to the Swiss frontier. Anybody who really wanted to could find him, that was a certainty, and the French police had already interrogated him three times.

In Genoa, he was still under the care of the American Counter Intelligence Corps, which was going to get him away to the Andes where it would use him again.

Like Adolf Eichmann, who had used the names Eckmann and Hartmann, Captain Barbie tore up photos of himself in SS uniform and had himself photographed as a refugee who had escaped the Soviet occupying forces. Despite the light-coloured jacket and spotted tie, the sly Barbie smile was still recognizable. He would need the photo for his passport to get him across the Atlantic.

Barbie alias Altmann would be following the same route as the notorious gas chamber merchant who was to escape capture for fifteen years. The Vatican as well as the

Americans knew the route well; they had sent many a genuine refugee along it – as well as a few war criminals from time to time. But to get onto that route, the Barbie family must keep acting the part of ordinary Germans nobody would take notice of; folks who just wanted to emigrate and build a new life for themselves in the pampas away from the wreckage of their own land.

Barbie had to knock on many doors. A month earlier he had cleared the first and most immediately vital hurdle: the Combined Travel Board (CTB), run by the Allied High Commission in Munich, had issued him with a temporary passport bearing the number 121 454. This would open all the other doors, starting with that of the International Committee of the Red Cross (ICRC) in Genoa. On the morning of 16 March 1951, he called on the ICRC, showing a special pass and a temporary visa, Number 1507, issued to him by the Italian Consulate in Munich on 21 February.

The official in charge of transatlantic travel documents handed Barbie a questionnaire; he set about filling it in. In 1972 the Altmann file was resurrected from the central archives of the Red Cross in Geneva, produced to show publicly that the ICRC had acted in good faith, and also 'to enable Mr Altmann to defend himself' in the event that he was not the Altmann in question. Paulette Tombet, assistant head of the archives department, said: 'We had no means of investigating all applications, of checking everyone's identity. We had to take them on trust. Perhaps a few war criminals slipped through, but those travel documents saved thousands of people's lives . . . In the post-war period we issued more than 150,000 travel documents.'

Hauptsturmführer Barbie had his alias committed to memory: Klaus Altmann, born 25 October 1915 at Kronstadt, Germany; engineer, Roman Catholic. He said nothing about his wife, Regina, but entered the names of his two children, Ute Maria, aged nine, and Klaus-Georg, aged four, and put down Kassel as their place of birth.

Asked to specify where he wished to go, Barbie wrote: 'Sud Amerika (Bolivia).' Possibly he kept his sun-glasses on; the official did not notice what his victims in Lyons had described as 'eyes you could never forget'. They were steel-blue, but on the form he put the colour of his eyes as brown.

Then he added his signature, 'Klaus B—,' catching himself just in time and correcting the B to an A and finishing the name Altmann rather awkwardly. That mistake could have cost him dear.

As for Regina, only the day before she had filled in an identical form in the comfort of her room at the Nazionale hotel – an appropriate stop-over. She described Frau Altmann as a refugee by underlining the word *profugo*. Her parents, she declared, were Matthias Wilhelms (instead of Mathias Willms) and Margaretha Mertens (instead of Mergens). The names were close enough to the real ones for her to feel confident of not making any blunders.

On Regina's form, as on her husband's, we find the usual signature testifying as to their moral standing: Professor K. Stef Draganovic. For the Nazi fugitives, Reverend Krunoslav Stefano Draganovic was God Almighty. A disciple of the Austrian bishop Alois Hudal, this Croatian priest was in direct contact with the American CIC. Most of the time he ran a seminary in Rome for young men from Croatia, but he was always willing to make a trip to Genoa to welcome the 'refugees' sent in his direction by the US secret service. There was a very good reason for this: every time he got an adult across the Atlantic he pocketed a bonus of $1,000 to $1,400, the rate varying with the quality of the merchandise.

In a detailed report on the Italian section of the Rat Line, US agent Paul E. Lyon wrote in April 1950 that Draganovic was a Fascist war criminal whose contacts with South American diplomats of the same persuasion 'are not generally appreciated by the State Department'. In spite of this, Draganovic took the Barbie file over from the

Americans and he did it so effectively that he was able to stand in for the 'anti-Communist refugees' in the corridors of the Genoa consulates.

The safe-conduct pass from the Red Cross was the Open Sesame to South America. Losing no time, on 16 March Barbie went to the Bolivian consulate where he had been asked a week earlier whether he had an Italian police record; a document dated 14 March certified that he had no record. This time he had to fill in form number 704. He gave his name as Altmann again, and then answered a few questions the consul-general, Jorge Arce Pacheco, put to him. The answers he wrote down were invaluable during the tracing-back process thirty years later:

> *Name and address of closest friend:* 'Padre Stefano Draganovic, Rome, Italy'
> *Employer for the last five years:* 'Firme Peter Hail, Dortmund, Germany'
> *Contacts in Bolivia:* 'Padres Roque Romao, Franciscan Community, Sacaba'
> *What work will you do:* 'Carry on my business'
> *Capital resources:* '$850 dollars'
> *How long are you expecting to stay in Bolivia:* 'Permanently'

But the road to Bolivia goes through Buenos Aires, and with the help of Reverend Draganovic's network Barbie acquired another visa from the Argentine Consulate three days later, on 19 March, signed by the consul, Rogelio R. Tristany. Klaus Altmann pledged in writing that he would not stay in Argentina any longer than necessary to reach the Bolivian frontier – even though Juan Peron tended to give German emigrés a good welcome.

Now all that remained was to buy the ticket, using a different fund from the $850. The Barbies found that the 12,850-ton liner *Corrientes*, run by the Dodero company, was due to sail on 22 March. (The name of this ship was curiously linked to Nazi criminals. Corrientes is the region on the border between Argentina and Paraguay where the sinister Dr Joseph Mengele, of Auschwitz fame, found refuge. And it was in Corrientes Avenue, Buenos Aires, that Adolf Eichmann was trapped by the Israeli secret service in 1960.) The liner's route was via Naples, Las Palmas, Rio de Janeiro, Santos to Argentina. The Barbies travelled third class. In the sixth spring since the war, they crossed the Equator at the comfortable speed of 17 knots.

Breathing a little more freely, they had a ten-day break in Buenos Aires, putting up at the El Dora hotel. Then on to the Andes in the company of three Croatian refugees and some Catalan nationalists.

They reached La Paz on 23 April 1951. The Bolivian capital is situated at an altitude of 12,000 feet and Klaus Altmann was not the first newcomer to suffer the effects, but he was delighted by the sight that met his eyes one morning as he emerged from the Italia hotel: a parade of Bolivian Socialist Falangists was filing past, wearing their black trousers and white shirts and giving the Fascist salute. They were singing as they marched along, just as it was in Germany before the war! In March 1973 Barbie recounted this scene to the Argentine journalist Alfredo Serra immediately following his interrogation by Public Prosecutor Gaston Ledezma Rojas; he also confirmed that Barbie and Altmann were one and the same.

Barbie said: 'I admire Nazi discipline. I am proud to have commanded the finest corps in the Third Reich, and if I were to be born again a thousand times, then a thousand times I would be what I have been. For Germany – for Bolivia!'

In Europe it was assumed the Nazi had not made his act of contrition. It was supposed that he had left Germany, but nothing definite was known. Four years after the second Hardy trial, the Sûreté chief in Germany submitted a report to Ambassador François-Poncet, containing two full pages on Barbie and concluding: 'From the latest information received, the person concerned is now in Norway, but it has not been possible to find out his exact address.' Well, only 8,500 miles out!

Klaus Barbie eluded the Nazi-hunters for twenty-one years. In the bosom of friendly military dictatorships, he lived a charmed life for a torturer, with just the occasional alarm.

The Americans gave him the most discreet support. If they were to use Barbie in Bolivia, he had to be washed whiter than white. Klaus Barbie needed to lie low for quite a while, like his neighbour Friedrich Schwend, who was one of the CIA's most valuable contacts across the border in Peru. Fritz Schwend, whom the Peruvians called Don Federico, had an impressive record; during the Second World War he was involved in the celebrated Operation Bernhardt, which flooded the market with twelve million counterfeit banknotes with a face value of £150 million, and produced by expert craftsmen at a deportation camp. Schwend, alias Kemp and Wenceslav Turi, had crossed the Atlantic in 1947, four years ahead of Barbie, to escape sentence by an Italian court; the Bolzano judge condemned him *in absentia* to serve twenty-one years for the murder of a Yugoslav soldier.

Klaus Barbie had graver charges behind him, which called for a longer stay in purgatory, so for fifteen years he led the quiet life of an ordinary engineer who once lived in a place called Kronstadt.

There were two reasons why this was an alibi he could not expect to keep up forever. Just as a criminal always returns to the scene of his crime, Barbie had an irrepressible desire to show off. His close friends heard the story of his wartime exploits, his service in the Gestapo. In the streets of Munich in 1947 his tales of Caluire almost caught up with him; in distant Bolivia he started to brag once more, far from the basement of the École de Santé Militaire in Lyons, far from the battlefield. In contrast to his wife, Regina, who could keep a secret for eternity, he spilled the beans to some of his most trusted acquaintances, pressing himself upon them in some cases. One of these friends was a German watchmaker in La Paz, J. H. Schneider, whom he met on most days in a café or at his workshop at 216 Calle Colon.

Schneider said: 'One afternoon we were strolling along together and suddenly he said, "You don't know who I am, do you?" I stepped aside and looked him square in the face. I answered, "I don't want to know, either."' He found out from the newspapers in 1972.

We can be sure that Klaus Barbie genuinely needed to take some of his contacts into his confidence, if only to impress them and gain status in the eyes of his Bolivian business partners. Naturally, it was the heroic side that he recounted. If Barbie alias Altmann could have kept control of himself and suppressed his yearning to boast of his rank as SS captain, if he had simply kept his mouth shut, there is little doubt that he would still be hiding somewhere in Bolivia or Paraguay today. But evidently he hated the idea of simply being forgotten for the rest of his life.

He was shy enough at first and spent two months looking for work. Unfortunately he knew neither Spanish nor the timber trade, but Barbie got his first job at a sawmill in Chulumani, near La Paz, in the *yungas* on the other side of the Cumbre mountains. Ironically, Eichmann was in timber as well – he had been a woodsman in northern Germany before he fled to Argentina. As June 1951 drew to an end, Barbie was feeding tropical wood to a saw; within a week he was promoted to foreman and found a place to live at Llojetas.

The boss happened to be Jewish, Ludwig Capanauer from Cologne, who arrived in Bolivia back in 1939. Capanauer, who is no longer alive, probably knew nothing of Altmann's past. Altmann buttoned his lip as far as Capanauer was concerned. A Jew was the last person he would confide in, and he was certainly not going to boast that he worked for one.

Over six thousand miles away in Lyons, he was condemned *in absentia*. On 29 April 1952 and again on 25 November 1954, he was sentenced to death. He may not have heard about this for some time. His own people in the Saar found out from the French press and wrote to him poste restante at La Paz, where he collected his mail under the name Altmann. Whether he knew at once or later, it made no difference to his day-to-day life, except that he could now start counting the days to prescription coming into effect: 7,300 days in the Andes sunshine until he was free from the risk of arrest. In those days he was not to know that De Gaulle would later decree that there could be no prescription for crimes against humanity.

Ute and Klaus-Georg now preoccupied Señor Altmann; for he wanted them to have a German-style education, even if they were to spend the rest of their lives in Bolivia. This was a very real prospect. Before the prescription applying to his two death sentences came into effect, he applied for naturalization. Altmann, his wife and later the children all applied. On 3 October 1957, Klaus Altmann and Regina Wilhelms de Altmann became Bolivian citizens with full civic and political rights. The act of naturalization was signed by President Hernan Siles Zuazo, who decided to expel Barbie twenty-six years later when he came to power for the third time. Ute automatically acquired citizenship in 1961 under the name Uta Maria Altmann Wilhelmes. They were all issued with Bolivian identity cards at Cochabamba.

Barbie now embarked on a tougher quest. He would not feel really free until he could go through customs and immigration checkpoints with an official passport in his hand, which would allow him to travel the world, even visit France, as a Bolivian civil servant.

In the wake of the August 1953 agrarian reform, the Llojetas sawmill was sold off, and Klaus Barbie settled in La Paz, starting his own small sawmill called the Maestranza Madera Alemana. The children could now go to Marshall Braun College with other German youngsters, for Germans had made themselves quite at home in La Paz with their own schools, co-operatives, chemist and cemetery.

These were good times for Barbie. Business was on the increase and his life was a far cry from the days when he walked off the boat from Italy and did the rounds of the German phalansteries looking for work. Now it was his party. Señor Klaus Altmann was a pillar of society at the head of the Santa Rosa sawmill. Timber was a profitable business, but the bark was even better, and Barbie was making a fortune out of quinine. Quinine was badly needed in Europe where antibiotics were not yet selling in great quantity. The sick and suffering of Europe were taken care of by the Hauptsturmführer from across the water, who shipped out wild quinine bark by the ton. He sent out no less than three million dollars' worth to the German firm Buehringer in Mannheim. This trade continued for four years. The Bolivians got wind of it and eventually set up their own factory to export quinine in powder form. The quinine venture was not to last, but the Bolivians were grateful to Señor Klaus for improving the plantations, and for planting out an area of young trees for the military pension fund in La Paz.

Barbie gradually moved into the sacrosanct world of the Bolivian Army, who held him in high esteem. These old colonels, formed by Roehm's SA men, had always dreamed of fighting alongside the Nazis. They were all of a kind, in their green uniforms, in their goose-stepping parades, with a German grandfather or grandmother, like Stroessner and Banzer.* If it were not for their Ray-Ban glasses, their black moustaches and their chiselled features, they could have been living twenty years earlier. This phenomenon was particularly common in Santa Cruz de la Sierra in the south, where the German community had settled well before the war and now held sway.

Klaus Altmann became a representative for foreign companies. He acted as a go-between in a uranium deal

---

* General Alfredo Stroessner, born 1912, has been President of Paraguay since 1954. General Hugo Banzer took over the Bolivian presidency in 1971 and remained in power until 1978 – one of the longest terms ever for a republic where there have been 180 revolutions since independence!

that involved the Bolivian Atomic Energy Commission and a German company in Frankfurt.

In 1960 the US Army had ideas of using Barbie, but they let it drop. The story in Washington is that the American secret service rejected the project. Probably Barbie knew nothing about it.

After the seizure of Eichmann, a wave of panic swept through the Nazi fraternity in South America in 1960 and lasted for two years, but the scare eventually subsided.

On the other side of the Atlantic the French legal machine continued its work, sending extradition requests to Washington – to no avail. France's military lawyers sought to make good the 1948 gaffe, and sent a team of gendarmes to make inquiries in the Triers area of Germany, in the French occupation zone. They probed around Kassel, Hesse, where Klaus-Georg was born. They questioned a foster cousin, Carole Bouness, who had married a teacher. She told them: 'I met Frau Barbie and her two children in the summer of 1957, when they stayed at Triers for two months. She said she was going back to Bolivia, and I acted as a post-box. After I'd read Barbie's letters I used to burn them, because I knew he had been one of the leading figures in the SS. I used to write to Regina Willms, or Müller, or Altmann, and Barbie told me the new post-box number each time he replied, because it kept changing.' The gendarmes dated their report 12 April 1961.

So, at last, ten years after reaching La Paz, Barbie had been located, but it seems the French authorities in Bolivia were not informed. The Hauptsturmführer continued to receive the latest news from Germany, since Frau Bouness handed the task over to a friend called Clara, who lived in the Rhineland.

In 1957, Anna Barbie, the torturer's mother, had been living for two years at 19 Dietrichstrasse in the centre of Triers, only a few yards from Karl Marx's birthplace. She felt safe from prying eyes in her two-room apartment overlooking an inner courtyard; she paid 40 Marks rent a month. She was a devoted Catholic and merely had to cross the road each morning to seek solace in the White Fathers' chapel. She kept to herself and never spoke of the war. If anyone asked what had happened to her boy, Klaus, she just said: 'He disappeared, I never saw him again. He was probably killed.'

It was not that simple, though, for sometime in 1957 young Ute came to see her grandma. She was sixteen at the time and chatted to some of the neighbours out of politeness.

Frau Christa Schmeling, the caretaker, revealed: 'She told us she had a small brother of ten. I said he must have been born after the war, and she grew flushed in the face.'

Two years after they found the Barbies' 'post-box', the French police paid a call on Frau Anna Barbie. They searched for incriminating letters, a clue as to the way he fled, where he was holed up. They got nowhere, not even a photo of any use; the only one his mother had was of him as a baby – understandably she preferred to remember him when he was little.

The police had a good reason for making the call. On 7 November 1963, the Palatinate Army Security Chief had sent a report to the Chief Commissioner of Police, head of the SA with the French Forces in Baden Oos. Stamped 'Secret and confidential', the report was about all the KdS leaders in Lyons in 1944, including Klaus Barbie. On the list were: Lieutenant-Colonel Werner Knab, Captain Heinz Fritz Hollert, Klaus Barbie and the head of the Sonderkommando and Section IV B, Karl Heller. The information was needed for an inquiry initiated by the Federal Office of Research into Nazi Criminals in Ludwigsburg.

Knab and Hollert were dead, the report said. Knab died in an Allied air raid on a Bavarian highway on 14 February 1945, and Hollert was killed in an attack on Lyons on 26 May 1944. As to Barbie, an investigation by the Wiesbaden Regional Office produced this information:

'After the German capitulation in 1945, Barbie was at once recruited by the United States secret service, who set him up and protected him in Munich, where his cover was that of a tradesman. Barbie had been living in La Paz, Bolivia, since 1961 or 1962 [in actual fact, as we know, since 1951], and his wife Regine *née* Willms joined him later. In Bolivia Barbie is believed to have a "cover activity" on behalf of the US and German intelligence services, the CIA and BND. He corresponds regularly with four members of his family living in Triers: 1. Paulinstrasse 8: with his daughter, Ute Barbie, born 30/6/1941 at Triers; 2. Dietrichstrasse 19: with his mother, Anna Barbie *née* Hees; 3. Dampfschiffstrasse 1a: with his aunt . . .'

It is stated that his mother-in-law, Frau Willms, 'recently made contact with a lawyer (so far unidentified) in Triers asking him to make discreet inquiries with regard to the search for her son-in-law that the authorities in France and in the Federal Republic might be conducting.'

The report recalls that two warrants for Klaus Barbie's arrest had already been filed: one dated 31 August 1945, issued by the military judge in Lyons for illegal detentions and killings; the other signed by Captain Vandoeuvre, a military judge in Lyons, dated 6 December 1950, on charges of murder, arson and looting. The author of the report, A. Battault, concludes with a recommendation that the French DST (Directoire de la Surveillance Territoire) and SDECE be advised of Barbie's presence in La Paz, and of his 'certain manipulation' by the CIA and BND. In compliance with the request of the director of the Bundeskriminalamt at Wiesbaden – who, the reporter says, wishes to avoid any contact with Interpol so as to guard against any possibility of Barbie's escape – Battault suggests the establishment of 'postal and possibly telephone surveillance of the four members of the Barbie/Willms family at the three aforestated addresses, also at the poste restante or post-boxes.'

So France knew as long ago as 1963 – at least France's secret services did.

It was only after the expulsion of Klaus Barbie that Maître Serge Klarsfeld exhumed this evidence. Who had an interest in concealing it? We do not know. Pierre Messmer, at that time Minister for the French Armed Forces, declared twenty years later when Serge Klarsfeld made this report public: 'It was an internal military security document not destined for the minister.'

So was Barbie to be forgotten in 1963? In 1964, not only were Jean Moulin's ashes solemnly transferred to the Pantheon in Paris, but General de Gaulle paid an official visit to Bolivia. How lucky for Barbie that the General preferred to go to Cochabamba rather than La Paz, because of the altitude. Could the French secret service, which was so expert at preparing the President's itineraries, have failed to re-activate the Barbie affair? Señor Altmannn could well have slipped in among the crowd of aymaras peasants and armed revolutionary militiamen when, on 19 September 1964, General de Gaulle, in uniform, said in Spanish from the Cochabamba government building: 'My Bolivian friends, today France has come to visit you . . .' If Barbie was indeed there to greet him, it would probably have been with a smile on his lips.*

One thing is certain: when the plain-clothes men accompanying de Gaulle shook the dust of Bolivia from their feet, Hauptsturmführer Barbie felt a lot easier. At this point he was still not really part of the Bolivian political and economic system, but he would become spectacularly so with the Transmaritima Boliviana.

Bolivia lost access to the Pacific nearly a century earlier,

---

* Altmann-Barbie, it is worth noting, was not 'put out to pasture' during General de Gaulle's 1964 trip, but in the previous year the Bolivian authorities had moved him away for a week when Marshall Tito stayed at Cochabamba in late September 1963.

and its people have always dreamed of getting their corridor through Chile back again. They still dream of it today; as evidence, you need only look at the Bolivian claim to the sea printed on the phone directories in La Paz!

Barbie smelled an opportunity in the air. He could not give them a port or a beach, but they would have their boat!

General Barrientos was in power. Barbie doubtless used his German friends to get inside the Quemado Palace – he has never said – but the General gave his full backing to the idea of a ship flying the Bolivian flag. As to financing, there was no difficulty, as it could be extracted from the pockets of the Bolivians; it was as simple as that. Early in March 1966, a subscription towards the first freighter was opened. The closing date of 23 March was announced, because on that date, every year, the Bolivians have marched through the streets demanding access to the sea. This 'Crusade for the Sea' would bring in four million dollars, the organisers announced. It actually produced no more than $50,000, but that was enough to form a company.

Gaston Velasco, ex-mayor of La Paz, says that Barbie put himself forward as a marine engineer and that he sold his idea so convincingly that he became the chief executive of the new firm, Transmaritima Boliviana S.A., with capital funds of 1.2 million pesos. Since the State also put money into the venture and was majority shareholder with 51 per cent, the firm ought to have been under the tutelage of a ministry. But that is not how it worked out, because Barbie started distributing $1,000 a month in royalties to the partners the State foisted onto him. In Bolivia money can buy anything, even the silence of the colonels. He had a fine office with the easily remembered address, 1616 Avenue 16 de Julio (if all its streets were named after *coups d'état*, La Paz would be quite a calendar).

You cannot buy much of a ship with so little money in the kitty, so it was decided to hire one. Barbie was handy with a paintbrush, and a few dabs of red, yellow and green on the funnel along with the initials 'TMB' took no time at all. Why upset all those people who had donated money?

In his capacity as chief executive, Barbie felt he was really going places. He acquired a new assurance, an arrogance that he had not known since the 1940s. We know that he was scared of nobody; an incident that took place in the German Club at La Paz in the spring of 1966 gives clear evidence of this. Dr Motz, the West German Ambassador, had just proposed a toast to the Federal Republic when there came a shout of 'Heil Hitler!' from the back of the hall. Everyone turned round to see Barbie giving the Nazi salute with a smart click of his heels. He was hustled out in double-quick time by three waiters, while crying out: 'Stinking ambassador! I was a Gestapo officer, and when the Nazis are back in power, I'll have you on my list –' The scandal subsided and he returned to the German Club some years later. Even as he gave his salute, he knew only too well that he had friends there as well as adversaries. Nazism and anti-Semitism were deeply rooted in some members of the German community.

There were also Jews in Bolivia, though many had left Europe not so much in fear of a revival of Nazism, but because they stood a better chance of making a living in Argentina or Brazil. In 1940 there were 11,000 Jews officially listed in Bolivia, mostly from Germany; they even had their own German Club. The club no longer exists today, through lack of members; now there are only about 1,000 Jews in the country.

Barbie had some French friends; one of them said later: 'Ah, the Jews, they used to say hello to Señor Altmann. So did the army officers. It seemed natural to everyone that he should have contacts at headquarters.' Monsieur Albert, as we had better call him, has been in La Paz for about thirty years.

Altmann told his friend J. H. Schneider: 'When the French no longer have anything against me over the war [the war crimes prescription came into effect on 26 November 1974] the Jews will still manage to think up something. They are very good at that. They have already done it with their propaganda about the gas chambers.'

There was no chance of the watchmaker contradicting him. J. H. Schneider had done war service in France and reckoned Barbie to be *'ein Mensch, der absolute korrekt ist, ein Kavalier'*. (A totally decent sort, a gentleman!)

Barbie has a French daughter-in-law, Madame Françoise Croizier de Altmann, whom I tracked down at Santa Cruz de la Sierra in the south, now a widow bringing up her three children. She said: 'My father-in-law always said he had nothing to do with the Jews. He had Jewish friends here, and he liked them a lot. Hunting Jews was not his job during the war. He was after the Resistance people.'

What else did Barbie have to say? Those he confided in remember a man who was fascinated by Hitlerism, but reluctant to talk about the Second World War and what he had done. However, he told several acquaintances that he admired Jean Moulin, and that the real traitor was René Hardy.

Monsieur Albert recalls: 'Altmann told me that for the arrest of the Secret Army members he had worked out a scheme with six civilians, three couples, whose job in particular was to mark a yellow cross on the house and on the room where Jean Moulin was.'

Watchmaker Schneider, Altmann's closest confidant, declared: 'De Gaulle used Hardy. He made the trip to London and de Gaulle told him the Communists had to be got rid of.'

Françoise Croizier said: 'Well, Hardy, that's all known. My father-in-law always said so. I'd rather not talk about that, it's very difficult . . . You know, I understand how someone ends up being a traitor when his family is under threat, his friends too. Who could stand that?'

Caluire is past history for Barbie. At ease with himself, Klaus Altmann of Bolivia decided to travel, and not only in South America. He wanted to see Europe again after fifteen years' absence. The war crimes prescription had not yet been brought into effect, of course, but nobody seemed bothered about him any more. His son, with the similar name of Klaus-Georg Altmann, had gone to and fro across frontiers without any trouble. Of course, he belonged to a younger generation, but at any rate the name apparently meant nothing to the police.

Barbie went to Hamburg on business in connection with the Transmaritima company. There was another reason for the journey: his mother had died. Born fourteen years before the beginning of the twentieth century, Anna Barbie passed away all alone on 26 September 1965, in Triers hospital. She went into hospital a first time, suffering from cancer, then returned to her two-room flat at 19 Dietrichstrasse. She told her old friend Frau Schmeling that her son, Klaus, had not disappeared in the war after all but was well and truly alive; then she went back to hospital to die. She did not mention that he was in Bolivia.

Frau Christa Schmeling recalls: 'She used to come down to us often and watch television. She was a nice white-haired old lady who minded her own business. When they showed war films on TV, Anna Barbie used to say she wanted to go up. She didn't like them.'

Barbie's mother-in-law, Margarethe Willms, was still living in Triers as well. She revealed that Klaus used to visit the second alleyway in the cemetery there and would weep at his mother's grave. This grave, today almost the only one without flowers, has three names engraved on a black marble cross:

—Nikolaus Barbie [his father] 21.1.1888–5.10.1933
—Kurt Barbie [his younger brother] 15.2.1915–29.6.1933
—Anna Barbie, *née* Hees [his mother] 26.11.1886–26.9.1965

But the real reason for his trip to Europe was to see his son in Barcelona, where he was studying law. In the summer of 1966, he spent a few days on the Costa Brava; it may well be that along with his Bolivian passport Barbie had a Mediterranean fishing permit issued by the French authorities.

Madame Thérèse de Lioncourt, formerly French consul in La Paz when Dominique 'the Gorilla' Ponchardier was ambassador, said: 'I remember that spring, there was this fellow always making a fuss in the consulate, refusing to wait, demanding that I see him. I went out into the corridor in the end to see what he was on about. He was shouting: "I asked for a fishing permit weeks ago. I have a place at Lavandou. I'm going on holiday to see my children who are studying over there. I asked for a permit for my boat at Toulon."'

Thérèse de Lioncourt found his application in her files, but there was no reply from the maritime people. He yelled: 'It's not much use being French. I am from the Saar, so I'm French. I like the country a lot, but with the French it's always the same mess!'

Madame de Lioncourt grew angry herself. She scolded him: 'In any case, how am I to know whether you are Altmann or not? And anyway you are no longer French since Germany took over the Saar.'

She remembers vividly: 'He went as white as a sheet! I told him France was prepared to forget past insults, but we weren't completely daft.'

Altmann retorted that he was not German but Bolivian, and stormed out like a madman. Thérèse de Lioncourt remembered a stack of old French passports still tied up with string ever since they had been collected in 1959 when the Saar went back to Germany.

She said: 'I found Altmann's passport and took it straight to Ambassador Ponchardier, who must have informed the Quai d'Orsay and sent over the identity photo.'

An investigation might well have begun from that point, but apparently nothing happened. Ambassador Ponchardier confirmed this incident in retirement at Nice: 'Barbie? They said he was somewhere around over there. I supposed he was in Paraguay. As to Señor Altmann, nobody at that stage saw any connection with Klaus Barbie, even the Quai d'Orsay people. If I had known I would have acted at once, naturally.'

Madame de Lioncourt's tip-off went the same way as the 1963 report: it was ignored or put aside.

The consul encountered Altmann again a few months later at the house of Señor Hermann, consular agent in Guatemala, well known at the French Embassy in La Paz. It was a strange embassy on the Avenida Arce less than one hundred yards from the Interior Ministry and the West German Embassy, and it employed two Germans. That evening in the villa between Obrajes and Calacoto, guarded by Alsatian dogs, Altmann felt very pleased with himself. He had asked Hermann to fix up the meeting to test whether Madame de Lioncourt had in fact learned something about him.

To return to the Barcelona trip, Barbie's son introduced Barbie to a young Catalan friend, Jorge Mota, a former treasurer of the Cedade, a Spanish pro-European outfit on the far right, who regarded Hitler as a hero.

Questioned in 1983, Jorge Mota remembered: 'Barbie came to Europe several times. He told me he had not been in the Gestapo but was an SS Obersturmführer. The last time I saw him, Barbie said he travelled across France to Germany and back again. When he went through Paris, he put some flowers on Jean Moulin's tomb at the Pantheon. He even showed me a photo of himself in front of the tomb.'

What would the Resistance say about that photo if they saw it?

The story of the flowers on the tomb of the head of the Conseil National de la Résistance has been confirmed by Barbie's daughter-in-law, Françoise Croizier de Altmann. When I met her at Santa Cruz de la Sierra she recalled: 'He used to speak of Jean Moulin with admiration. He said Jean Moulin was one of those people you feel are like yourself. They were similar to one another in character.'

Barbie told the story to a reporter from the West German magazine *Stern*, adding: 'I know that may seem strange – ' He recounted that he then 'went to West Germany to the Ubersee [overseas] club where I dealt with Hapag on business and with the German-South American Bank.'

Santa Cruz, some four hundred miles from La Paz, is a colonial town, a sort of Bolivian Texas, where the dollar rules, a land of cocaine, oil, and soldiers doing the goose-step, as in Chile. People speak Spanish or Guarani and you hear more German than English. Françoise Croizier taught French there, at the give-away rate of a dollar a lesson, hardly enough to feed her three children: Corina, aged fifteen, Nadine, twelve, and Nikolaus, ten, who was the spitting image of Barbie. His name carries on the five-century-old tradition of Barbie sons called Nikolaus or Klaus.

The Barbie that his daughter-in-law and grandchildren knew was not the man who tortured Jean Moulin, nor the officer who killed hostages by the hundred and despatched Jewish children to the death camps in cattle trucks. No, for Françoise, Barbie was not that man at all. Possibly he had committed some atrocities, she thought; but it was forty years ago and 6,000 miles away, and it was during the war 'when men are turned into killers'.

Weighing every word, she said: 'We miss him awfully, especially the children, who keep asking for him. They call him Opa. Klaus Barbie was the ideal grandfather, kind, full of attention. If they hadn't taken him away, he would have come to live with us here at Santa Cruz. Now he needs our help. He writes to us from his prison in German, in block letters. He says he is well treated, but feels very much alone.'

Françoise Croizier joined the family in 1966. She had met Klaus-Georg in Paris, where he was studying law. That summer Françoise went with him to England, and then to Barcelona, where the older Barbie visited them.

The wedding took place at Cochabamba on 6 April 1968, but their parents were not present. Françoise explained: 'My future father-in-law was not too keen on our getting married: he thought we were too young at twenty. But above all I loomed as a danger to him – imagine, a French national in the family. It could mean big trouble for him, that was what he thought.'

So Klaus Barbie senior was not told and found out only afterwards. Little did he suspect that the details set down a year later, on 24 July 1969, on the 113th sheet of the wedding register at the French consulate in La Paz, would in time lead to his downfall. For the details relating to Klaus-Georg's father were strangely similar to those on a search sheet that had been circulating for years, originated by the French judicial machinery against one of the biggest of all war criminals. Certainly the surnames were different, but the first names and dates of birth were exactly the same.

French Consul Paul Colombani was surprised at the coincidences and mulled them over for quite a while. The idea that he ought to do something nagged at him, as France did not have a permanent SDECE official at La Paz.

At the close of his diplomatic career, Paul Colombani told me: 'I noted that the names and first names were fairly similar. So I went to see the Germans [Ambassador Dr Hampe was just along the street] and they said they knew nothing about Altmann.' Curiously the following year they knew everything about him, though it is true there was a new ambassador.

Paul Colombani raised his scruples with Ambassador Joseph Lambroschini, his superior. Lambroschini later told me: 'I learned, of course, that Barbie was in Bolivia. But at that time we had the Régis Debray business on our hands, and his life was at risk. That was more urgent than Barbie. We couldn't go to the Bolivians and say we wanted both Debray and Barbie!'

Joseph Lambroschini sent a message to his director at the Quai d'Orsay, Monsieur Jurgensen. There was no official reaction but it was clear that the French diplomats in La Paz could not chase two hares at once. Debray had been caught, and he was in danger of being skinned.

So in the autumn of 1969 it was perfectly well known that Barbie was in the neighbourhood. One of my colleagues in New York went to investigate the death of Che Guevara. He had a coffee with the ambassador in Avenida 16 de Julio, and was told in confidence: 'This place is where Barbie comes for his *cafeito*.'

France decided to lie low on Barbie; and Debray, jailed for thirty years by the Camiri military court, was freed in 1970.

With that over, France could go for Altmann-Barbie. Lambroschini was in poor health and Jean-Louis Mandereau took over, but he did not take action because nobody informed him about the Butcher of Lyons.

Paul Colombani said: 'There was no reason to mention it to Monsieur Mandereau directly he moved in. High up, they had decided to let it rest, and it was over my head.'

A few weeks or months after his arrival, the consul eventually told Mandereau of his suspicions. Barbie had gone off to Lima. The ambassador told me: 'I immediately notified Paris but got no response . . . I made a few inquiries among our West German colleagues, and thanks to a keen anti-Nazi, a young counsellor married to a French girl, I became convinced that Altmann and Barbie were one and the same person. The German embassy had known it for ages.'

That was in the summer of 1971. My New York colleague was busy with other material and was held to secrecy. Neither Beate Klarsfeld nor even the best informed journalists yet realized that Klaus Barbie was commuting, so to speak, between La Paz and Lima.

Françoise Croizier takes up the story: 'At that time, I was none too sure who my father-in-law really was, but I kept thinking that, after all, he was a German who had settled in South America after the war. My husband knew, but he had said nothing except "Maybe one day we'll have a bombshell burst here!" Whatever the truth, I had accepted the risk, I wasn't the only Frenchwoman who married a Nazi's son and, after all, I married the son, not the father!'

The Transmaritima company chartered as many as nineteen freighters at one point, flying Greek and German flags. The *Argolis* and *Argonautis*, for example, would berth at the port of Arica, Chile, with wheat for Bolivia and weapons for Chile.

Although not a single piece of written evidence has been produced, it is widely known in diplomatic circles that French arms were delivered to Israel after the embargo decreed by General de Gaulle in 1967 in the wake of the Six-Day War. Barbie, chief executive of Transmaritima Bolivia, is said to have persuaded a French arms manufacturer that Chile would buy the consignments intended for Israel. Chile got its arms, Bolivia took its cut on the way, and Tel Aviv had the rest, the story goes. It seems everyone was happy.

Some diplomats go further and assert that this shipping operation explains why the Israeli secret service showed no interest in the Barbie case. The observer may well ask why the story had no backing in written form, in South America, at any rate. The reason is that the Bolivians simply do not keep that kind of record; documents would be far too dangerous and there are times when it is better to rely on a bad memory. Who knows the damage a document might cause in years to come!

Klaus Barbie travelled more and more. He was seen less and less frequently in La Paz and Cochabamba and more often in Brazil, Peru (in early 1967), Mexico and the United States, especially around Miami, Atlanta, San Francisco, Galveston and New Orleans, where his son was an agent for Transmaritima.

He was a man flirting with danger. He risked his neck in Brazil, which had granted West Germany extradition in the case of Franz Stangl, the ex-commander of Treblinka concentration camp, where 700,000 people perished. Stangl was seized in February 1967 after tip-offs from Nazi-hunter Simon Wiesenthal, and handed over to the West Germans five months later on the understanding that he would not be executed. Franz Stangl, now dead, was sentenced to life imprisonment just before Christmas 1970. But it must have been in Brazil that Barbie met up with a man named Sassen, South American representative for the Austrian firm Steyr Daimler Puch. Barbie was to make a lot of money out of this meeting . . .

The Transmaritima company enabled Barbie to travel, but normal trade was not his strong point; he was no desk man. Barbie preferred a quick killing, as they say in business circles. One or two deals a year, the occasional profit from speculating on the dollar, and he was happy to go back to his piano in the La Paz apartment and play Beethoven.

Regina, whose Nazi sentiments remain intact, meanwhile wrote stories for children and drove shop-keepers mad trying to bargain with them. She never went out for a drink with her husband; in this regard she was very Bolivian, since husbands go alone to cafés in Bolivia.

Señor Altmann himself was an abstemious customer; at the Caravelle and the Confiteria La Paz he would always sit at the same table with his back to the wall so that he could see the door, drinking neither whisky nor *pisco sauer*, the local rot-gut. The slightly built man in a tweed jacket and Tyrolean-style hat was a familiar sight and people used to shake him by the hand, respect him, envy him because of his connections with the big shots, among them the army chiefs.

Amazingly, he managed to creep right under the wing of the colonels, acting as their adviser. There was not a German family in Santa Cruz who did not know that. Klaus Barbie alias Altmann was among those who engineered the coup by General Hugo Banzer on 21 August 1971, the 185th in one hundred and fifty years.

Barbie procured the necessary weapons and helped train the private militia groups, who so naturally turned into paramilitary forces when the time came. Banzer never forgot. He saved Barbie from the French three years later when President Georges Pompidou, albeit somewhat half-heartedly, demanded his extradition.

It is well known that America has a political hold over countries like Bolivia, but close scrutiny reveals an especially strong German influence over the South American state; in those days the German oligarchy would quickly arrange the ousting of any general who had left-wing inclinations. It could intervene effectively since half Bolivia's economy was controlled by German families, and that was how Hugo Banzer came to power.

A Santa Cruz businessman, Erwin Gasser, admitted: 'We paid dearly to get this regime. You don't carry through revolutions with Bratwürstchen [small sausages]!'

But as the 1970s drew near, the former SS officer began to lose his grip. A few leaks sprang in the Transmaritima company. One Bolivian considered Altmann to have lost influence to such an extent that he took Barbie to court for debt, in September 1971, when Judge Carlos Terrazas Torres issued an arrest warrant for Altmann. But it did not stick, thanks to the intervention of Rear-Admiral Orlando Roca Castedo, who testified on Barbie's behalf. The relevant document includes the sentence: 'The plaintiff dared to seek the arrest of Don Klaus Altmann as if he were a common delinquent, without thinking of the possible consequences.' The plaintiff in question was a Bolivian quinine dealer whose name was not divulged at the time. Deeply vexed, he strode into the French Embassy in Avenida Arce and declared outright that Don Altmann was none other than the sinister Klaus Barbie. The Embassy doubtless knew that already, but all the same the quinine dealer left them what he said was a photo of Altmann.

Barbie may have sensed the danger, for he called back

his son from the Transmaritima offices in New Orleans and sent him and his wife, Françoise, off to Hamburg. Françoise was happier there, and Klaus-Georg was able to make the acquaintance of a friend of his father, Roberto Quintanilla Pereira. Forty-three years old, Quintanilla had lately been rewarded for special services; he had been an ex-chief of the anti-guerrilla police and played a part in the preparations for Che Guevara's execution. It was also said that he was well acquainted with the circumstances of General Barrientos's death. Quintanilla was now consul-general in West Germany. The young Altmanns were frequent guests at the Quintanillas' Hamburg residence.

Françoise recalls: 'He was a wonderful man and the children adored him; they called him Toto . . . He used to get phone threats in the middle of the night. "We're going to get you," the callers would say.'

And they did. He was gunned down on 1 April 1971 at his apartment, the killer, a woman, pumping several 9 mm bullets into him. Quintanilla's wife grabbed her, and the killer lost her wig and her Colt Cobra before escaping. Quintanilla just had time to tell his wife, 'Look after the children', then he died.

A few minutes later Klaus-Georg Altmann burst in, and took the consul's wife in his arms. He attended the cremation nine days later and accompanied the ashes in the Lufthansa plane that took her and the children to La Paz.

The description of the killer, the wig and, above all, the Colt pointed to Monika Ertl, thirty-five, as the suspect. The gun's number was especially helpful. It appeared that she got the gun from a leftist millionaire publisher in Italy, Giangiacomo Feltrinelli, who financed the operation and had bought the gun. The Bolivian Interior Ministry affirmed that two guerrilleros with the false names of Chato Peredo and El Gordo planned the slaying in Santiago, Chile; Imilla (Monika Ertl) was picked to do the job.

Austrian police officers caught sight of Monika and Feltrinelli subsequently at a hunting lodge in Styria. Monika Ertl was the daughter of a Bavarian ski and kayak champion, a mountaineer and cameraman who had led an expedition into the Bolivian jungle and mountains in 1946. Monika went to school in La Paz, where she married Señor Harjes, of German origin.

A year after Quintanilla's murder, on 16 February 1972, Feltrinelli blew himself up in Milan with a bomb he was fixing to an electricity pylon. Next year, it was Monika Ertl's turn: she was gunned down by police in a La Paz street, having returned with an Argentine passport bearing the name of Nancy Molina. Her body lies in the German cemetery near the Miraflores district.

Her murder was doubtless a vengeance killing for Quintanilla. But there have been other murders involving people known to Barbie: General Barrientos (a helicopter 'accident' on 27 April 1969 – the police report was made out by Colonel Quintanilla); his rural trade unionist friend Jorge Soliz (found dead on 26 November 1969, on the side of the road between Cochabamba and Santa Cruz); the *Hoy* newspaper managing editor Alfredo Alexander (blown to pieces with his wife by a booby-trap parcel said to have been planted by an upholsterer who worked for Altmann); journalist Jaime Otero Calderon, who had been working on these stories and perhaps knew too much (strangled in his office on 16 February 1970).

General Torres, who later headed a democratic government in Bolivia, suspected his predecessor Ovando of these killings, and strove to wrench the lid off these mysteries. He never managed it, and was himself assassinated.

Considerably more worrying from Barbie's standpoint was the killing of Peruvian millionaire Banchero Rossi on 1 January 1972 . . .

The Transmaritima business had collapsed and Señor Altmann skipped off to Peru, finding a welcome just outside Lima from his friend Don Federico Schwend, the forged pound-note expert, who was his partner in a curious firm named La Estrella. ·

Schwend's history was tortuous. He was seized by the Gestapo in 1941 on the grounds that he tried to give the Mexican consul, who was working for the English, forged plans of a submarine. He was about to be tried when Dr Grobl, head of the German intelligence service, who realised he could use a crook like Schwend, intervened, got him released and took him on as a financial adviser. He was offered a 30 per cent commission, had his name changed to Wendig, and was told to spread around forged pounds sterling. The operation was tagged 'Bernhardt', after Sturmbannführer Bernhardt Kruger, who thought up the scheme to inflict damage on the British economy.

'The worst part of the job was not forging the pound notes, but producing the paper,' I was told by Dr Hottl, a top man in the Amt VI spy service, now in retirement at Alt-Aussee, Austria, near the celebrated Lake Toplitz where whole crates of forged sterling were found. He said: 'In the end we came up with a mixture of paper and old rag just like the English paper. All we had to do was print on it. That was done by experts, many of them Jews from the concentration camps.' The counterfeit money was worked into any circuit involving trade with London. The money went via Istanbul to Santiago and other cities. Posing as a Yugoslav refugee from a village razed by the Nazis, Schwend reached Peru four years before Barbie came over on the *Corrientes*. But Peru kicked him out after three years, and he moved to Ecuador, where he teamed up with another Nazi named Sassen. Three years later he was back in Peru, under his real name. He settled in Santa Clara to the north-east of Lima, raising chickens; in 1970 the farm run by Don Federico was producing 200,000 chicks a month. By now he was a CIA agent, and the chicken farm was a good cover. He contributed financially to the building of a commissariat at Vitarte, half-way into Lima, and fixed up security around his property, although he avoided giving it the appearance of a blockhouse. A llama called Gretchen was kept in the grounds. Another job he performed was to run, unofficially, Peru's first mail censor scheme.

He was arrested several years later and charged with various rackets, including black market dealing in dollars – a sum of $350,000, it was rumoured in Lima. Schwend had a framed photo of Martin Bormann at his place. When the police asked him about it, he said: 'Bormann is alive. I have met him frequently!'

In fact, Bormann was killed just after he fled the Berlin Chancellery in May 1945. His bones were found in 1972 when there was digging on the Friedrichstrasse. Anthropometric analysis of the jawbones and teeth, when checked against his medical file, established formal proof. So why did Schwend claim the devil was still alive? Simply to show off, not only among his ex-Nazi buddies who contacted him as part of the Odessa escape network, but also among the local Germans, and various South Americans he wanted to impress. Bormann was used as a kind of scarecrow; sometimes he was said to be a tourist, sometimes Padre Augustin of the Franciscan order – an appropriate disguise for a ghost.

Don Federico Schwend made quite an impression in prison, too. The warders and other inmates at Lurigancho never forgot the crates of eggs he had brought in for them. When inspected, they were found to contain two yolks, and could not be hatched for that reason. The Peruvian police gave this old diabetic Nazi with a bald head and an eagle's profile the nickname *Doble Jema*, meaning 'double yolk'.

Earlier in 1966, when Klaus Barbie made his first trip to Europe, Don Federico gave him a message for his friend Otto Skorzeny, who had freed Mussolini in the famous Operation Cicero, and who was then living in Madrid. The message read: 'Klaus Altmann, bearer of this message, can be trusted. He was Hauptsturmführer in France and was condemned to death after the war.' We can be sure that Skorzeny gave him a big welcome when he turned up at his Madrid home, well known to other comrades of the Third Reich.

In July 1976, Friedrich Schwend was expelled and later arrested in West Germany, unable to settle a hotel bill of 50 Marks – thirty years previously he could produce millions of forged banknotes. He was released and went back to Lima, where he died in 1981 at the Ricardo Palma clinic. His son-in-law's mother observed: 'Hm, not surprising. They were all Jews in that clinic and they got rid of him.'

So thanks to 'Double Yolk', Klaus Barbie holed up in Peru in 1971 at a moment when the funds of Trans-maritima were so depleted that his son never got his last pay cheque; he let his beard grow, vowing: 'I'll shave when I get paid!' Barbie thought it prudent to quit La Paz until the storm blew over and people forgot that the ships had never actually been bought.

Schwend, who said he knew Altmann as far back as 1942 in Amsterdam, which seems likely, found him a house within smelling distance of the chickens at 200 Calle Malicon, Chacalcayo. (An error by the Peruvian secret service at one point led to the belief that Altmann lived at number 210, which is the El Carmen villa. Consequently, for years, this villa's photo kept appearing in the press. Actually, for a very long time now, this charming residence has been occupied by Japanese.) By coincidence it was Bavarian-style; ringed with high walls, it had a garden, swimming pool, terrace-balcony and small vegetable plot. The area was known as California. Barbie was in his element, a stone's-throw from ex-Nazis whichever way he looked. His wife Regina adapted well, but had been happier in Cochabamba.

The house faced a hill on the other side of the Rio Rimac ('the murmuring river'). On the hill was a fantastic villa, the property of the fish-processing magnate Luis Banchero Rossi, a publisher like Feltrinelli. He was found dead on 1 January 1972. The rumour was that Rossi wanted to publish the truth about the Nazis and the noted

Odessa network in South America. The police moved fast and detained the gardener's son, who confessed to killing his employer by stoning him. There was only one snag – the boy was mentally deficient, a small fellow who could never have murdered someone like Luis Banchero on his own. Juan Vilca was also the gardener at Barbie's rented house, and he and Barbie had been seen together at the Vienna bar only a few days before Banchero's death. Vilca – the father – was later convicted of the murder, but let out of jail after five years.

While no accurate picture of what happened has emerged, it does appear that the billionaire wanted to get back at Klaus Altmann and threatened him. This at least is the view of the French ambassador in Lima, Albert Chambon, who chatted freely to me after he resigned. 'Luis Banchero was trying a bit of counter-blackmail. That was the belief of the examining magistrate, Jose Santos Chichizola, who was taken off the case when he held evidence of the Germans' guilt. When a search was made at Schwend's place, he found weapons, drugs, and so on. It was his belief that the way Banchero was tortured and killed was SS-inspired. [On 12 April 1972, the magistrate personally forced open the door of the study where Don Federico was burning the last of the files. He also found two rifles with telescopic sights and a $5,000 cheque.] The newspapers in Peru said: "According to first reports, Banchero was a blackmail victim of war criminals." Refusing to be manipulated, the fisheries king reportedly "threatened to reveal their true identity, which was the reason they eliminated him".'

Don Federico Schwend responded to the magistrate with the following words: 'Altmann was not at Banchero's house on 1 January, he was with me at Santa Clara, in my home. As to the dollars you found at the house, Altmann left them behind.'

One evening 'Double Yolk' phoned direct to the ambassador's residence, and told him: 'This is Colonel Schwend. You claim I'm a war criminal. Well, you'd better be very careful.'

A few nights later a blast wrecked the entrance gate to the embassy at San Isidro.

Did the French Government actually know where Klaus Barbie was hiding? And did they feel it was better to forget about him, since he must have been in a sorry state, living in exile, suffering agonies of anxiety? It was a question a lot of people were asking even after the trial.

We have a confidential memo from the Foreign Ministry in Bonn, dated 20 September 1969: 'He [Barbie] and his family reached Bolivia in May 1951 via Argentina . . . Our inquiries made little headway because Altmann has close links with the Bolivian authorities. Unconfirmed rumours are that they entered the country on foreign passports (Vatican). . . His daughter Ute [naturalised on 31 January 1961] asked us for a residence permit for the German Federal Republic, where she would act as representative of the Boehringer company in Mannheim, for which her father was an agent. She gave her father's previous nationality as Polish. We recommend that inquiries be conducted with prudence, as Klaus Altmann has good relations with Bolivian government circles and with other ex-Nazis living in South America, such as Fritz Schwend, now at Lima.'

There was an enclosure with this memo compiled on the basis of data from the West German Embassy in La Paz, an excellent photo showing Altmann with a group of businessmen. This means that the cat was out of the bag in the autumn of 1969. No action was taken, however, that might lead to the extradition of Klaus Barbie. We shall never know what General de Gaulle might have done; by then he had withdrawn to Colombey-les-Deux-Églises. His successor was meanwhile preparing to grant amnesty to Barbie's best friend in France, the head of the Lyons militia, Paul Touvier, also twice condemned to death, at Lyons in 1945 and at Chambéry in 1947; in 1983 the magistrate Christian Riss issued another international arrest warrant for Touvier on the grounds of crimes against humanity.

Everything was happening at the same time: the German memo, the Bolivian businessman's legal action, the mystery surrounding the marriage register – it all coincided with the very instant when West Germany was filing away the Barbie dossier for good. (Moreover, I turned up a curious fact when going through the files at La Paz central prison: Klaus Altmann was jailed on 23 November 1971 for a debt of 54,207.60 pesos claimed by the COBOFO [the Bolivian Development Corporation]. The detention warrant exists but there are no details in the archives about his release. However that may be, he was definitely in Peru a few days later.)

Suddenly Nazi-hunter Beate Klarsfeld emerged from the wings. Still very active today, this young German woman from a military family, wife of a French Jew, has spent years digging out Nazi war criminals, not for money, but because she wants to see justice done. Beate Klarsfeld vowed to fight negligence, not with the motive of vengeance but to root out slackness by the courts, weakness in officials, compromise at all levels. She is not against forgiving but hates tricks and impudence on the part of the former SS men who have fooled the military courts. Not a Jew herself, she nevertheless feels horror at the persecution the Nazis conducted. Born in 1939, she probably did not have experience of the war in the 1940s. She will not agree that her generation should simply wipe the slate clean. The philosopher Vladimir Jankélévitch has said: 'Of herself she is the conscience of a country without conscience.'

It goes without saying that Beate Klarsfeld does not work on her own. She is assisted by her husband, Serge, lawyer and historian, president of the association Sons and Daughters of the Deported Jews of France. (Serge's father died at Auschwitz.) She also gets backing from Jewish organizations, and from Israel. Only Barbie and his close defenders see commercial interest in the campaign conducted by this impassioned woman. She is outspoken, she does not mince words, and is not afraid to name names. She physically assaulted West German Chancellor Kiesinger and has chained herself to trees and railings in West Germany, Poland and Bolivia in a bid to mobilise the press. She has a taste for the spectacular, and can be irritating.

But if it were not for the Klarsfelds, the quiet Señor Altmann, killer, torturer and then arms dealer, would doubtless still be living a tranquil existence in the shadow of the Andes dictatorships.

In June 1971, as Barbie's crimes were about to evaporate in France with prescription – on 25 November 1974, in the case of the second death sentence – the Munich Public Prosecutor's office decided to drop the new proceedings started in 1960, because of lack of evidence. This meant that Klaus Barbie would be rehabilitated, possibly indicating to other West German prosecutors the line to be adopted for three hundred other similar cases.

Beate sprang into action, came up with witnesses, rallied the Resistance people, and successfully persuaded the German Prosecutor Ludolph to reopen the file that his colleage Rabl had just closed.

Beate Klarsfeld had more than ideas; she also had courage and tremendous energy. Once the Munich Public Prosecutor was convinced that Barbie took an active part in the extermination of Jews, her task was to gather evidence, and above all to show that Altmann and Barbie were indeed the same person. It seemed obvious, but it was not easy to prove. As material evidence, the authorities had only a few photos of Señor Altmann and just two of Klaus Barbie, a full face shot and one in profile, taken in Germany just after the war. Professor Ziegelmayer of the Institute of Human Genetics in Munich had the photos enlarged and obtained a good contrast. In a 16-page report he went through each trait, each angle, each feature of the two faces, in minute detail, Barbie in 1948 and Altmann twenty-one years later.

'Face taller than it is wide,' the report said. 'Left eye slightly higher than the right eye.'

But where was the old fox? The answer reached Beate Klarsfeld through the mail. She was contacted by an employee of the millionaire Luis Banchero, a German named Herbert John, who worked in the publishing house Editoriales Unidas. Through a contact in Munich, journalist Peter Nischk, John sent a description of the Nazi organisation in Peru and Bolivia. He also gave the real name of Don Altmann. He wrote: 'Klaus Barbie alias Altmann is living with Fritz Schwend at Santa Clara near Lima, Casilla No. 1, Carretera Central 14 kilometres.'

This letter came through the door of the Klarsfeld home on 29 December 1971. Three days later – by a strange coincidence – Luis Banchero Rossi was murdered.

The hunt for the Hauptsturmführer was on, and the Klarsfelds were not the only ones ready. My bags were also waiting in the hall.

10

A T FIRST THE CHANCES of my finding Barbie at all
seemed remote.

The Altiplano suddenly stopped short, flush with the
mountain; from above, the city looked like an ant heap. La
Paz, I thought, was a kind of Bab-el-Oued in the Andes,
with the cold sun reflected from the tin roofs everywhere
you looked. It had been misty at Lima, but here in the
limpid high altitude it was like being an eagle, you could
see for miles.

El Alto airport is at an altitude of 13,385 feet, which
means your heart beats wildly at the slightest movement,
the tiniest emotional upset, while your blood thumps
somewhere inside your temples. It's called the *soroche*,
mountain sickness.

A slight panic grips you in the taxi as it careers down to
La Paz itself. One day there will be a good highway, they
say, but meanwhile all they have is hairpin bends and a
picture of the Holy Mother of God screwed on to the
dashboard. It is an old American automobile with a
star-spangled windshield and tyres as smooth as a baby's
elbow. Some of the tackle and baggage is in the boot, the
rest on the roof. I have fun counting the crosses marking
previous accidents, anticipating the one we are heading
for. The driver is getting 50 pesos per passenger and extra
for the baggage. He whistles cheerfully, his elbow poked
out of the window.

'*Cine*, stars . . . good good,' he prattles in Bolivian
English. But somehow we cling to taxi drivers as we do to
air hostesses on a long flight. They are our instant link
with a new world; we need them.

'You know Señor Klaus Altmann?' I venture.

'Señor *como*?'

We let it drop, checking the time: 3.00 p.m. on 31

January 1972 and well into the Bolivian summer. In Paris it was chilly, and right now the French capital's millions are relaxing over dinner. Somewhere in this bustling city is Klaus Barbie, alias Nikolaus Altmann Hansen, phoney son of the equally phoney Peter Altmann and Anna Maria Hansen. Official passport Number 588-71.

Once again my fingers slip inside my pocket for the results of the latest German investigation. Apart from the resemblance between the two photos, Barbie in 1940 and Altmann in 1970, there are some exciting comparisons in that document: Señor Altmann's wife is called Regina, born 7 December 1915, at Osburg near Triers, maiden name Willelms. Klaus Barbie's wife is called Regina, *née* Willms. His daughter, Ute, was born on 30 June 1941 at Kassel. Barbie's daughter is called Ute too, and she entered this world on exactly the same day at Triers, in the Rhineland. His son, Klaus-Georg, is marked down as having been born at Kasel bei Leipzig (Kasel with one s only) on 11 December 1946. There is no such place as Kasel. But at Kassel some 120 miles west of Leipzig on that same date Klaus-Georg Barbie was born at Dr Kuhn's clinic.

For Beate Klarsfeld it was a race against time to get the Hauptsturmführer arrested while he was still in the Santa Clara area. Not as wealthy as French Radio-Television (ORTF), she had to get the money for her fare to Peru from her friends. Loaded with documents, she barged in on French Ambassador Albert Chambon, who had been deported during the war.

When an urgent request to Peru for extradition was sent by the Quai d'Orsay, it was in the knowledge that Ambassador Albert Chambon would do everything possible to procure it. He had served with the Noyautage des Administrations Publiques, one of the Resistance networks and had been deported to Buchenwald. The French government knew he would stretch diplomacy to the limits. In fact, the very same day he received it, he went to the office of the Interior Minister, Richter, but

Richter was in no hurry to disturb the *excellentissimo* Señor Altmann, against whom he had no complaint so far.

Monsieur Chambon told me: 'How could you expect him to know anything about the case? They had no idea what was involved. The easy-going attitude of the South Americans has some link with their language. In Spanish the word *'deportacion'* has nothing to do with concentration camps or gas chambers. For the Peruvians and the Bolivians it simply means temporary exile, 'being locked in the cupboard', as they say. It signifies a comfortable stay in a friendly neighbouring country, where you cannot harm the government in power, while you still receive your salary.

He added: 'In any case it's our own fault that the South Americans kept on shielding the Nazis. They knew nothing of the Vel-d'Hiv horror in Paris, had no familiarity with the atrocities. We ought to have spelled it out to them. Manifestos were no good, we should have run information campaigns with films, photos, witnesses' statements. That would not have cost more than a few ex-servicemen's gala evenings.'

Chambon was sure that if France had been more forceful in putting its case Barbie and his friends would no longer have an easy run with their story that Jean Moulin was just a *guerrillero*; that his Resistance comrades were a bunch of thugs and dangerous leftists who shot valiant German troops in the back; that deportation was the lesser of two evils. The German colonies in South America, so ready to stand by the SS settlers, would have carried much less weight with those governments.

Monsieur Chambon recalled: 'When Maurice Schumann was Foreign Minister, I told him there was no hope of Bolivia giving us Barbie.'

In the fight against Barbie it was going to be one down for Beate. Barbie won the first round by crossing the frontier before the authorities decided to take up pursuit. Señor Altmann had influence and he had friends like

Fritz Schwend, who was calmly raising his chickens and tending his llama. With their help he went through the frontier post of Rio Seco, escorted by two men from the P.I.P., the Peruvian secret police, in a white Volkswagen with a false number plate. Whether it was bravado, a sick joke or chance, the number happened to be the same number as that of the Hungarian Ambassador.

At the frontier, Señor Altmann just disappeared.

I knew a little of the Bolivians from a trip I made to Camiri in 1967 when I interviewed Régis Debray at the Casino Militar prison for *France Soir* and the TV programme *Cinq Colonnes à la Une*. But five years had gone by and if anyone ever mentioned Che Guevara it was only to tell the story of how his severed hands had been sent to Fidel Castro. Régis Debray had been released just before Christmas two years earlier, and he returned to France for a time. In La Paz the presidential chair had yet another occupant, General Banzer, who gained power partly through Don Altmann, as was later discovered.

There was no point in trying to pull a fast one on the Bolivian authorities. Yes, I said, I was here to contact Klaus Barbie. Yes, he was the only person we were interested in just now.

On Monday I had confirmation that other foreign newsmen were in on the hunt, and my juices started to flow because on a story like this it's no holds barred. My deadline, it seemed, was mighty close, for the First Channel in Paris had booked a programme on Barbie the following week for the feature *'Une Première'* (Page One Lead Story). Barbie was a lead story, if I could get it.

French officials held out little hope. One diplomat warned: 'If you find out where Altmann is living, take it easy, it will be guarded. They don't know you and they're trigger-happy.'

We scoured the streets of La Paz, especially the Sopocachi district, where we knew Barbie had friends. Our driver, Rafael, kept his ears and eyes open, too; he was a Quechua – from the Altiplano – and had a broad weatherbeaten face with prominent cheekbones and rather slanted eyes. He asked his Quechua acquaintances, though he ignored the women, who slowly munched their coca leaves, wearing bowler hats, with their children on their backs wrapped in grey or black capes. 'No ask women, waste time,' growled Rafael.

Our cameraman, Christian van Ryswick, was restless and kept stamping his feet. His 16mm camera and set of lenses were all ready, cleaned and checked over. He was not optimistic, I could tell, but he tried not to show it. Sound engineer Jean-Pierre Ajax was his usual calm self. He had done it all: the Congo massacres, the Vietnam war, Cambodia. René Larmagnac had his batteries fully charged and was constantly checking his lamps.

'Blue or artificial, which light to do you want?'

'Can't tell yet, wait till we've got Barbie.'

I could have hoped for a better beginning. I closed my eyes and tried to commit to memory the photos of Barbie that I had. We received a good luck telex from Paris from Jacques Alexandre and Jacques Olivier Chattard, producers of the 'Plein Cadre' programme; the idea that we were not a forgotten army boosted our morale.

I went back to room 505 at the Sucre Hotel, and found someone had searched by belongings. They had put everything back neatly, except for the copy of Playboy I had bought at Orly Airport.

To console myself I studied a list of Barbie's friends that I had in my possession, along with notes on where they fitted in, how much clout they had. I reflected on the story that one night at a German Circle meeting a few years ago, Klaus Altmann started firing a gun into the air, yelling: 'I'm the Gestapo, nobody scares me.' Whether or not it was true, he scared me, especially as rumour had it that Barbie was as safe as the invisible man for as long as there were Germans in Bolivia. The all-powerful German colony in Santa Cruz de la Sierra was backing Barbie all the way; they would never let him down, even if the

Bolivians had a full, authentic account of his crimes in Lyons, the Jura and the Netherlands. Altmann provided the weapons that brought Hugo Banzer to power in place of Juan Torres, and Banzer owed him a big favour for that. I began to realise how reticent they were going to be in high places.

Tuesday came, with nothing to report, just inquiries greeted with smiles and no answers. Only a hint of a promise here and there. 'Tomorrow you come back, Señor, tomorrow . . .'

In Paris the Cognacq Jay studios were wondering why there was not a single foot of film when we had been there four days. They knew we might well miss Barbie, but if we could not get him we should get some film of his close acquaintances.

Then I learned just after midday that French Ambassador Jean-Louis Mandereau had submitted the extradition request to the Foreign Ministry. I immediately asked for an interview with President Hugo Banzer Suares. I was informed: 'If it is for the Altmann affair, the President is far too busy.'

I followed up with: 'Oh no, not just that. I'm interested in Bolivian policy, its international relations.'

Not a hope. So we moved on and the four of us ended up with a Chinese man who spoke Spanish with a Bolivian accent. Like Paris and New York, La Paz is also very cosmopolitan; we even saw a bullfight poster featuring a *torero* from Japan.

On Wednesday we got a break – a middle-aged woman who ran out of money at the middle of every month. But not this month, thanks to a small consideration from me, for which she said she could arrange a meeting with Altmann. I found out that the Bolivians planned to arrest Altmann, whether to satisfy France's extradition request or to protect him, I could not tell. I noted a story in *Hoy* about a commando group arriving in La Paz, under the cover of a French TV team, to kidnap or eliminate Altmann. We live and learn.

The Bolivians intended to keep Klaus Barbie in the Panoptico Nacional, the equivalent in La Paz of St Peter's jail, on the grounds that for several years he had owed the sum of 54,237.26 pesos – repayments to the Bolivian Development Corporation. But first, they were to interrogate him, even though they must have known every detail of his life. It was plain that Barbie had lost control of his destiny, at least for the time being.

My contact obtained the authorisation to see Barbie from a friend in the civil service. I hurried along to the Interior Ministry a few yards from the French Embassy and stuck the chit under their noses. They searched me three times, then decided the chit was not dated correctly. I spent another five hours getting the date fixed, and then went back to the Ministry.

'*Mañana*' was all I got from them.

Pending *mañana*, we took some reels of Beate Klarsfeld, known here as the '*cazadora de Nazis*'. Two hours later she was expelled, and packed the reels in her bag, but she was not allowed to take them with her even into the French Embassy, because they felt that her procedure was not compatible with protocol. She had physically assaulted Kiesinger, the former West German Chancellor (and former Nazi). God knew what she would do in La Paz!

More filming, this time in the German cemetery in the capital. Some of the graves had swastikas on them, and there was a 1914–18 war memorial at the entrance. Barbie might yet, I feared, end his days here, 5,500 miles from Berlin.

We took views of the city and did an interview with a Jew who had onced lived in Lyons. He said his wife was deported and died at Auschwitz. He knew all about the German oligarchy here, but he didn't know Barbie.

We ran a few feet on Father Rivals, a French priest who had a front seat during the recent clashes in La Paz in

August, when 200 people lost their lives. In a strong Perpignan accent he told us: 'The Nazis were given a big welcome in Bolivia, and elsewhere in South America. The ruling class needed good organisers, with a knowledge of discipline, police procedures, counter-guerrilla tactics. They don't care about World War II. The SS refugees are regarded simply as excellent leaders of men, and they were given positions of responsibility.'

He was right. The army uses the goose-step here, even though Nazism is not rated too highly. When you mention the Germans to a Bolivian, the chances are he thinks of those Germans who founded the phalansteries prior to 1914 and did such good work. After all, La Paz is a far cry from the battlefields of World War II. It's like telling a Breton schoolteacher about some South American war.

Thursday, 3 February. At last I was inside the Interior Ministry. But maybe that was all I was going to see. The walls were a miserable grey, with a few calendars, and a man in khaki with a tommy gun every three yards. They looked about sixteen years old. Another search took place, and an officer informed me: 'It has been arranged. The Minister agrees in principle to an interview.' I swallowed hard, and then he said: 'Provided Señor Klaus Altmann agrees.'

For days I had waited for this chance, and the goddamn camera team wasn't there! They were roaming the city taking shots of the scenery for lack of anything better.

The officer said: 'We are going to blindfold you, and put you in a police van with your equipment. For security reasons, nobody must know where Señor Altmann is.'

Of course. It dawned on me. When the Israelis grabbed Adolf Eichmann in Argentina it made big headlines. The Bolivians remembered that, ten years after he was hanged.

There was another wait for two hours, with a lieutenant and his twelve-year-old son who thought France was somewhere in the Middle East.

Then they said: 'It is too dangerous. We shall bring him here. Come back at 3.00 p.m.'

I managed to get Christian on the phone and told him to move it and get over to where I was. I asked the Bolivians if they wouldn't mind if we started setting up our equipment. If we could only show how professional we were, if they could actually see the lamps in place, maybe we would have won half the battle. We got the tackle into a third-floor office, skipped lunch and waited. We ran over the facts as we knew them; I read through the material I had: Lyons, Jean Moulin, the coincidences about the names, dates and places for the Altmann family and the Barbie family. I prepared my questions in German, knowing I would not be able to look down at my notebook, because if it went as I expected I would not have time to mess about with bits of paper, just the time to confront Barbie eye to eye.

Christian van Ryswick loaded a few 16 mm magazines, and lined them up on an officer's desk. With his lamps all ready, René was slumping in the chair where Barbie was to sit. Jean-Pierre prepared a long-play tape so there would be no gaps, and connected up a standby recorder and two extra mikes just in case.

I told them: 'No clapper board. We start filming the moment the door opens.'

The door opened soon after that, and again and again, and each time we started filming, wasting yards of reel. Our nerves were frazzled. Three whole hours we sweated it out, and the ashtray started to look like Mount Etna. The Bolivians came in, disappeared, came back.

'Señor Altmann not like.'

'Has he arrived?'

'Next door.'

'All we want is a few words.'

'I go see.'

A colonel entered: 'You must submit your questions in Spanish. This is not censorship, just to know in advance. Señor Altmann prefers it that way.'

By now my notes and the photos of Jean Moulin and Barbie were under the blotting-pad on the officer's desk. The colonel waited, but I didn't want him to see the pictures, or I would lose the surprise on Barbie's face when I showed them to him. I pulled over a typewriter and bashed out five questions in Spanish. Easy questions.

'This is French TV with Klaus Altmann. Questionnaire. 1. Could you possibly tell us who you are, your name, where you were born, the names of your family? 2. The German authorities . . .'

Just before 6.00 p.m. the door opened once more. Half a dozen officers came in, behind them was Klaus Altmann. I was scared there would be lawyers too, but there weren't any, unless they were waiting somewhere.

Altmann was shorter than I expected, dressed in a white turtleneck sweater and a brown jacket. His gaze was gentle, his smile a little flabby, but he had a certain arrogance about him. He appeared tired, resigned. He looked around him as if to say 'This is indeed an honour.'

The tape had been running since the first officer entered. One of them said: 'You have five minutes.'

René aimed the lamps at full power. An officer tripped over a cable and the mike fell to the floor. Jean-Pierre had it back within three seconds. Altmann sat there like a prince.

I said: 'Tiene Usted la posibilidad de decirnos . . .'

But suddenly I turned to the Bolivians and told them I was starting again, that I would translate into German.

'Wie heissen Sie?'

Altmann answered in German, his voice weak, almost a murmur, in a steady tone: 'I am Klaus Altmann Hansen, born 25 October 1915, in Berlin . . . I have a wife and two children. My wife's name is Gina, my son's Jorg, my daughter's Ute.'

'Is your son married to a Frenchwoman?'

'Yes, a Frenchwoman.'

The Bolivians shuffled their feet. They did not

understand German, this was not what they had expected, not playing by the rules. Quickly I switched back to Spanish: 'Second question. The German authorities and the Munich Prosecutor . . .'

Then I went into German with the same question. Señor Altmann continued quietly, with the tone of a misunderstood victim. He had his answers ready.

The photos? He said: 'Chance plays a big part with photos.'

The same first names? 'There are plenty of coincidences like that.'

The war? 'I was a lieutenant to begin with, then captain. I took part in the invasion, in Holland, in Belgium, then I went to Russia from 22 June 1942 to late '43. I was in the Ruhr with the 12th Armoured Corps and then the war ended on 8 May, as you know . . .'

We had established communication. I dared not glance at my watch, but I knew that at least ten minutes had gone by because Christian had changed a 16 mm magazine. The Bolivians were reluctant to cut Altmann off. Then I asked him in French: 'Have you ever been to Lyons?'

'Nein. Ich bin nie in Lyon gewesen, aber es ist so . . .'

He fell right into the trap, answered quick as lightning when he was not supposed to know any French! Whether he realised it I could not tell. All I knew was that he went on talking, although his eyes had a harder look to them. I now had proof that he knew French. I pushed my luck.

'Tercera pregunta . . .'

'I was never a member of the Gestapo.'

Was he a Nazi? 'Naturally I was in the National Socialist Party, the Hitler Youth.'

The SS? 'I was not in the official SS. I belonged to the Wehrmacht, 126th Infantry Division.'

I heard clicking at the end of the reel. Christian changed his 120-metre magazine deftly, minding his own business; he did not understand a word of German.

'Did you ever know Klaus Barbie?'

'Er, no, I can't recall him. I reckon he just carried out

orders as a soldier. Like the French, I suppose, in Africa, North Africa, or the American troops now in Vietnam, like the Israeli troops and the Arabs, the Pakistanis and the Indians.'

The fourth and fifth questions, for the Bolivians. Señor Altmann's grey eyes were looking at his shoes; his gaze rose furtively. I realised that I was the cop now. There was something crazy about it but I couldn't stop myself, I had to go for the kill. I thrust the photo of Jean Moulin at him, the one with the hat and the scarf masking his scar. It was in black and white.

Altmann shrugged it off. 'No, I don't think . . . Didn't they publish something about him in *Paris-Match*? I believe I read that this Moulin died on his way to Germany.'

'So you know about that?'

'Yes.'

'Are you afraid of dying?' In 1972 the death sentence has not yet been abolished in France. I hoped he would jump as an innocent man normally would.

He replied: 'I do not understand this question. I went through the war and I was not afraid to die then.'

The interview looked as if it were over. But I told Señor Altmann that none of what we had was of any use, and that we ought to have another 30 seconds, in French this time, so that everyone would know what he was saying.

'I don't know much French,' he said.

'I'll help you: "I am not a murderer." '

'I am not a murderer.'

I could feel a clammy hand on my back; that's how it seemed. I slowly turned round to Jean-Pierre, who gulped audibly when he heard Barbie talk in French. His hand quivered on the volume knob. Christian came in close and was holding his breath.

The Nazi repeated submissively after me: 'I never practised any torture. I do not know Jean Moulin [he pronounced it *Mouline*, Spanish-style]. I was never with the Gestapo in Lyons.'

I mentioned the Eichmann seizure and asked if he

thought the same could happen to him.

'That would naturally be a very bad thing for France.'

I raised my eyebrows: 'Do you like the French people?'

'My son married a Frenchwoman, so you will realise I have nothing at all against the French people.'

Did he ever meet Bormann or Dr Mengele? Never knew them, he said. But I saw his face tense up for an instant, his lips tremble. Now he wanted to cut the interview short, and he appealed to the officers in the shadow on my left. Everyone felt ill at ease. Altmann got up, said goodbye in German and bowed his head.

Without realising we were still recording, the colonel said: 'Let this be clearly understood. This meeting was not arranged by the Bolivian police, of course.'

I was so preoccupied that I did not even notice that Barbie had quit the room. There were a thousand other questions I should have asked; you always think of them afterwards.

Afterwards my chief concern was to conceal the film and the soundtrack. I slipped them among my files and strode confidently towards the colonel's office, then went right past it without stopping. I was almost outside, and the risk of the Bolivians asking to hear the tape lessened with every step. 'Hasta luego, hasta luego.' I smiled as I emerged from the Ministry. The French Embassy was only 150 yards away. I got there and went straight to the consul, who opened the safe; we laid the reels and tape inside. Finally, I collapsed in an armchair, and stayed like that for a few minutes, saying nothing. Christian and René came in a quarter of an hour later, angry because I ran out on them but glad to see me there. The Bolivians took their passports and poked around in the equipment boxes, looking for the reels. The consul, Colombiani, came to their rescue.

We sent a telex to Paris: 'Meat in the can, two and a half reels. Prefer to send baby instead of nursing it here.' No answer. At Cognacq Jay there was nobody in the studio – Paris was asleep.

Friday came. As they said they would, the Bolivians jailed Klaus Altmann.

Meanwhile here is the *Hoy* report on our interview: 'The journalists at *Hoy* have learned that agents from the Sûreté (French police) recently interrogated Klaus Altmann before his detention in St Peter's prison. These French agents were disguised as French television journalists, assuring the authorities that they had a questionnaire available for Altmann's guards. However, the journalists did not put the agreed questions. On the contrary, they carried out a veritable interrogation using English, French and German, assuredly to record Altmann's voice; they asked him to write something, probably to analyse his handwriting. Finally, when they asked Klaus Altmann to walk a few steps, he refused outright. Thus ended the work of the French Sûreté agents.'

We were summoned to the Interior Ministry.

Walter Morales, Secretary of State, spoke into the camera: 'The Bolivian Constitution recognises the independence of the judiciary. Klaus Altmann is a naturalized Bolivian citizen. Until the contrary is demonstrated in law, we cannot make a decision.'

The proceedings were to last an eternity. That afternoon I slipped 150 dollars to the governor of St Peter's prison, asking him to let me see Barbie. He said it was all right, but no cameras, and no talk about his having the money. Curiously, he issued me with a receipt.

Altmann's cell was the lieutenant's office, with clean walls, a statue of Christ on a plinth, artificial flowers. He even had a phone and could ring up the outside world, his wife, for example, who was still in Lima, or his lawyer, or his friends, who were soon to give him help. He could stroll about at will in the prison yard, but he kept away from the other inmates. For security reasons, he had his meals in the office.

I noticed at once that his bearing was more haughty than it had been the previous day. This did not surprise me; not only had he realised he had failed to convince us, but he was now confined. And, although he was certain to be out before long, prison was the starting-point for his clashes with the tax people.

Barbie told me: 'I am fond of Paris, you know. I was there last year in late February. Went through Orly and seized the chance of a few hours in Paris. It has changed a lot.'

I tried to get a photo of him from the side, to compare it with the pictures the Americans took in 1948 when he was in their care in Munich. Barbie knew what I was up to and turned when I turned.

The warders were watching us like hawks. For their benefit Señor Altmann put on a smile, relaxed, seemed to take it as a joke.

But underneath he was furious about something. He whispered to me, lisping: 'You watch your step, mind how you go. Oh, I've got nothing against you but I have lots of friends.'

I was thinking that this was how he spoke as he stroked his celebrated grey cat before torturing Simone Lagrange, aged thirteen.

I left the jail and contacted the consul, Paul Colombiani. He warned me: 'Get out as fast as you can. Take the first plane. They'll kill anyone here for fifty dollars.'

On to Lima, where I tried to contact Barbie's wife, Regina. No luck. Friedrich Schwend had her safe inside his fortified farm at Santa Clara, where the Nazis congregate in this part of South America. Schwend agreed to see me, and I went with the Agence France-Presse man in Lima, Albert Brun.

He had Spanish furniture, two-colour curtains, whisky on the table.

Schwend said: 'I can assure you, Altmann is not Barbie. I met Barbie personally in Egypt. He must be about eighty by now.'

I asked him to put that in writing. He refused.

Back in Paris, they put new developer in the bath to get the best from the reels. Three copies were run off. Jacques Alexandre, chief editor, got in two interpreters, a German and a Spaniard, to handle the interview.

He sent me a telex: 'Have seen rushes of your material. Fantastic. Perfect interview. First-class material. Hearty congratulations. Good luck.'

For the *Plein Cadre* programme, he got some more reports: inquiries in Switzerland at the International Red Cross headquarters to find out how Barbie got a safe conduct in 1951 when France was already seeking extradition from the Allies; an interview in West Germany with the Munich Prosecutor General, Manfred Ludolph, who re-opened, on Beate Klarsfeld's insistence, the official inquiry after Prosecutor Franz Rabl closed it; a report from specialist G. Ziegelmayer of Munich University who produced the anthropometric report; and, most importantly, an inquiry in Lyons in the basement of the Sipo-SD at the École de Santé and the Fort Montluc jail, with accounts from witnesses.

But before the programme, Jacques Alexandre really went to town with a special slot lasting twenty minutes on the evening news, broadcast on 8 February: a confrontation between Altmann and his victims, a two-way link with Rome bringing in Raymond Aubrac, who had been arrested with Jean Moulin and tortured a dozen times by Barbie; a live statement from Dr Frédéric Dugoujon in Lyons; in the Paris studio, Simone Lagrange and Monsieur Fusier. Madame Lagrange was categorical – Altmann was Barbie!

Raymond Aubrac was overcome with emotion: 'It was terrible watching him, like the times I was in Barbie's office. That way he has of lowering his eyes and bringing them up again smartly. . . Between that man and Barbie there is the same resemblance as between a father and son.'

The programme, which won a prize for reporting in Cannes, had such an impact that our competitors on *24 Heures sur La Une* had to cancel the sequence they had scheduled for that evening in their news magazine.

Much has been said about this live confrontation. Let me simply quote a passage by Roger Bouzinac of *Nice-Matin*: 'Television is dedicated to live testimony. For once we cannot accuse it of reducing us to complacency. It has awakened our minds and appealed to our consciences.'

That was 1972.

Left: The Ecole de Santé Militaire in Lyons. (TALLANDIER)

Below left: Inspector Louis G. Bibes, who tracked down Barbie in Germany after the war and questioned him on three occasions in 1948. (D.R.)

Below: Erhard Dabringhaus, a US counter-intelligence officer. He claims that Barbie was paid $1700 per month working for him. (UPI)

Left: Klaus Barbie alias Altmann (behind microphone), director of the company Transmaritima Boliviana S.A. (D.R.)

Below left: Altmann (second from left) in June 1967, when he was exporting large quantities of quinine. (D.R.)

Right: General Hugo Banzer, President of Bolivia, who came to power with the support of the German community in Santa Cruz. (KEYSTONE)

Below: One of the 17-tonne Kurassier tanks, built in Austria and equipped with French 105mm guns, sold to the Bolivians with Klaus Altmann acting as broker. This photograph was taken in San Francisco Square, La Paz, during a military coup. (D.R.)

Left: Serge and Beate Klarsfeld in their office in Paris the day Barbie returned to France. (UNCUOGLU–SIPA)

Right: Klaus Barbie and René Hardy (left) in La Paz, July 1972. Their meeting lasted three minutes. A proposed second meeting never took place. (GAMMA)

Below: When Barbie was confronted with a photograph of Moulin in the course of the interview televised on 3 February 1972, he said: 'I do not know this Monsieur Moulin. I am not a killer. I have never tortured anyone.' (ORTF)

Left: Françoise Croizier, Barbie's daughter-in-law, who is French. She lives with her three children in Santa Cruz de la Sierra, in southern Bolivia. (DE HOYOS-SYGMA)

Below: Barbie in San Pedro prison with the prison governor. (D.R.)

Right: Barbie being interviewed by the author. (GAMMA)

Below right: A photograph of Klaus Barbie taken by the author in La Paz central prison the day after the televised interview in February 1972. (DE HOYOS-SYGMA)

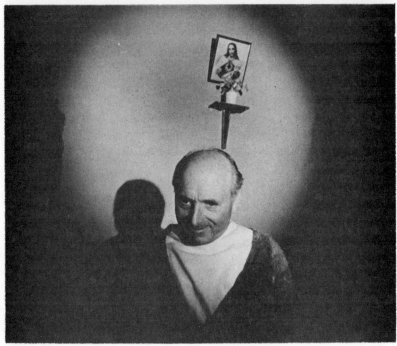

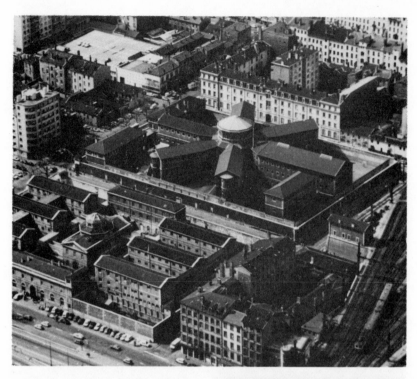

Above: Saint Joseph prison on the banks of the Rhône, where Klaus Barbie was incarcerated in 1983. (AUTHOR'S COLLECTION)

Below: Christian Riss, who has been preparing the case for the prosecution of Klaus Barbie for crimes against humanity since 1980. (D. BARRIER-GAMMA)

11

KLAUS BARBIE DID NOT stay long in prison. On orders from Rolando Kempff, the department controller, he was allowed to walk out on 11 February with a transistor radio under his arm. No doubt he thought his German colleagues in Santa Cruz had supported him, and the Bolivian officials dared not touch him now.

Back in France that same day, a shocked President Georges Pompidou wrote a personal letter to General Hugo Banzer: 'You are certainly aware of the immense impact in France of any news relating to the name under which Klaus Barbie is living. Time effaces many things, but not everything. The French people will never accept that crimes and sacrifices be lost in indifference, or that the notion of justice be tarnished.'

The Bolivian President replied two weeks later: 'I can assure you that the Bolivian judges required under law to consider this affair will give justice the final word.'

In less diplomatic terms, the local press backed Banzer's reply with front-page stories attacking 'the new French insolence in regard to Bolivia's national dignity'. Papers recalled that General de Gaulle had invoked 'noble and Christian sentiments' to get Régis Debray spared in 1967. In fact General-President Barrientos replied at that time: 'If for Your Excellency the main concern is France and the French, my prime duty is towards Bolivia and the Bolivians.' Banzer's response was a little less huffy than that, but nonetheless signified that there would be no political decision, and since there was no extradition agreement, it was in the lap of the gods.

Altmann was sick of being presented with incriminating documents, and realised that his disclaimers were increasingly hopeless. But it dawned on him that he could make quite a bit of money out of his story. Consequently he went so far as to admit that he had indeed belonged to the Sipo-SD in Lyons, but in an interview obtained by the Brazilian correspondent Ewaldo Dantas Ferreira and published by *France-Soir*, he said that the name 'Barbie' was just a pseudonym he used.

Henri Noguères wrote: 'Publication of these Barbie pseudo-memoirs was neither historically useful nor morally desirable.' But what would the readers have thought had they read the entire 'confessions'? For not everything was actually published; not solely because the story got bogged down in details, but also to avoid kindling the flames. In the hands of the editorial people at *France-Soir*, certain passages were cut.

One passage that failed to see the light of day read: 'Today the guerrilla fighter attacks indirectly, without uniform, without showing his identity as an enemy, without being subject to the laws of regular warfare . . . so the methods to be used against guerrillas answer to no law . . . In our army [Barbie does not say whether this means the Wehrmacht or the Bolivian Ejercito] "Che" Guevara would not even have reached the rank of sergeant. He was ineffectual, he committed only errors.'

And to get at France more directly, he threw out a challenge; he said that those who were after him had already had their lesson from the Régis Debray affair. To obtain the release of the young revolutionary theoretician, 'they paid General Juan José Torres and his entourage the sum of $300,000.' Reading these lines in Argentina where he had fled, General Torres immediately protested to the French Ambassador; he also complained to the President of the Assemblée Nationale. But since the passage was not published in France, no denial was deemed necessary.

Of more direct concern to Resistance people was the accusation of 'cowardice' against General de Gaulle, for being out of France while others fought there. This mixture of hate and excuses did not need to be circulated in France in 1972 to provoke indignation in certain quarters. We have a comment from Claude Bouchinet-Serreulles, who was Jean Moulin's deputy for five years: 'Thirty years afterwards Barbie is discovered and, for the first time, being tracked down. He is wondering to what extent the Americans will protect him in view of his services to them after the liberation of Lyons. Today he can still pull the old strings and, in an attempt to sow discord among the adversary, he is trying to set Frenchman against Frenchman.'

In the National Assembly in Paris, Secretary of State Jean de Lipkowski told Parliament that France had been assured that 'surveillance of Klaus Barbie will naturally be reinforced,' while the courts checked whether Altmann was really Barbie and whether extradition was feasible.

Communist politician Virgil Barel, whose son Max was tortured to death either by Barbie or his men at Montluc in July 1944, called for the dossier to be handled by the United Nations. He declared: 'It is vital that the international body should adopt a stance on the business, which is an international matter. I say that not only as the father of a hero and martyr but as a French democrat. We must carry this through.'

In reply, Monsieur de Lipkowski said it was a bilateral, not an international, issue. He added: 'Extradition, Monsieur Barel, signifies that we are not satisfied with expulsion, and I record that solemnly at this rostrum.' Nevertheless, the French government drew attention to a resolution voted unanimously at the United Nations on 13 February 1946, recommending that all member states co-operate in the search for war criminals and aid their extradition to the countries where they committed their crimes.

Let us also take a quick look at the strange death of one of Barbie's friends, the French count Jacques Dugé de Bernonville, who was done away with in Rio because he knew too much about the Nazis.

Formerly a 'cop' appointed by the Vichy regime, he was

condemned to death *in absentia* by a Toulouse court on 8 October 1947. He flew to Canada using the name Benoît. France called for his extradition in 1951, and he sought refuge in Rio de Janeiro in the arms of the Bragance family, which had reigned in Brazil since 1889. Like Touvier and a host of others, he went into a convent for a few weeks. Four years later Brazil still refused to hand him over to France; the death sentence was still in force in France, though not in Brazil. On 27 April 1972, a few weeks after Klaus Barbie had been officially identified, the old count's strangled body was found in the Lapa district in Taylor Street, lying under a picture of Marshal Pétain. Bernonville had a teacloth as a gag and his hands and feet were bound with his own neckties.

After inquiries the Rio police came up with a suspect, a young man named Wilson, son of the count's servant, but too mentally handicapped to have committed this crime. He confessed all, telling the judge that the police had convinced him it was a ritual crime which he carried out in a state of possession. It was all the fault of the Macumba, the god Exu and a few others, he said. Four months earlier the Peruvian billionaire Luis Banchero Rossi had died in somewhat similar circumstances.

How does Barbie come into this? Bernonville had made some trips to Bolivia despite his modest means, and at Rio he said he was willing to do a biography of the Butcher of Lyons, bringing in other Nazis now in South America.

The Bolivian Supreme Court took its time deciding on the extradition request.

Meanwhile Don Altmann was back at his table in the Confiteria La Paz. Magazines to which he was a subscriber were sent to him at the café. He would sit with a cup of coffee, wave to a passing colonel and smile, and chat with his buddies. The French Ambassador, Jean-Louis Mandereau, crossed over to the other side of the street whenever the Butcher of Lyons approached.

Altmann was arrested again on 2 March 1973, doubtless

as a result of impatience on France's part combined with his own lack of caution. It seems diplomatic overtures plus Altmann's cocky interview with the Brazilian journalist did the trick, and the idea of expulsion started to take root. The Soviet news agency Tass said that he had sent 100,000 French Jews to the gas ovens, and also that he admitted involvement in the supply of arms to Israel after the war.

So the Nazi was once more cooped up in his cell, but he also had access to the stores inside the prison. There was a direct view from the first floor on to the Plaza Sucre, and any competent sniper could have eliminated him when he leaned against the window.

The affair began increasingly to irritate the Bolivians, and they could have got rid of him. Nevertheless, he spent six months in the cell, enjoying facilities not customarily allowed the average Bolivian inmate: he did not need to queue up in order to see his family in the corridor. His detention order mentioned 'libro correspon-diente', meaning he could receive anyone he liked, even a journalist, and have meals brought in from outside, which he did.

He was questioned a week after his return to jail. Prosecutor Gaston Ledezma Rojas came in, having read the series of articles published by Ewaldo Dantas Ferreira that constituted a confession Barbie had agreed to make for a few thousand dollars. Using prepared questions, the prosecutor kept at Barbie for two hours, with no magistrate present. He emerged from San Pedro to tell the La Paz press that, for the first time, the five sheets obtained 'contain enough evidence to affirm that Altmann is indeed Barbie'. This was ten months after the newspaper announcement. (In the summer of 1980 Prosecutor Ledezma was to say publicly that his government had always kept the Barbie file open to the extent that it was unnecessary to make a new application for extradition.)

Barbie immediately asked to appear in court, pleading habeas corpus. His counsel, the aged Constantin Carrion, did his best, soft-soaping the *'Excelentissime'* Supreme Court, but it was no good. Barbie stayed in jail.

Carrion protested that the detention was totally illegal. He came to regret this; two weeks later he was sharing his client's cell, charged with 'using a document ruled counterfeit by the judiciary', though the document had nothing to do with the Barbie affair. As he went to join Barbie in the Panoptico jail, he made a short statement to the press. He said his arrest stemmed from remarks he had made to the press two weeks earlier when he complained at the workings of justice in Bolivia.

Barbie acquired another counsel, Adolfo Ustarez of Santa Cruz, who protested vainly: 'I appeal to the President, for he is the ultimate hope of justice!' He too was in jail when Barbie was expelled in February 1983. His argument was that 'diplomatic missions cannot plead or be cited', and that the French Embassy had violated this rule by joining in the procedure against his client. He claimed: 'The embassy appointed an agent and two assistants for the translation of documents, paying one of them the sum of 50,000 pesos.'

Thereafter Barbie appears to have been forgotten, at least in Bolivia. The next thing we learned was that he was to be released, on 18 June. Paris found out, and the French government, at a cabinet meeting in the Elysée, called for Klaus Barbie to be kept available to the judiciary.

The Ambassador in La Paz, Jean-Louis Mandereau, commented: 'It would have been easy to roll him up in a blanket and ship him out, but what a scandal!' – thereby ruling out the idea of kidnapping.

He sent a sealed memo to the Latin American Section at the Quai d'Orsay revealing that a Supreme Court member had called on him and promised to get consent for extradition for the sum of 5,000 dollars!

The proposition was conveyed to the Elysée. Mandereau was informed that Georges Pompidou simply wrote *non* in the margin. The French foreign office instructed him to grant no further credit for any reason.

Naturally he complied. The Bolivians came back at him with a reminder that they were still waiting for the reward for freeing Régis Debray in 1970.

French lawyers were sure that the Supreme Court would issue a refusal, and they wondered what other courses were open to them. Peru looked like a promising angle, because France has an extradition agreement with the Lima government. Paris and Lima were disputing the question of nuclear tests in the Pacific, but they both wanted Barbie.

The Peruvians had done nothing to keep Barbie in January 1972 and even gave him an escort to the Bolivian frontier when Beate Klarsfeld reached Lima demanding his arrest. Now a year had gone by, and Peru wanted Barbie on a charge of currency-trafficking with Friedrich Schwend. Peru made an official request to Bolivia for Don Klaus. The Supreme Court Chairman, Dr Hernan Ayala Mercado, consented to extend Barbie's detention. That day the French Embassy was celebrating Bastille Day.

What did General Banzer think of it all? He realized he owed much to the German community, but this business was driving him mad. Diplomatic sources were saying that he would prefer to cease protecting the war criminal whose presence was harming Bolivia's image internationally.

The Supreme Court rejected the Peruvian application on 25 October 1973; it was plain that it would also turn down the French extradition request.

Jean-Louis Mandereau told me: 'Banzer knew the judges in Bolivia were far from possessing the necessary competence and honesty, so he revoked the powers of three-quarters of them, including the entire Supreme Court.' However, just before they quit, in the few days still left to them, the Supreme Court hastily issued its definitive judgment on 11 December 1974: no extradition for Barbie. Ambassador Mandereau expressed his astonishment, and he was told: 'What do you expect? The magistrates had to come over with something: money or the ruling. So they issued the ruling; it was far easier!'

Without even waiting for the decision, Klaus Barbie went

off to Paraguay on his official passport, spending a week in two Asuncion hotels. He was well aware that Paraguayan President Alfredo Stroessner was friendly to anyone who remained loyal to the Nazi cause. Barbie returned to Santa Cruz de la Sierra in Bolivia on 15 February. The Quai d'Orsay was extremely bitter.

A whole new career opened to Barbie, now convinced he could trust his friends. The veteran SS lost no sleep over the past, and the future was no cause for concern. Things were looking up in Bolivia, where colonization was entering a new phase. For example, there was a project – though it was gathering dust due to intervention by the Church – to bring over thousands of South Africans, Rhodesians and Namibians to settle in new townships near Santa Cruz. They could expect a hearty welcome if they were white and anti-Communist. Behind the project was Under-Secretary of State Dr Guido Strauss, a leading light in the Bolivian Socialist Falange. The news got around that West German contacts had issued a $150 million line of credit for the absorbing of 150,000 whites by Bolivia in a six-year period – exactly 1,000 dollars per head for this immigration programme 'to improve the race'. The man with the job of liaising between the Bolivian government and the African whites was none other than Señor Klaus Altmann.

When the Transmaritima company went bankrupt, Barbie's son Klaus-Georg left Hamburg and took over a postcard business in Barcelona, while he fixed up a job in Austria. He and Françoise and their three children settled there, at Niedendorf in the Tyrol, a few miles from Ute's home. (Ute was a bookseller in Kuftein. Her father had been against her marrying a Bolivian, even one with German blood; he had asked his friend Hans Rudel, the famous Nazi aviator, to find her a husband.)

Françoise worked as a tourist guide, but the couple failed to get regular employment in Austria, so they made their way back to Bolivia, confident that the Supreme Court had delivered the final word on Barbie's extradition. Klaus-Georg Altmann landed in Santa Cruz de la Sierra representing the Austrian firm Steyr, selling farm machinery and mopeds.

Steyr-Daimler-Puch also made tanks, light 17-ton Kürassier vehicles equipped with French 105 mm guns; the CN 105-57 was mounted on a modified turret of the kind used on the second generation AMX 13 tanks, enough to make a Bolivian general's mouth water, a highly manoeuvrable armoured vehicle, fully suited to the steep streets of La Paz. The shells could pierce 6 inches of armour. In all, just the job for fighting the guerrillas or keeping street demonstrators in check.

The Bolivians bought 34, with the approval of France, who, under the contract, had to be consulted each time a Kürassier was sold, the weaponry being French.

With no questions asked, Barbie senior took a one or two per cent commission, which normally would have gone to the regional agent. Since each tank with its armament sold at five million French Francs, Klaus Barbie netted about two million francs for using his influence with the Bolivian military. He acquired a comfortable villa at Santa Cruz with a fair-sized garden, ringed with a wall that was cemented with bottle fragments. The house at C-6 Oeste Final in the Equipetrol district was worth $80,000, Françoise Croizier reckoned.

The arms dealing business was shrouded in secrecy. Many in the sector were fidgety about Barbie's entry into the arena. Letting Klaus Barbie in was overdoing things a bit. In February 1979 several protest letters were exchanged in the armaments industry. A hand-written letter addressed to a certain 'D6' said it was surprising that Klaus Barbie was allowed to negotiate the sale of the first 34 tanks supplied to Bolivia, but the Austrians went through with the deal. The agent was Mr Brodnik.

Nineteen months later, the deal came to the attention of the Nazi-hunter Simon Wiesenthal, who runs the Jewish

Research Centre in Vienna. In March 1983, the *Miami Herald* reported that the sale of these tanks had been one of Altmann's biggest business killings. Wiesenthal wrote to the Generaldirektor of the Steyr company, Michael Malzacher, protesting about the deal. Malzacher said he knew nobody called Barbie.

In April 1979, Michel Goldberg-Cojot, whose father was deported to Auschwitz on the orders of the Sipo-SD in Lyons, arrived in La Paz. (He and his son had been taken hostage by a pro-Palestinian commando group on an Air France plane that was hijacked to Entebbe in 1976 in a completely unconnected incident.) He wanted to dispose of Barbie, and calculated he would receive a jail term of five years.

It is hard to say whether he really wanted to kill the Nazi or whether he was simply running after a story, but he posed as a journalist, and got to meet Barbie in Bolivia, which he called 'the scrapheap of European history'. They had a curious interview, about everything and nothing, mentioning, among other issues, the Americans and the Russians.

Barbie said: 'We were the front-runners in the struggle against Bolshevism. Look where they've got to now! If the Americans had not caused us to lose the war, that would never have happened. Anyway, I prefer the Russians to the Americans; they are more cultivated, more intelligent, more courageous. I mean the Russians, not the Communists.'

Of the Caluire affair, he said: 'I had more power than a general had. I changed the course of history when I arrested Jean Moulin. Had he lived, it is he and not de Gaulle who would have presided over France's destiny after our departure. France would doubtless have become Communist.'

After the interview, Michel Goldberg-Cojot no longer had the heart to kill Barbie.

In the mountains of the Tyrol, Klaus-Georg discovered a passion for hang-gliding. He took the machine he owned to the Santa Cruz villa and used it at weekends, when he would launch out over the Andes above Cochabamba. On Labour Day, 1 May 1980, he made his last flight, crashing to his death under the gaze of his horrified parents.

Françoise Croizier described the event: 'He jumped off Mount Tunari, and it was the first time Klaus Barbie and his wife had watched him do it. He had waited for the wind to spring up, and about midday he launched himself off the mountainside. He did a turn to the right, circled widely, and finally crashed against the rocks. The Bolivian Army helicopter arrived an hour later. He was already dead, but his father kept giving him mouth-to-mouth resuscitation to make his wife think he was still alive.'

Françoise was not there. She was at a friend's wedding: 'Later I went there and saw the rock; the Indians had already washed the blood away – they're superstitious.'

Klaus-Georg was buried in Cochabamba, and Barbie had a notice put in the paper. It was misunderstood; in Europe, for a couple of days, it was assumed that the Lyons torturer was the one who had perished.

A rumour went the rounds in Bolivia at one stage, to the effect that, although Klaus Barbie was unwilling to become directly involved in drugs, the son had fewer scruples. The young man was said to have worked with the *narcotraficantes* and had set up his own route to Brazil, for his own benefit or for that of the so-called 'fiancés of death'.* It was believed that this business escaped the control of the drug bosses, who rid themselves of the new boy by arranging the hang-gliding accident, mafia-style, with the parents looking on. A *leyenda* (just a story) perhaps, but it does seem strange that no autopsy was done on Barbie, which could mean a pot-shot was taken at him in flight. It is also curious that the glider was not properly examined.

Françoise said: 'I had tried to get French nationality for

* Nazi instructors brought in to train right-wing paramilitary groups.

my husband, although living in France, even under the assumed name of Altmann, was risky; someone could have kidnapped one of the children with the idea of provoking my father-in-law, challenging him, forcing him to come out into the open and give himself up to the French.'

The Butcher of Lyons dared not visit Europe. He was safer in Bolivia, where he had plenty to keep him busy and where he still acted as adviser to the military.

In July 1980 Barbie was one of the architects of the Garcia Meza putsch that expelled from power Meza's cousin Lidia Gueilier, who had attempted to introduce a new democratic system in Bolivia. Still fiercely anti-Communist, he is believed to have had Nazi instructors brought in from Paraguay to train paramilitary groups. These Germans, taken on by the Bolivian police, included Manfred Kuhlmann and the well-known Joachim Fiebelkorn, detained in West Germany, whose extradition was requested by Bolivia. The instructors were known as 'the fiancés of death' and included a Frenchman, Jacques Leclère, who was expelled after Barbie.

Some journalists covering the Garcia Meza coup described it as a joint operation by the 'Fascist gangs and the drug godfathers'. The Fascists supplied the brute force and the drug men supplied the dollars.

An instance of Altmann's power at this time is shown in the misadventure that occurred to Bolivian Peter MacFarren, a *Newsweek* correspondent who wanted a background story on Barbie and sought him out at Cochabamba in August 1981. He found his house at Calle Atahuailpa and rang the bell. Nothing stirred inside. He hung around for a while with a colleague, Marisabel Schumacher, taking a few photos of the villa. Then a car and a jeep roared up loaded with troops and paramilitary men.

'We are the SES, Servicio Especial de Seguridad,' an officer declared, and the two journalists were taken off to the 7th Army Headquarters, where the boss was Guido Vildoso Calderon. MacFarren and Schumacher were separated and threatened with torture unless they revealed how they got Altmann's address. After four hours' interrogation, they were released with the advice: 'If you had come straight to us, you would have had an interview with Señor Altmann.'

They subsequently learned that Barbie went to the Cochabamba headquarters twice a week. The SES organized the mercenaries who had planned the Garcia Meza putsch. When he entered the building Barbie got a salute worthy of a general. In due course he told the West German magazine *Stern*: 'I have a good reputation here. Every time the army needs help, they call me in.'

Once in power Garcia gave the Interior Ministry to the redoubtable Luis Arce Gomez, head of the Headquarters Number 2 Section, who sought out Don Klaus for his expertise in advanced interrogation. Barbie had access at all times to the Miraflores Headquarters and the offices in Avenida Arce. This pass, made out in the name of Klaus Altmann, is in the vaults of Secretary of State Gustavo Sanchez. He is wary that it will fall into the hands of military figures who treasure souvenirs of Klaus Barbie. The Butcher of Lyons is shown in the photo with greying hair, and in uniform! Wearing a Bolivian colonel's jacket with gold buttons, he is credited with the rank of honorary colonel, and his number is 33300252. The pass also bears his right thumbprint and gives his blood group, O. It is valid until 21 December 1985. The presence of the Lyons Butcher at the Miraflores Headquarters has been confirmed by the French military attaché in Lima, who saw Barbie twice when he visited La Paz for talks with military leaders. He recalled: 'He was just sitting there at a small desk like a junior official, insignificant, with white hair.'

We may well ask whether Barbie kept in touch with the CIA, or at least its agents in the United States Embassy. Nobody seems to remember seeing Don Altmann take the lift to the third floor of the American building in Murillo Square, although of course he did not need to go there in person to sell his information. His close friend Alvaro de Castro says he had no contact with 'the Yankees', but usually reliable sources suggest the Americans obtained Barbie's analyses through their contacts in the Interior Ministry. This implies that he handed over to the Ministry information that was made use of elsewhere.

Drug dealer Garcia Meza was swept from the Quemado Palace by Torrelio, who was soon chased from the presidency by Guido Vildoso Calderon from Cochabamba Headquarters. Barbie was quick; within twenty-four hours General Vildoso had a visit from the Obersturmführer, offering his services.

As he left the Plaza Murillo building on 22 July 1982, a reporter from Radio Panamericana challenged him: 'You owe the sum of $10,000.'

He got no further, for Altmann snapped: 'That was to do with Transmaritima; it is not my personal affair.'

'Have you offered to work for the government?'

'No, never!'

'What are you here for then?'

'I am here for special reasons. You know that I lost my son.'

'They say you are in touch with a terrorist group in jail in Brazil.'

Altmann answered: 'I do not know those people. I left Cochabamba a year ago and I pulled out of everything. My wife is ill and I am grieving for my son. Leave me alone.'

It is true that Barbie hardly left La Paz at that time. Every day he could be seen going down Avenida 16 de Julio, back to his home in the Jasmin apartments, or on his way to see Regina who had already been in hospital for several weeks. After a long and painful illness his wife died of cancer on 6 December 1982, the day before her sixty-seventh birthday.

For Barbie's enemies there was comfort in the fact that in having survived the death of his loved ones, at least he had known a sense of loss.

At the German Club there was speculation about whether the torturer would be buried in the German cemetery one day.

A diplomat recounts: 'Nobody wanted Barbie alive, but his corpse would be different; he would embarrass nobody. He could be interred with the others, though a slight distance away.'

One wet miserable morning, about thirty people from the German community stood by Regina's grave after a short Mass in the chapel. The coffin was lowered into the grave. Everybody threw in a few clods of earth, except Barbie, in dark glasses, who threw in some roses and said *'Liebling'* (darling). Ute was there from Austria, as well as his cook, his best friend, Alvaro de Castro, and a man named Carboni. These three took him back home.

The cross bears the name Regina Willelms de Altmann; only the first name was correct. Behind the cross, about twenty yards away, lay Monika Ertl, the woman who killed Quintanilla.

A young Bolivian woman, Mary-Flores Saavedra, was at the ceremony. She was fascinated by the Nazis, particularly Barbie, whom she had known for a short while. He was willing to chat with her.

She said later: 'He adored his wife, recalling that she had been a champion tennis player. Señor Altmann was *muy emocional* as a man, persecuted. He was well in with the CIA and had been since the war. Of Jean Moulin, he told me: "Moulin was the strong man of France, and next to him de Gaulle was *una simpla figura sin poder*. I did not kill Jean Moulin; he tried to commit suicide. I transported him wounded from Lyons to Paris, where I went to Colonel Boemelburg, who was waiting in a room with two doctors." He also told me that he laid flowers on his tomb after the war. On 9 November he came to see me and declared: "This is a great day today! It's 9 November, the day I received my insignia from the Führer." [On 9 November 1944, Klaus Barbie had been promoted to the rank of captain in the SS.]

Mrs Saavedra made an extraordinary observation regarding Barbie. One day in the Copacabana Hotel she asked to see a telephone directory. On the cover was a colour picture of Pope Jean-Paul II. Mrs Saavedra took a small cellophane-wrapped photo of Don Altmann from her handbag. On the back were the words 'Loyalty until death'. She put Barbie's photo next to the Pope's picture and said: 'Don't you think they look alike?'

After Regina's death, the old Nazi wanted nothing better than to go and live in Santa Cruz with his grandchildren in the Barrio Equipetrol house, where his young Alsatian dog, Axel, had been found poisoned a short time before. He talked about removing the photos of Hitler from the La Paz apartment and hanging them up a couple of miles away, ending his days as a nice comfortable grandfather.

He was widely respected, admired, envied, even achieving a certain nobility – which counts so much in Bolivia – by becoming godfather to several children. 'Uncle' Barbie had several godchildren, all Catholic, whom he helped with presents of money and also with his influence. An example was one young man whose father bought him a taxi-cab but could not get him registered with the drivers' syndicate. Don Altmann, in a paternalistic gesture, fixed it up in his own inimitable way.

Opa, as his grandchildren called him, did not leave La Paz at once; he was too busy. And yet he must have sensed the danger, for he said to his daughter-in-law Françoise, whom he nicknamed Fanny: 'You'll see, Fanny, your President will buy me soon!'

He knew that with the election of President François Mitterrand in May 1981 and the advent of Siles Zuazo as head of state in Bolivia, the question of extradition was bound to come up again. He could have fled to Paraguay, but he was still convinced that Bolivian justice would count for more than political considerations.

He was to prove quite wrong.

For the strategists of the French Left, Barbie was a big target, but not a priority. In 1973 Pompidou's France had waited a year for a reply to its extradition request. A group of men resolved in the end to try their luck where diplomacy had failed, either through slackness or adherence to the rules of the game.

A secret plan was drawn up at that time to seize Barbie. The idea was to bring Barbie back just as OAS colonel Argoud had been brought back, that is, without the French authorities' knowledge. The plan was to seize Klaus Altmann-Barbie in the streets of La Paz when he went to collect his mail at his post-box on a Sunday morning. He would be taken by car to an airfield where a two-engined plane would be waiting. He would be flown to Chile's Arica airport, where the Allende government would gladly co-operate in his transfer to Paris. He could be handcuffed, tied up in a sack and left in a van somewhere in Paris, the Place Vendôme for example.

On the financial side, Serge Klarsfeld came up with the necessary funds. A certain person had written to him in August 1972: 'Can you fix the purchase of a hire-car, it comes to $2,500–3,000.'

Three days before Christmas, with a borrowed passport on which he personally swapped photos, Maître Klarsfeld left on a recon flight with his mystery contact. They flew over the Andes and touched down at Arica. There they met up with two opponents of the Banzer regime; one of them, who was back in a position of influence late in 1982, was to be a key figure in Barbie's expulsion in February 1983. The two visitors from France pretended to be tourists, posing for blurry photos against the parched mountain backcloth. The four commando members smiled for the black and white pictures: Serge Klarsfeld, two Bolivian refugees and the mystery contact – who was none other than Régis Debray!

Thus, three years after being freed (the Camiri military court had sentenced him to thirty years, along with the Argentinian Ciro Bustos) Régis Debray was prepared to do a kidnap job with Bolivian accomplices; in the event of failure, a major diplomatic row would have ensued. There would have been little chance for Debray then.

Régis Debray, as Counsellor at the Elysée Palace, confirmed the story to me: 'It was a thing of the heart. Personally I have nothing against Barbie, but it was a good plan to demonstrate the similarity between the struggles, the Bolivian Resistance and the French Resistance. In any case, the idea originated from my friends in the Bolivian Resistance. It was not a Socialist project.'

So why was the plan abandoned? First, because the Bolivian opposition was not ready. Their infrastructure of hide-outs, arms and vehicles had been dismantled by the La Paz government. A better opportunity was needed – for example, Carnival time, with disguises, lots of rowdy celebrations, as in an old crime movie. The Carnival went by, and the date was put back again, to March. Just their luck – Barbie went back into jail at the beginning of March as a result of the extradition request submitted by France. Was this a ploy on the part of the special services who did not want the Barbie business springing up when the first round of the parliamentary elections were held in France? Perhaps. Anyhow, when he emerged from St Peter's jail, Chile, on the other side of the Andes, was paralyzed by an ITT truckdrivers' strike, and Pinochet was eyeing La Moneda. So help from Chile was out. Barbie joined his wife at Cochabamba, and nothing was done.

'By chance the return to democracy in La Paz in October 1982 was to coincide with Régis Debray's presence at the Elysée,' Serge Klarsfeld noted.

The next opportunity came when Herman Siles Zuazo was returned to power.

Siles, a democrat, had been swept away by the colonels. He sought asylum for three weeks at the residence of

French Ambassador Raymond Césaire. The French managed to get Siles across the border to Peru via Lake Titicaca. Then, a month before he regained the presidency – an inevitable event with the colonels in a panic after they had raided the State coffers – Hernan Siles Zuazo had several meetings with Raymond Césaire in Lima in the San Isidro district, in the presence of Luis Barrios, a Peruvian diplomat.

The focal point of their conversations was Barbie. It was on this occasion that an expulsion strategy was worked out. The starting date was 6 October 1982 when Siles would re-enter the Quemado Palace.

The timetable was:

1. Siles would give a press statement to the effect that Barbie was undesirable in the new democratic Bolivia.

2. The President would revamp the Supreme Court of Justice, which would re-examine an extradition request from West Germany and also a new request from France, citing 'crimes against humanity' (war crimes were now prescribed).

3. The Bolivians would arrest Barbie; there was certainly no lack of grounds.

4. The Bolivians would expel Barbie.

On paper it looked fairly straightforward. What happened was to prove less simple – almost clownish.

Barbie, as cocky as ever, saw no reason to cringe and did not sense the hunters on his trail. He was not even armed, although procuring a gun in Bolivia is simple enough. General Ovando had publicly declared that Barbie was covered by prescription, and that the distinction between war crimes and crimes against humanity did not exist in Bolivia. 'Many years have gone by, and this business is not worth attending to,' he had said. In July 1972 René Hardy had paid a lightning visit to La Paz; Professor Michel Goldberg had left to write his piece 'Why I did not kill Barbie'; the men from French television were no longer hanging around disguised as commandos; and the Nazi-hunter Beate Klarsfeld had no plans to come back. There seemed to be nothing to fear and Altmann kept on smiling when people said he was an ex-Nazi. 'I am not an ex, I am still a Nazi!' he would say.

Beate Klarsfeld wrote: 'People may well say Barbie was not on his guard – why didn't you kill him? But none of them would have done it themselves.' She said her role was to try and persuade the legal experts to put the criminals on trial and prevent the rehabilitation of Nazi crimes committed in France.

Many times the question arose as to whether the whole matter should be dropped after forty years. President François Mitterrand rejected this argument, giving the go-ahead to those who wanted Barbie back in France: Robert Badinter, Régis Debray, Serge Klarsfeld and many others – even if the price was high.

The Césaire plan got off to a flying start. President Hernan Siles Zuazo scarcely had time to take office before he told the magazine *Newsweek*: 'People like Barbie are undesirable in our country. He has been involved in drug-trafficking and we have no intention of protecting those who act against the interests of the Bolivian people.'

That was in October 1982. Barbie showed no reaction. He must have seen the comment, for he had a subscription to *Newsweek*, but he was constantly at his dying wife's bedside.

The French realized that there had been no arrest warrant out internationally since the failed extradition request in 1974. The procedure initiated in Lyons for crimes against humanity was an internal dossier; the matter had to be put right at once. On 27 November Judge Christian Riss signed another arrest warrant; it was up to the diplomats to re-initiate extradition.

Bolivia now had to change the make-up of the Supreme Court. Democracy implied that members of the Supreme Court could no longer be designated by the military, but were to be recommended by the Senate and ratified by Parliament. Hernan Siles Zuazo set about organizing this, even though he might end up with a Supreme Court against him; of the twelve new members appointed on 25

January, eight were on the opposition side. But at least the extradition request made a few months earlier by West Germany could be examined again. The German case was based on the murder of French Resistance fighter Joseph Kemmler, head of the Secret Army in the town of Saint-Claude. The Bolivians thought this constituted flimsy grounds, but it had a basis in law. The inquiry had been re-opened in 1977 after the 1975 ratification by the Bundestag of the Paris-Bonn accord allowing West Germany to try war criminals already judged *in absentia* within France.

Next, Klaus Barbie had to be detained. The Bolivians resurrected an old unsettled debt to the mining company COMIBOL dating from the time Señor Altmann was chief executive with Transmaritima.

Everything seemed to be going like clockwork. But as a precautionary measure the French Embassy had an opinion poll taken by its agents. They learned that Barbie seemed to have less clout than in the past, and that some of his friends had dropped him because he was getting on in years and was no use to them because of his record. In addition, it was generally agreed that the Obersturmführer was losing ground psychologically in the wake of his son's death and the loss of his wife. He appeared to be more resigned than before.

One morning the baited hook was cast, a blue official document signed by Dr Lozada calling on Señor Klaus Altmann to settle the sum of $10,000 at the Controleria General de la Republica. The authorities could have summoned Barbie on other issues, but there was no point in picking him up on a charge that would inevitably finish up in court. Above all he must not end up with a prison sentence. The $10,000 was bound to irritate Barbie beyond measure, and it did, as it turned out.

'You stay here,' his colleague Alvaro de Castro ordered. 'I'll go and see what all this is about.'

Barbie, however, was getting pig-headed in his old age. This wretched business was riling him and he would tell them so himself. In the early afternoon of 25 January 1983, he strode into the Controller's office to settle the eleven-year-old debt concerning the reimbursement of a down payment on shipment of ore from Chile to Europe. Naturally, an argument developed as to the exchange rate, whether the official rate should be used or the black market rate, which was exactly double. By luck or good judgment, the argument was not resolved, and Barbie was back in jail in his first-floor cell for the third time, close to the office of the Governor, Colonal Juan Bustillos. For the third time he placed his thumbprints on the identity sheet with details of his assumed identity. Barbie even added that he went to university, that his wife was born in 1923 (it was actually 1915), that his father died in Berlin (instead of Triers), that his mother's name was Anna Hansen de Altmann (Anna Hees) and so on.

The very next morning, the French press, which had been silent about him for years, announced that the Butcher of Lyons had been caught.

Barbie's defending counsel, the agent Constantin Carrion, could do little. He affirmed to a Mexican journalist that Régis Debray, now Adviser to the Elysée, was 'jointly responsible for the deaths of two hundred Bolivian soldiers and seven officers who fell in battle against Che Guevara's guerrillas in the Nancahuazu region to the south.' Barbie was on record as saying late in October 1982: 'In 1967 President Barriento had to fight [Régis Debray]. I had to fight the guerrillas in France, except that at the time Germany and France were at war.'

Carrion went further, indicating that the La Paz authorities could shortly ask France for the extradition of Régis Debray.

In La Paz there was no time to lose, for Barbie's friends were preparing to pay the $10,000. In France, things were taking time, the process was complicated and all the details needed to be firmed up. French officials feared a repetition of the Pagliai fiasco.*

* Pagliai was an Italian extremist who was thought to be one of the authors of the Bologna massacre of 1980, in which a suitcase

The decision to detain Barbie had taken long enough for the French to start trying to hustle events along. Raymond Césaire had the idea of going through Parliament. If Parliament found that the head of state in 1957 had granted naturalization to a fictitious Altmann instead of Barbie, the rest should be easy. Through diplomatic channels the French envoy impressed on Siles Zuazo's aides that getting rid of Barbie would help Bolivia enormously. Nobody abroad would invest in Bolivia if it failed to demonstrate its democratic basis. There was an international crisis on, and the IMF could withhold assistance – soft loans would not be forthcoming. Raymond Césaire seems to have done some plain speaking in a bid to shake up the aged President.

The other 'viceroy' at La Paz, the US Ambassador, presented the arguments of the American Jewish lobby to the Quemado Palace, backed up by financial arguments, at exactly the right moment. Since President Siles Zuazo clearly sought to clean up the drug-trafficking, a tricky task in view of corruption at all levels, the United States was prepared to finance the operation. The United States was the biggest market for these evil products, and it provided $45 million towards monitoring and eliminating coca plantations and replacing them with other crops. With the colonels in their foxholes, Washington was keen to help Siles Zuazo, but it had to dump Barbie, who was part of the criminal fraternity.

No doubt La Paz got the same message from Antoine Blanca, adviser to French premier Pierre Mauroy. Blanca was appointed roving envoy and his first assignment was

---

exploded in a station waiting room, killing 85 people. Friends came to his aid and a gunfight broke out in Santa Cruz. Pieroluigi Pagliai, whom the US secret services suspect of participating in torture sessions conducted by Bolivian military personnel while Barbie was advising them, was taken back to Rome, badly wounded, on 9 October. He died without revealing anything of his organization.

to Bolivia, from 24–30 November, where he hoped to have talks with Siles and his Interior Minister Mario Roncal. He seems to have got the message across. In January French financial expert Jacques Friedman arrived in La Paz, and reported back that Bolivia's external debt was four billion dollars.

Events followed fast. Siles Zuazo cancelled a trip to France, where, at the Socialist Party's invitation, he was to have represented Latin America at a conference on The Authors of Change. The Bolivian regime was in a state of turmoil with the resignation, accepted 20 January, of six MIR far left ministers who wanted quicker results in the drug clean-up and the eradication of the far right paramilitary groups.

Soon, French President François Mitterrand gave consent for a task-force to be set up, involving Foreign Minister Claude Cheysson, ex-Resistance; Defence Minister Charles Hernu, also ex-Resistance; and Justice Minister Robert Badinter, whose father was seized in Lyons but never returned from Auschwitz. Badinter suggested a cell be prepared at Montluc and caused some delay by insisting that everything be done legally, which did not prevent Maître Jacques Vergès from later challenging the legal basis for the transfer of Barbie.

Meanwhile Altmann's lawyers were no longer allowed to see him, and even less so, Alvaro de Castro, who tried to deliver meals from outside.

Like most prisons, the Panoptico has only one gate, and dozens of newsmen gradually assembled there, hoping to get an exclusive interview with the prisoner; they were also afraid that he would creep out unnoticed. These journalists, about sixty on the final day of the vigil, did not know that among them were two agents from the French DGSE counter-espionage service whose job was to evaluate the extent of any support Barbie still had, while also making sure he was not kidnapped, either in a rescue bid or with the intention of murdering him. Three or four other people were checking Don Klaus's friends carefully, watching the route to the airport and protecting the neighbourhood of the French Embassy and Raymond Césaire's residence in the valley township of Obrajes.

The $10,000 debt was finally paid, as an entry on 2 February at the Central Bank shows. Barbie's lawyer was disappointed because Barbie would perhaps still be in the Panoptico San Pedro if the outstanding sum had not been settled.

At the Elysée in Paris, Jean-Louis Bianco and Secretary Jean-Claude Colliard received reports several times daily. The Bolivian authorities had no wish to start further proceedings against Barbie, even though there were plenty of misdemeanours they could fall back on; as far as they were concerned, Barbie could go free. Further arguments were needed in order to gain time, because the transport arrangements were not complete yet. Out of the blue, the Controller was inspired to seek interest on the $10,000, an amount of 755,964.45 pesos including 681 pesos for legal costs – i.e., an extra $3,000.

Barbie knew nothing about this. He simply learned through the grapevine that he might be expelled, perhaps across the border of his choice.

The think-tank at the French Embassy had come up with three possible developments:
1. Barbie could be kidnapped without difficulty, chloroformed and whisked off by plane to Peru, just as Adolf Eichmann had been extracted from Buenos Aires in 1960. With precise timing, the Nazi could be switched at Lima to a regular Air France Boeing 747, five minutes before take-off, and stowed on a specially prepared upper deck. The stone walls in La Paz did not a prison make – for money could remove anyone from a Bolivian prison.
2. The normal expulsion process could be awaited. The Bolivians would send Barbie out on a regular flight, for example, via Lufthansa to Frankfurt, making a stopover in, say, Bogota or Puerto Rico, where a reception committee from the French special GIGN squad would hijack him. The West Germans were prepared only to ask

for extradition; they certainly did not want delivery just ahead of the parliamentary elections. Monsieur Mitterand had two discussions on the matter with Chancellor Helmut Kohl.

3. Barbie could be flown out directly to France. This was the method ultimately decided on.

On 31 January a DC 8 from the French COTAM military transport service was positioned at Rochambeau Airfield at Cayenne, which is French territory. The plane had been used for an official visit by Monsieur Mitterand to Morocco and was to have flown Premier Mauroy to the West Indies. Flight-Sergeant Tardot stood by, ready to get Barbie from La Paz in the DC 8; the ground staff had concealed the words '*République Française*' and done a repaint job on the fuselage. However, unknown to the DC 8 crew, a group of four DGSE men was also standing by with similar instructions at the Novotel hotel in Cayenne. The taskforce considered that if the COTAM DC 8 paid the visit to La Paz, the expulsion would be regarded as a kidnap. Better to use a C 130 Hercules. There was a temporary hitch when the Bolivians demanded to know who would pay the aviation fuel.

Transport was not the only problem. Public opinion had to be prepared, especially in Bolivia. On 27 January Agence France-Presse news agency carried a report stressing the excellent relations between the two countries. With the word 'expulsion' studiously avoided, it said: 'The decision by Bolivia to detain the war criminal Klaus Barbie and seriously consider his extradition, at the request of Paris and Bonn, confirms the intention towards democratization by the new government in La Paz, and should further improve its relations with Europe . . . The arrest is bound to promote in Europe the new image Bolivia is attempting to present . . . An informed source says that France is willing to grant "substantial aid" to Bolivia, as are West Germany and the EEC.'

The story was picked up right away by the Bolivian

newspapers. But in Bolivia itself the approach was less direct. Israeli Ambassador Arie Avidor lent documents, photos and films on World War II and the extermination of the Jews; the idea was to influence public opinion and create a suitable climate of opinion. January 30 was the fiftieth anniversary of Adolf Hitler's assumption of power. For several evenings in a row, Bolivian audiences waiting for their Dallas-style TV soap operas, were given scenes of the Nazi atrocities, complete with Klaus Barbie as an 'inset' throughout the programme! The horrors of the war, plus Barbie, were enough to ensure that nobody would dare to say: 'Oh, that poor Señor Altmann, such a respectable man . . .'

While the Supreme Court in Sucre was taking its time over the West German extradition request, Raymond Césaire was going back and forth between the French Embassy and the Quemado Palace. For it was not enough to get verbal agreement from the President of Bolivia; the correct procedures had to be gone through, with all the right signatures on official paper. There were delays on more than one occasion. After the resignation of the six MIR ministers, the government met to study the Barbie case just before the 25 January incarceration. Siles Zuazo called for a vote within the Cabinet. They voted unanimously for Barbie's expulsion.

But the question was where to? The Bolivians considered three possibilities:

1. Expulsion to Peru, which had an extradition agreement with France. The snag here was that Barbie might be held there for a long period, as the P.I.P. police had orders to present him before a magistrate in connection with currency dealing and ballpoint-pen trafficking.

2. Expulsion to Brazil. But the Bolivians judged that any competent lawyer could get him released.

3. Expulsion to Cayenne or the West Indies.

Later, Information Minister Mario Rueda Pena, who was playing hard to get with the special envoys, said: 'In law, we ought to have freed him. But what an outcry there would have been. Twice, in 1972 and 1973, he had got away with it, leaving prison and toddling off home.'

He was asked: 'Why did you not begin by trying him here in Bolivia, for example, on a charge of backing the armed militia or having links with the cocaine traffickers?'

He said: 'We lacked evidence. Barbie left no tracks at all. He was very smart.'

Pierre Viaux, First Counsellor at the French Embassy, hardly got a wink of sleep. There was a constant flow of telex exchanges with the Quai d'Orsay, but the Barbie business found Viaux in his element as a diplomat. The ministry kept seeking the latest position, bombarding him with orders. On 4 February Foreign Minister Claude Cheysson ordered a news black-out. On the seventh floor of the modern Embassy building, newsmen could hear Raymond Césaire thumping his desk: 'I don't wish to see them!'

For once the Bolivians were equally quiet. They realized that Barbie still had valuable contacts, some of whom were close to Siles Zuazo. They seemed to enjoy keeping the international press on its toes, especially as Bolivia stood to rake in useful royalties from an exclusive interview with Barbie in the aircraft planned by Carlos Soria of Bolivia's Channel 7.

Guards were strengthened at the Panoptico prison. The Nazi was watched by five heavies from the Interior Ministry. From 27 January on, secrecy was more than strict. Officials indicated to certain newsmen that they would each have their exclusive interview with the Lyons Butcher – for a financial consideration. Some journalists, poor fools, advanced a deposit. Barbie's lawyers hinted that the prisoner would be freed, arguing that extradition could be ruled out and that expulsion was unlikely.

The matter of plane seats added to the confusion. A certain Altmann reserved a seat on various flights from La Paz to Peru, Brazil and West Germany. On 4 February at 3.00 p.m. the Information Minister started working up a TV crew. The Bolivian reporter and his engineers were told 'to take what you need for several days'. A camera was sent to the Interior Ministry in Avenida Arce.

The 755,964.45 pesos in interest was finally paid to COMIBOL – by a special fund in France! That Friday around 6.00 p.m., two persons fluent in Spanish went to the Controleria General, offering the sum in cash. The Comptroller hesitated, not knowing who was settling the account. He telephoned a colleague, and then declared: 'OK, I'll take it.'

He counted out the notes, offered a receipt and asked to whom it should be made out. The two visitors said not to bother, and Assistant Controller Jaime Urcullo signed an order for the release of Klaus Altmann Hansen. The legal procedure went ahead and an official accompanied one of the two persons to the Panoptico jail, leaving a subordinate at the Controleria wondering what the hell he was going to do with all those banknotes until the Central Bank opened on Monday.

On the first floor of the prison, a warder opened the cell door (the padlock was broken, anyway), took Barbie out onto a veranda, put handcuffs on him and prepared to take him down to the empty yard. There was only one exit from the prison and vehicles could not be parked there because of the steps.

At 8.50 p.m. waiting newsmen and doubtless some of Barbie's pals watched as a smallish man with a hood over his head was thrown into a jeep that roared off with an escort. The journalists chased it. The area round the gate was now almost empty, with just a few clever newsmen waiting, along with some who had no transport. Then, the real Klaus Barbie emerged and was taken away.

At El Alto Airport, after the departure of the last Aero Peru plane for Lima, the shiny grey C 130 stood alone with full tanks, safely in the military zone of the airport. Already aboard was Carlos Soria's TV crew with Hugo Roncal.

Barbie had already made a stopover in the basement of

the Interior Ministry. This was more than a formality; it took place in the presence of Under-Secretary of State Gustavo Sanchez, the best contact for the French and the Americans. Barbie, still handcuffed, was brought into a room bright with Bolivian television lamps and faced four or five people standing in line. One of them was one of Barbie's lawyers, Adolfo Ustarez, jailed on 24 January just before Barbie's arrest and charged with organizing paramilitary groups.

Sanchez had been looking forward to this moment, the farewell he had arranged. He asked Barbie if he recognized his old companions. Barbie gazed at them one by one, saying each time: 'No, I don't know him.' French journalist Claude Critton was also there – the Bolivians had said he would have a scoop and promised he would fly with Barbie in the plane. However, not only would Critton be stuck in La Paz, but he was not allowed to have the video cassette that recorded the scene – the cassette has never been made public and lies in a safe at this moment. Various witnesses signed a document and lawyer Ustarez just had time to inform Barbie that, according to policemen, Minister Mario Roncal Antezana had been visited three times that day by the French Ambassador.

Gustavo Sanchez recalls: 'After that I took Barbie to the airport. Up to that point he still did not believe he would be expelled, and supposed he was being transferred to the Tarapaca Barracks on the Altiplano. He was counting on his lawyers' finding a loophole for him. I asked him: "What do you feel about dying?" He answered evasively: "War is war, the people I killed were guerillas." Then I told him: "You are going to Germany."'

At the airport was Information Minister Rueda Pena, fresh from a stay of several months in East Germany, and proud of his fluent German. With the other Bolivians looking on, he began chatting with Herr Barbie without introducing himself. The conversation took place in a hangar where Barbie was being kept from journalists. The newsmen were in the VIP hall, which had blankets over the windows and troops standing outside. Inside was the man the journalists were supposed to think was Barbie, whom they had earlier seen emerge from the prison, and drive off in a jeep.

It was a miserable wet and windy night, with the thermometer at 45 degrees Fahrenheit. Barbie did not even have a jacket. A policeman was ordered to hand him his green parka coat.

'*Und?*' the Minister was saying.

'*Ich bin zufrieden,*' Herr Barbie said. ('I will be very happy to see my German homeland again.')

Then he started patting his pockets, his trousers and the parka. 'I haven't any money at all. How will I pay my hotel room?' he said, embarrassed, smiling wanly.

The journalists were all invited to a reception by Interior Minister Mario Roncal. The day before, at a cocktail party, he had created what he called 'the greatest diversion in my career', by maintaining 'for a joke' that Barbie was on his way to Frankfurt in a German military plane.

But there was one journalist still at the airport, Philippe Vieillescazes from the French TF 1 television channel, who witnessed the take-off of the C 130 at 10.28 p.m. precisely, heading north-east.

On board were two pilots, a doctor named Abularach, who was mysteriously killed in a plane crash in June 1983, three Bolivian policemen, who were to travel as far as France, the Bolivian TV crew, who had just learned the destination, and, very discreetly at the back, two or three DGSE agents. There were no seats. Barbie sat on the deck of the plane wrapped in his parka. The C 130 was still over Bolivian soil on its way to Brazil when journalist Carlos Soria began setting up makeshift deflectors in aluminium foil to light up the expelled Nazi. 'I haven't had time to do any research,' he wailed.

Another document he had not seen was the new extradition request from France, referring to 'crimes against humanity' that had just arrived at the French Embassy in La Paz, intentionally late.

At his press conference Mario Roncal was saying: 'Why did we expel him to France? Because that was the only country willing to take Klaus Barbie.'

French premier Pierre Mauroy had been paying an official visit to Guyana and the West Indies. It was important that he leave Guyana to avoid giving the impression that the French Prime Minister had come to supervise Operation Barbie. Pierre Mauroy had left Cayenne that Friday morning. At Fort de France in Martinique that same evening he referred to François Mitterrand's symbolic gesture at the Pantheon in Paris after his election in May 1981: he had laid a rose on the tomb of Jean Jaurès, another for Jean Moulin, and a third for Victor Schoelcher, the parliamentarian who did away with slavery in the French territories in 1848. Mauroy lingered a little when he mentioned the second rose, but it was the third that won the loudest applause.

Leaning against the side of the C 130, Barbie chatted, while the Bolivian television people fussed about.

'This is a kidnap!' he protested. Nobody felt like arguing. Barbie was leaving behind two graves: his wife's in the La Paz German cemetery, his son's in the other German cemetery at Cochabamba. He complained he was dirty and said he should have been given the small case he had in prison with his toothbrush, razor and some Deutsche Marks. He had been hustled about too much and was still living in the immediate past. Barbie seemed unable to focus on the future and the Germany he thought he was heading for. Carlos Soria kept at him, but he clammed up on anything connected with Bolivia, at least to begin with. Then he found he was back in the 1940s without knowing it.

'Vae Victis,' he said with a little smile. 'We had to win the war, don't you see, otherwise we lost everything. At the Nuremberg trials they accused the vanquished of many crimes, but only the vanquished, there was nothing about the Allies' crimes.'

Of the rejected extradition request in 1974, he said: 'I felt easy, because my lawyers had always said that law, justice, would prevail in Bolivia.'

Soria asked him if he was afraid of dying. He answered: 'Death is cruel, of course. It always was, throughout the world's history, starting with Adam, and Cain, who killed his brother Abel.' He gave a little shrug.

'If you had to sum up your life?'

'I would say, really, that I have suffered a lot.'

The C 130 touched down just before 6.15 a.m. in Guyana. It was still raining. As a security measure, the control tower was informed only 22 minutes before the plane landed. A white Renault 4L shot out to fetch Barbie and rush him to the Rochambeau airfield terminal. There he was awaited by the Commissioner of the Republic, Claude Silberzahn, Prosecutor Bertrand and a crestfallen Flight Sergeant Tardot who had just been told he would not be flying to La Paz to pick up the Nazi. Also in the building was a German interpreter from the Foreign Legion barracks in Cayenne.

In French, the Prefect informed the prisoner of the arrest warrant issued on 27 November 1982. The interpreter told Barbie and the Flight Sergeant read out the charges drawn up by Judge Riss in Lyons. Barbie frowned; it had just dawned on him that he was in French hands. He said in a level voice: 'I admit to being Klaus Barbie in time of war.' Gendarmes typed out the customary affidavit, and the various papers were transferred to the waiting DC 8 with Barbie.

Meanwhile, Edmond Frédéric, correspondent for the *Le Monde* newspaper, was chatting with the crew of the C 130.

'When do you take off again?' he asked.

'When we've been paid, and not a moment before.'

A group of passengers waiting for a regular West Indies flight watched the DC 8 sneak out, with no idea who was aboard.

Barbie asked the time. It was 11.25 a.m. Paris time, he was told. A look of resignation spread over his face at the start of the long journey. The SS Obersturmführer was shown to a seat, and a mealtray was placed on his lap.

The camera moved in on him again.

'So you think your crimes should be forgotten now?'

'Absolutely, yes. Because so many new crimes have been committed, more than one hundred wars since World War II.'

'How can you justify what the Nazis did?'

'Napoleon was condemned, too, by virtually the whole of Europe. Two hundred years later he was a hero.'

'What do you think of Hitler?'

'He united the people. In a year and a half he eradicated six million unemployed.'

'But the methods?'

'You must examine both sides to find out if it was justified or not. The former foes should get together and clear themselves in the eyes of history.'

When the camera drew away, Barbie rasped: 'I have lost my life!'

Someone said: 'Come now, the guillotine has been done away with.'

'It makes no difference. I am in death's waiting-room.'

The DC 8's destination was a well-kept secret. It landed at Orange military air base at 8.15. Well to the north at Evreux, journalists were stamping their feet, and also at Lyon-Satolas airport, where airport police had to detain a young woman whose parents had been deported decades before; she had a .22 long rifle carbine under a plaid blanket.

Gendarmerie General Louis Bernadac told me: 'We knew there would be a lot of people at Satolas airport. It was risky, for Barbie was supposed to be tried, not lynched. So we kept the whole thing secret and I was asked to carry out a veritable military operation to protect the prisoner.'

His subordinate, Colonel Le Gouil, said: 'In addition I had a reserve squadron of mobile gendarmes standing by, just in case.'

To avoid all risk of assassination the military top brass decided that the final stage between Orange and Lyons would be made by Puma helicopter. Barbie, visibly exhausted, got out of the DC 8; the gendarmes had him on a cord attached to his handcuffs (cabriolet model 83).

Carlos Soria later said that an expression of panic gripped Barbie's face when he entered the helicopter, as if he realized only then what was happening to him.

The Puma settled onto the tarmac at a small air base just south of Lyons, and the prisoner was transferred to a van with blanked-out windows, covered on the inside with cloth. At normal speed the convoy of fourteen vehicles travelled to Lyons. And at precisely 10.15 p.m. on 5 February 1983, Klaus Barbie entered the prison yard at Fort Montluc, forty years after he had left it.

There was only one top-level statement, which came from Premier Pierre Mauroy, now in Guadeloupe. He said: 'The French government has not acted in any spirit of vengeance.'

Back in La Paz, this view was not shared by all. Siles Zuazo's adversary, Vice-President Jaime Paz Zamora, head of the MIR party, protested that Barbie should initially have been put on trial in Bolivia, if only because he had taken part in various military *coups d'état*. General Banzer's party, the ADN, also said Barbie could have been brought to court in Bolivia.

The newspaper *Presencia* said: 'Whether we like it or not, guarantees in law also apply to Nazis. It would have been logical to await the decision of the Supreme Court . . . Bolivia has succumbed to the distasteful lure of money.'

Ultima Hora commented: 'The Government has sold Klaus Altmann, a Bolivian citizen, for a reward so far undisclosed to the people.' Only the tip of the iceberg will probably ever be disclosed – the officially announced 100 million francs and 3,000 tons of flour, aid, it was stated, that was part of normal French assistance to Bolivia. Ninety million francs was for the military hospital at La Paz and the rest for the customs service.

Once Raymond Césaire had completed his mission, he was named ambassador to Peru and left Bolivia without the usual honour awarded to ambassadors when they leave, the Condor of the Andes, the equivalent of the Légion d'Honneur.

President Siles Zuazo seemed none too happy when he went home in late March after a visit to France. He told newsmen: 'I have not come to present the invoice for Barbie.' The presidency in La Paz publicly issued a financial statement: 'Withdrew $40,000 US for official visit to France, returned to Central Bank $25,980.43, expenditure $14,019.57.' This is not much, even for a small official delegation abroad.

In mid-May the newspapers carried advertisements headed 'Bolivian TV Informs the Public . . .' In six paragraphs readers learned that 'photos sold to *Paris-Match* by Hugo Roncal, producer of Channel 7, did not implicate the official TV network'. The ad was signed by the top man, Julio Barragan Calvimontes. Roncal, who was in the DC 8 with Barbie, was brother to the Interior Minister.

With Klaus Barbie safely in his cell at Montluc, François Mitterrand wrote to Hernan Siles Zuazo and lauded his courage and integrity. True to form, the Bolivian Supreme Court continued to examine the German request for extradition! There were still a few loose ends. Minister Mario Roncal, for example, had to reply to the parliamentarian Carlos Valverde Barbery, former head of the far right Bolivian Socialist Falange. Roncal, who had been openly accused of building up a lucrative account in Switzerland with the earnings he made from cocaine, told parliament: 'Bolivia contravened no laws by expelling to France a person who had violated the immigration law in obtaining Bolivian citizenship under a false identity.'

And so the curtain finally went down on Barbie's long stay in Bolivia.

The controversy now switched to France, where graffiti began appearing on walls along the lines of 'Barbie will win!'

A weekly publication commissioned a public opinion poll, carried out by IFRES between 5 and 7 February 1983, and covering a sample of 1,000 persons representing French people eighteen years of age and older.

The question asked was: 'Would you restore the death penalty for Klaus Barbie if he were found guilty of killing thousands of French people, and in particular Jean Moulin?'

The result was: YES 56 per cent; NO 40 per cent; DON'T KNOW 4 per cent.

12

A s I WRITE THIS in March 1984, the Barbie story is not yet over. Barbie's return to France was intended as the beginning of a victory for justice. It may turn out to be a 'triumph for democracy', an electoral gimmick, or a plain old-fashioned political shambles. We shall see.

Safely behind bars, Barbie was news again. It was hard to believe he had actually been caught. The lawyers, magistrates, jailers and fellow prisoners registered the event, and then a curious disquiet seemed to overtake them.

The lawyers nattered among themselves about who would handle this major trial for the defence, openly affirming that they would never dream of pleading for the Butcher of Lyons. The magistrates asked for time. When Judge Christian Riss was handed the case he was relieved of about 100 small dossiers, leaving only 130 on his desk! A variety of minor investigations involving small charges, rogatory commissions and experts' appraisals were hawked round the corridors in wicker baskets to be shared among colleagues already overworked, who welcomed them with the enthusiasm of a schoolboy faced with a pile of extra homework. The prison warders groaned, because the jail was bursting at the seams and because the arrival of Klaus Barbie instantly ended an experiment involving the introduction of more humane prison conditions for inmates. The inmates were understandably not enthusiastic at the prospect of tighter discipline.

People also started wondering whether Barbie might not prove to be a bigger problem than he first appeared, in his borrowed coat and with no luggage. In particular, just how good was Barbie's memory? What hidden secrets did he have about his stay in Lyons? What revelations would he make? More recently René Hardy has talked of possessing a 'suitcase full of documents'. Could Barbie also have one? The former SS officer had felt more at ease since the decision of the Bolivian Corte Suprema a decade ago, but he could not be absolutely sure that he was safe, and no doubt he had stashed away some evidence somewhere. It is hard to imagine that a Nazi of his calibre would neglect to keep evidence concerning the French and Dutch collaborators who worked for the Gestapo, a reserve of calumnies that would keep people at a distance if the need should ever arise. He may have a trunkload of ghosts from the 1940s, like a Swiss bank account, safe from prying eyes.

That was exactly the question being pondered on by his first counsel, Lyons barrister Alain Compagnon de la Servette, who had saved a French collaborator from the death sentence shortly after the Liberation, in the course of the second trial of Barbie and his friends in 1954. As he waited for Barbie's arrival, he wondered what documents might come to light.

He told me: 'That evening we were all in the Palais de Justice, Prosecutor Berthier, Judge Riss and myself. There was a great air of mystery and nobody would say when or where I would get to see Klaus Barbie. Suddenly we were whisked off to Montluc and taken into the clerk's office, where we confronted him standing under a first-aid box on the wall. Barbie – at last!'

Legal requirements were strictly adhered to. Although the office was within the outer perimeter wall, it was external to the prison itself. An official read out to the SS captain the same phrases he had heard at Cayenne airport. 'You are charged with . . .' An interpreter handled it nice and slowly, so that the clerk could get it all down.

Barbie said: 'It has been a long journey, I feel tired from the flight and rather ill. I am suffering from polyneuritis and prefer to wait before making a statement.'

The exact time was inscribed – 11.20 p.m. – and Barbie was booked in at the very scene of his crimes. He was the

996th inmate of Lyons' jail, the 239th name on the list of war criminals compiled in London forty years earlier.

The barrister called his counsel the next morning, and it was unanimously decided that he should not appoint another lawyer but designate himself. Barbie consented.

The reactions were not slow to follow in those first days of February 1983. Serge Klarsfeld declared: 'Mission accomplished,' which was not strictly true, for he did not surrender the file on the child victims of Izieu. Former Prime Minister Jacques Chaban-Delmas deemed that the jailing of Barbie brought to an end the scandal of his continued freedom. Defence Minister Charles Hernu said: 'How can we fail to hope that justice be meted out to those reponsible – ' The mayor of Lyons, Francisque Collomb, emphasized that up-and-coming generations would at last discover the terrible consequences of dictatorship. He thought in terms of History. Others were more interested in the guillotine, with left-wing radical Senator Henri Caillivet and Gaullist Member of Parliament François Léotard calling for the death sentence to be restored in the case of crimes against humanity; to that Daniel Meyer, President of the International Federation of Human Rights, replied: 'That is an instinctive reaction rather than a carefully thought-out one.' The Ministry of Justice responded with unusual speed, recalling that 'any bill aimed at the restoring of the death sentence in France with regard to a charged person ignores the basic principle that criminal law cannot be altered retrospectively.' It seemed Barbie would not meet the same fate as Eichmann, and Simon Wiesenthal remarked that 'the sentence cannot be anything but symbolic'.

Politics came to the fore. A section of the French left hastily produced Jean Moulin's widow, Madame Marguerite Stork-Cerruty, and shoved her onto a platform, where she cried: 'I've bought champagne. This is an unprecedented victory!' Just as fast, the Resistance people cut her down to size – she was divorced and had remarried; she had left Jean Moulin in 1927; she knew nothing. For the French Communist Party, Gaston Plissonnier welcomed the news.

Serge July, managing editor of the newspaper *Libération*, observed: 'The French authorities have started up a symbolic machine and it is hard to imagine all the effects of this . . . It is indeed a devil that France has captured, quite legally. Klaus Barbie is in truth the archetype of the Nazi devil; he is neither a collaborator like Touvier, nor even a bureaucrat like Eichmann, but a butcher-in-chief . . .'

There were other demons in the wings. Pierre Messmer, another ex-premier, recalled the settling of accounts by the 'ardent purgers' of the Liberation, and hoped that the forthcoming Barbie trial would not wake sleeping dogs. Colonel Rémy made no bones about it: 'The extradition [sic] of Klaus Barbie is a deadly gift!' Historian Henri Amouroux warned: 'Let us not make this executioner the arbiter of Resistance quarrels and dramas, or the judge of our history and our passions.'

Perhaps it was already too late. Who was going to place the Caluire enigma under lock and key? When Barbie set foot on French soil again, so did Jean Moulin. There is no prescription when it comes to History.

Paris Mayor Jacques Chirac, ex-premier Raymond Barre (who said, 'After thirty years you leave God to judge the criminal'), leader of the Front National Party Jean-Marie Le Pen, the pro-Communist General Labour Confederation, the Germans, the British, the Tass news agency in Moscow, Israeli public prosecutor Gideon Hausner, who dealt with Eichmann – everyone had their say. Tass denounced the way the United States had helped Barbie in 1947, Le Pen said Barbie's return was an election ploy before the local government ballot of March 1983.

Madame Simone Veil warned of the squabbling that could arise: 'When it has been shown that France under the Occupation comprised collaborators, quite a few skunks and a lot of weaklings nobody could have expected to be heroes, do you really think anything will have been achieved?' Simone Veil had herself fallen victim to Hitler's madness. She, like others who had suffered, wanted a trial of the Nazi ideology, a broadening of the debate.

As to the West Germans, who had sought Barbie's extradition, officially they did not rule out the idea of asking France to hand over Barbie after the Lyons trial, but most Germans wanted this historic trial of Nazism to take place on the French side of the Rhine.

French Foreign Minister Claude Cheysson recalled the Nazism of the pre-war years during a press luncheon: 'None of that would have occurred without unemployment and the despair of a whole society. We should reflect on that when we argue purely economic factors in relation to the present crisis. Even the most civilized of societies can be thrown into fearsome turmoil if it is condemned to unemployment and a population that survives only by virtue of government subsidies.'

Scarcely had Barbie entered Montluc than we began to look for René Hardy. Hardy was living in Melle, in the Deux-Sèvres in Western France. Hardy had crossed the Atlantic with a journalist and reached Bolivia, where he confronted his Nazi accuser; he had given his story to a weekly magazine and posed for pictures. Surely he would have something to say for himself now. Some people advised us to leave him alone, implying that we had no right to stir the whole thing up again, since we had not been involved.

I honestly believe it was right to give Hardy the chance to speak. He could have got out of it, but he did not. He said: 'They were like boy scouts, they didn't wage war, they were playing at boy scouts . . . I couldn't care less now.'

On two television channels and on radio, René Hardy said: 'They are trying to pin it on me; let them try. I've got a suitcase full of documents!'

The idea of televizing the trial was going the rounds. Justice Minister Robert Badinter set up a committee to examine the question of TV coverage for all trials, not just Klaus Barbie's. The committee was headed by a trusted magistrate, André Braunschweig, former examining magistrate and assize court president, a moderate trade unionist and currently President of the Criminal Appeals Court. Along with some colleagues, I said I was in favour of covering proceedings on television; if we were allowed to take notes and make sketches there was no fundamental reason to ban video cameras from court. It is my feeling that something better is needed than a static picture of a court reporter giving his report from prepared notes on the steps outside the courtroom, which is almost like radio. If the Barbie trial went on TV, everyone could 'attend', provided the jury and witnesses were not hampered in any way and the rights of the defendant were safeguarded. The matter was discussed in Lyons.

Meanwhile the prisoner's counsel thought it appropriate to call in a representative of the Church to help him. The obvious person was the lawyer-priest Robert Boyer of the Jesuits, member of the Bar Council and the only man in France who was a prison chaplain as well as a lawyer. But this choice of defence counsel was not confirmed. The Archbishop of Lyons, Monseigneur Albert Decourtray, issued a statement saying it appeared contradictory that the Church should defend a man who had not publicly admitted his crimes. He said: 'The presence of a priest at the preliminary examination, as at the trial, could feed the powerful and worrying contemporary trend towards underestimating the full horror of Nazism, to which Christians cannot consent.'

Unwittingly Monseigneur Decourtray was leaving the terrain free for Maître Jacques Vergès, 'the terrorists' friend'.

Judge Christian Riss, born in Algiers of parents from Belfort and Alsace, was not even half Barbie's age when he took over the dossier in 1982. This young 'first magistrate' read up on the Occupation years, delving into rare books in an attempt to get under the skin of Klaus Barbie, and at the same time to prepare himself for an inquiry that few have to tackle, into crimes against humanity. He also had available the fastidious reports on the interrogations in the 1952 and 1954 trials. His difficulty was that, until 1983, there had only been four people charged with crimes against humanity: Paul Touvier, whose whereabouts are unknown; Jean Legay, who was police *délégué* under Vichy in the Occupied Zone; Maurice Papon, who was once Prefect of Bordeaux and in March 1984, at the time of writing, has been waiting fourteen months to be examined by a Bordeaux judge; and finally, Klaus Barbie, the only one actually in detention.

The French criminal code defines crimes against humanity as murder, slavery, extermination, deportation or other inhuman treatment committed against civilian populations during war or occupation – all persecutions carried out for political, racial or religious reasons. But Barbie's lawyers will certainly remind us that there is no 'scale of sentences' and that this recent legislation dating from 1964 under de Gaulle cannot be applied retrospectively, on the grounds that a crime does not exist if the law against it has not been passed. In 1943–4 the French criminal code made no reference to the concept of 'crime against humanity'.

This has given Christian Riss something else to consider. In 1954 the court in theory had sentenced Barbie to death for deliberate homicide of 'numerous French nationals' with premeditation. Barbie's defence could claim that this encompassed the entirety of the crimes, that one cannot pick out the victims of Saint-Genis-Laval, for example, that one cannot remove the 'victim of war' label from them and turn them into victims of racism, and political or religious persecution. Barbie has already been tried for all these crimes, it could be argued, even though he has not been punished.

Barbie was eventually moved to Saint Joseph jail in the centre of Lyons on the banks of the Rhône. Montluc does not provide full medical surveillance and security; Lord knows what would have happened if, when he arrived, someone had aimed a rifle with telescopic sights at him instead of a camera with a zoom lens. At Saint Joseph he is less likely to be killed. He was transferred one Saturday evening in a mere four and a half minutes with police motorcycle escort. He emerged from Montluc from under a black tarpaulin that used to hide the guillotine from nearby houses.

At Saint Joseph, the ex-SS captain was placed on the first floor in I Block, on the north side; other inmates had been moved out to make room for him. That is where he is at the time of writing, in a cell three times larger than the one at Montluc. Half the first floor is reserved for him. At the end of the corridor is a big gate with two locks, one opening from inside, the other from outside. Barbie is completely on his own, and never sees his fellow prisoner Roger Rocher, who used to run the AS at Saint-Étienne and is incarcerated in the same block. Like the other prisoners, Barbie gets his meals from the prison kitchen, and can have little extras, which he has to pay for. He can watch television in an adjacent cell, where he is allowed to receive visitors. When people come to ask him questions and discuss his case, he is taken down to a 'praetorium' on the ground floor where he sits opposite the visitors at a table covered with green baize.

One of those visitors was Elie Nahmias. Barbie told Nahmias: 'Why would you have been arrested? You don't look like a Jew.'

Madame Simone Lagrange confronted him, formally accusing him of torturing her in 1944. Barbie said he was pleased to see her: 'I haven't seen a pretty woman for six months.'

Barbie is allowed a daily walk on his own in the yard, which is covered with a corrugated plastic roof, in case someone should get it into his head to shoot the prisoner.

His daughter Ute Messner came from Austria to see him. When she arrived by train on 5 March 1983, she was assailed by newsmen. As she emerged from the prison, wearing a leather coat and sporting a mauve scarf, she told them: 'I learned only a month ago why my father was sentenced to death in his absence . . . Yes, he is well treated . . . He considers he is being detained in conditions of dignity and honour. . . No, he has no suicidal tendencies. . . No, I could not kiss him, there is a glass partition. . . He is tired and ill. . . Yes, he has been a good father to us.'

Maître de la Servette intervened before the news-hounds could become more specific. He said: 'Do not ask a daughter to judge her father!'

The day after her visit, Barbie was rushed to Edouard Herriot Hospital, complaining of acute stomach pains. He was put in Ward G, and had a hernia operation, performed by Professor Lombard-Platet. He was in hospital for a week and recovered. He spoke fluent French while he was there. Journalists reminded Maître de la Servette that some accused had been freed for medical reasons; he replied: 'There's no reason why he should be, he's just fine.'

Servette also said: 'Barbie is not a great intellectual, but he's not a poor sap or thickhead, as some papers affirm. He was only a minor officer who would certainly not have been tried with the big fish, if he had been caught immediately after the war. The arrest of Jean Moulin was the big event in his career.'

Barbie has applied for release, which is not as outrageous as may seem, in the light of French legal procedure. This is the only way he has of getting his case examined by the Appeals Court. His counsel seeks to demonstrate that Barbie is the victim of 'covert extradition' on the part of the Bolivians; the sole means of presenting the case before the top court in France, and thus before the public, is to apply for release. Judge Christian Riss rejected the application, as will the Chambre d'Accusation on appeal, before the plea reaches the Appeals Court on the Quai de l'Horloge in Paris. Judge Riss turned it down partly on the grounds that Barbie's safety cannot be guaranteed if he is free on French soil.

Enter Maître Jacques Vergès. Jack-in-the-Box, we might call him. Barbie's defence counsel sought out the West German 'collective', a group of lawyers specializing in the defence of Nazi criminals. Vergès, who happens to be the 'friend of Carlos', the terrorist chief, has an Asian smile, a leather jacket, and rolling eyes behind oval-shaped spectacles. He sat down on the other side of the glass partition to ask a few questions about the Bolivian aspect of the affair, and then took over the whole file!

He set about handling Barbie's case so dramatically that Barbie appears to have lost control of it. The Barbie case has become the Vergès case, in a sense, Barbie can do little about it, and must console himself reading crime stories. Jacques Vergès's father is from the French Pyrenees; his mother is from Vietnam; his twin brother is a Communist in La Réunion. For today's youngsters he is known as the man who acts for Nazis; for the family of the French Labour Minister Robert Boulin who killed himself; for Magdalena Kopp and Bruno Brequet, who were lieutenants to the terrorist Carlos; for the members of Action Directe; for Princess Tsutsumi; and so on. But for the preceding generation Vergès is the defender of the Algerian National Liberation Front, the man who dared to confront the French State and act for the independence fighters. In all his cases there are two common features: none of the clients is a Jew and none of the cases is run-of-the-mill. That means press coverage.

He is highly intelligent, crafty, and courteous when he feels like it, a man who shines in explosive situations. He is quiet enough in his office but can rudely clap his hands for service; he can maintain a smile for hours while blowing cigar smoke at his fellow lawyers during a TV programme.

'I was born happy,' he is fond of saying. But if you look at his hands, his fingers, his lips, you will notice that they quiver.

Mystery shrouds Maître Vergès. It seems he

disappeared from the face of the Earth during the 1970s. He evaporated so completely that it was widely believed his body lay in a concrete coffin on the bed of a Spanish creek. Neither his brother Paul nor his Algerian wife Djamila Bouhired, whom he married at the same time that he switched to Islam and took the name Mansour, would say where he was.

People recalled that he was at one time a chum of the Cambodian Pol Pot, that he had lived for a while in Prague, that his friends and enemies often called him 'Infra-red'. Where was Infra-red in the 70s? Some suggested that he had shacked up with Castro or Khaddafi, that he was in the Palestinian camps around Damascus, or in Moscow or Cambodia. My own information leads me to believe he was in China.

When he resurfaced he merely said: 'I'm back again and brimming with hope, hardened too. Note that word!' The rest he kept under his hat. In 1978 Vergès donned his robes again at the Paris bar to defend another Klaus, his colleague Klaus Croissant, lawyer to the West German Baader-Meinhof gang, who was expelled from France.

When Vergès moved in on the Barbie case in 1983, I was not the only journalist to wonder who had appointed him and who was paying him. 'It was Monsieur Barbie who asked me; he sent me a note in the usual manner,' he asserted.

That is all very well, but as far as we know, Jacques Vergès was not the first name on anyone's lips in the Cochabamba mountains of Latin America, or in La Paz. If Barbie was aware of his reputation, he must have received a sign from Heaven. It was certainly not Maître de la Servette who advised him to take Vergès. Possibly Ute mentioned his name; she might have had a chat with Third Reich admirers such as the Swiss banker François Genoud, ex-treasurer of the Algerian National Liberation Front and a friend of Vergès. Ute Messner has told *Stern* that neither she nor her father were paying a thing for Maître Vergès's services.

Full of his own importance, Infra-red proceeded to turn Barbie's defence into an attack. Dragging Maître Boyer into it, *pace* the Archbishop, the barrister commented quietly: 'There is a mistake about Barbie. This is the trial of a man, not of a system.' Alain de la Servette's view was that defending does not mean whitewashing.

Maître Vergès brought in Ute Messner's former 'interpreter', his colleague François Heckenroth of the Evreux bar, who speaks perfect German. Vergès became the driver of a powerful legal steamroller. He appealed to the judge and the Appeals Court, lodged a plaint against 'kidnapping', denounced 'repressive international law' as evoked by the Lyons court, claimed forgery and use of forgeries (the Izieu message), and went to the European Court of Human Rights. Attack was certainly the best form of defence in this case, for the Appeals Court had to dig out the texts of the London and Moscow Conventions and of the United Nations. It worked – until the Advocate-General of France, Henri Dontenwille, warned in the Criminal Appeals Court on 26 January 1984: 'The method of the plea for release . . . may be compared to a type of hijacking of procedure.' In other words, enough is enough.

Barbie and his advocate had already switched the case to another front, reversing the roles: 'If Jean Moulin died, it was because he was betrayed by people who are still alive and basking in the aura of heroes.' Not a new idea, of course, but when Vergès published a book, the media gave him plenty of exposure and the attack hit home. The problem was not so much that the matter of Jean Moulin's suicide was raised yet again – after all, it was not to his dishonour, when we recall that Pierre Brossolette jumped out of a window to escape the Gestapo. What hurt was the idea that Moulin wanted to kill himself 'when he *realised* that he had been *betrayed* by members of the Resistance'. Without proof, that kind of statement was bound to rouse the ire of Resistance leaders like Frenay, Pineau and de Benouville.

Vergès kept his cool, ready to hit back. He was obliged to complain after Henri Noguères, with Resistance backing, deliberately called him a liar.

Meanwhile, in Lyons, the complaints grew in number as the pleas for Barbie's release became known. In early summer 1983, Madame Mireille Bertrand of the Communist Party Politburo told the Lyons court that, while her delegation had no wish to interfere with procedure, it wanted the charges to be broadened to include the prescribed war crimes and the Caluire betrayal. The Communists requested of the Public Prosecutor 'that, through Barbie, the inhuman regime that gave birth to many Barbies should be judged'. The reply was: 'This plea from a party that is represented in the Government appears inappropriate to me.'

The B'nai B'rith Jewish community staged a demonstration outside Saint Joseph prison, with placards reading: 'No to freedom for the executioner!'

Vergès warned of the risk of an accident. What accident? Vergès explained: 'I have reason to fear that certain persons might be inclined to think that Klaus Barbie's death is the only possible outcome. It is to be feared certain persons will not be content to await his death, but will be tempted to speed up the process. I am afraid the death of Klaus Barbie would be the most shameful solution, but the easiest way out of this hornets' nest.'

Barbie demanded to have a 'neutral' doctor, independent of the prison administration. There have been worrisome rumours concerning medical treatment in the prisons. The former SS captain said he had circulation trouble, so the judge had him examined by specialists. Since the medical file is part of the dossier on the case, along with the interrogations, it is being kept secret under Article 11 of the law designed to prevent leaks during a legal examination.

A fan club has developed around the Butcher of Lyons,

but the letters he receives are not answered. The judge is keeping them, he doesn't want to let 'France's top prisoner' read them if they amount to an apologia for Nazism. Soon after Barbie returned to France, an elderly American woman, obviously not short of money, took up residence at the Sofitel hotel near Saint Joseph. She stayed three weeks in Lyons hoping to see him and give him her support and protection. She claimed she had had a son by Barbie and declared she wanted to leave everything to him. She managed to get in touch with Barbie's lawyers, who questioned Barbie. He was tickled pink. The American admirer eventually left to console some other Nazi somewhere else. The tabloids would have had a field day with that story, had they known about it!

Within the dirty grey prison walls that once housed a convent, Barbie paces the cell, the man who got away in 1950, was forgotten in 1963 when police reports had already located him in La Paz, whom no one wanted in 1969, and who could not be bought in 1973. Ten years later he is an embarrassment.

The cold wind from the Rhône beats against the prison, shaking the weeds growing at the foot of the walls. Barbie is no more than a few hundred yards from the former École de Santé Militaire across the Gallieni Bridge, where they are planning a Museum of the Resistance.

In Bolivia Barbie once compared Lyons to the massacre village of My Lai in Vietnam: 'I fully understand Lieutenant Calley [who carried out the slaughter]. He saw what I saw ten times over, a hundred times, during the war. The Germans were being killed all the time, and Calley saw his men killed, four or five Americans. That is why he did what he did, because things were tough in wartime.'

He has further said: 'I have never considered myself to be a criminal. If we had won the war perhaps Mr Truman or Mr Eisenhower would have been war criminals. I'm even certain of it!'

We shall see if the jury at the Rhône Assize Court is

prepared to go along with arguments like that. If there is a trial, that is.

Why must Barbie go on trial forty years after the war? Because, for some, Hitler lives on. Because History must be set down as it was. Even the parts some would prefer to forget.

Appendix

FRENCH COMMAND HQ GERMANY

RECORD OF EVIDENCE

Trial of Lieutenant-Colonel Hardy, René. Examination of witness Barbie, Klaus, with the K.D.S. Lyons during the German Occupation of France.

In the year one thousand nine hundred and forty-eight on July sixteen.

I Bibes, Louis, Chief Commissioner of the Interrogation Centre of the Surveillance du Territoire (SDT) in Germany, auxiliary criminal police officer of the Prosecutor of the Republic,

Assisted by Inspector Chapuis Amedee of my service,

And by Lieutenant Whiteway, French liaison officer with the military authorities of the United States occupation zone of Germany,

In view of the Rogatory Commission herewith dated 23 June 1948, of Military Justice Commander Gonnot, Examining Magistrate at the Paris Military Court, concerning proceedings against Lieutenant Hardy, René, charged with acts liable to harm National Defence and failure to disclose crimes comprising the interior or external security of the State,

I ordered the transporting to Munich (Bavaria) in the US occupation zone of Germany, and had appear before me, the witness Barbie, Klaus, former SS Hauptsturmführer of the BDS Frankreich,

Who, having declared himself neither relative nor ally nor servant of the accused and having sworn to state the whole truth and nothing but the truth and affirmed he knows sufficient of the French language to dispense with aid from an interpreter, gave evidence as follows:

My name is Barbie, Klaus, nationality German, born 25 October 1913 at Bad Godesberg (Rhineland). I served in the German occupation troops in France from May 1942 to 28 August 1944. I held the rank of SS Hauptsturmführer and occupied a post in the BDS Frankreich. More particularly, in the rank of Obersturmführer, I occupied as representative of AMT VI of the RSHA a post at Gex and then at the KDS Lyons in Section IV. Was subsequently promoted Hauptsturmführer.

Pursuant to my previous statements and in particular the statement you obtained on 18 May 1948, I am willing to answer all questions you wish to put to me.

Question 1: Do you know the person shown in this photograph? (Witness was shown photo of Multon alias Lunel)

Answer: I clearly recognize in this photo the man Multon alias Lunel who was brought to me in June 1943 by Hauptsturmführer Dunker, our Marseilles representative. Multon had been arrested in Marseilles in connection with the Flora affair. He had agreed to work for the Gestapo. After agreeing this, he was released. In the Flora affair Multon had revealed the mailbox used by Didot in Lyons and that was why he was brought to Lyons. When presented to me by Dunker, he agreed to carry through in Lyons the offer already made in Marseilles. This related to contacting Didot.

Question 2: Do you know of the circumstances surrounding his arrest in Marseilles on 28 April 1943 and his despatch on a mission to Lyon during May 1943?

Answer: I know nothing about the Flora affair or the circumstances in which Multon alias Lunel was arrested in Marseilles. I can only say that he was recruited by Dunker and he consented to serve our cause. He could serve us in Lyons to contact Didot and I must say right away that it was he who gave us the real name of the latter, Hardy. It should be said here that the KDS Marseille agreed that Lunel, also called Multon, should go to Lyons. This agreement was effected between the two local KDSs.

Question 3: Can you say how Multon knew about the mailbox of the rail sabotage group in Lyons? (Address: Madame Demoulin, 14 rue Bouteille) Was it through information received from Lecouster, arrested in Marseilles?

Answer: I do not know how Multon came to know about this mailbox. I do not know the name Lecouster. I can only say that Multon came to Lyons with Dunker and that our concern was to exploit information in his possession. I did not concern myself with the origin of this information. Having in my hands the reports of our Marseilles service, I accepted their accuracy and I was obliged to take advantage of them as early as possible.

Question 4: What was the date on which Madame Dumoulin was arrested? Was it 24 May 1943? Was Claire, Hardy's liaison agent, at 14 rue Bouteille, also arrested on that date?

Answer: I cannot say what the date was. However, I believe this arrest could not have occurred before the Caluire arrest because it would have deprived us of important intelligence sources.

Question 5: Tell us about the trailing of Hardy by Multon in the city of Lyons.

Answer: We merely had the maildrop watched. Multon did not trail Hardy in the city of Lyons. He only waited near the mailbox because he was certain that orders reached this point.

Question 6: What do you know of Hardy's activity in Lyons before Multon arrived. Did you know the cover names? (Carbon, Didot, Bardot, which?)

Answer: I knew only Didot, I knew no other name; he was ordered by the Resistance to sabotage railways. I also knew he was an engineer, as far as I recall. It was through a report sent by the BDS Frankreich that I knew that fact. Additionally the BDS Frankreich and senior personnel in the RHSA guided me in the action against railway sabotage.

Question 7: Was it through the Dumoulin mailbox that you learned of the existence of a Didot-Vidal rendezvous in Paris, set for 9 June at 9.00 a.m. at the metro station La Muette?

Answer: Yes. In early June 1943, or perhaps late in May, Multon, who was watching the Dumoulin mailbox, brought me the document that set the Didot rendezvous in Paris on 9 June 1943. As far as I recall the paper read: 'The general awaits you at such a place, such a date, such an hour.' Multon told me himself that he was sure it meant General Delestraint.

Question 8: When this message was intercepted, did you know of it, and if so, through whom? Was it put back in the box? What was the exact wording? Was it in plain words or in figures or code?

Answer: I state that the original of the message was brought to me by Multon. I noted it and copied it and had it put back in the mailbox. This message was in plain words. I clearly remember that the expression 'the general' was in this message.

Question 9: On 7 June 1943, Didot-Hardy left for Paris. Did K 30 (Moog, Pierre, known as Moog, Robert, called Bobby), whose photo we will now show you, and Multon receive orders from you to arrest Didot-Hardy, who was going to Paris? What exactly were those orders?

Answer: After interception of the message fixing the rendezvous mentioned in the previous question, I asked Multon how we should proceed. He told me we should have the train watched because he was practically certain Hardy was in Lyons. I said to go ahead and had Multon accompanied by K 30, whom I recognize in the photo you are showing me. I do not recall how one of these two men told me that Hardy was in the train. What I do recall clearly is that I personally phoned our Chalon-sur-Saône service to have Hardy arrested in the train in conjunction with the Customs.

Question 10: June 8, 1943 at 1.00 a.m. Hardy was seized when the train reached Chalon-sur-Saône. Were you notified by Moog or Multon, by phone from Moulins, about Didot-Hardy's presence on the train, or did Multon tell you from Chalon-sur-Saône about Didot-Hardy's arrest and that of his travelling companion Cressol?

Answer: As I have already said, I gave advance warning to our Chalon service that Hardy was on that train, and I also said Multon alias Lunel was in charge of trailing him. So our local service did the necessary and Hardy was seized along with another person whose name I do not know. It is obvious that Multon was at our Chalon service when they phoned to say that Hardy had been arrested. But Moog (K 30) carried on to Paris because we did not want to miss the meeting with Hardy arranged by 'the general'. The next morning I went to Chalon myself by car to get Hardy and bring him back to Lyons. At Chalon prison I interrogated Hardy's travelling companion. It was my view that he did not count in this business, and I had him freed. This man was held by the customs as a precautionary measure.

Question 11: Were you not told of Didot-Hardy's arrest at Chalon by the station master over the phone?

Answer: If I remember rightly, it was our service, I mean the Chalon Gestapo, that notified me of Hardy's arrest. I do not think the station master came into this. But it is possible that the station master's phone was used. It was not Multon who called me but a German, perhaps Kruger, the local Gestapo chief.

Question 12: Is it true that Didot-Hardy and his travelling companion were transferred during the night of 8 June 1943 to Chalon-sur-Saône prison?

Answer: That is correct. I took delivery of Hardy at Chalon prison and that is where I questioned his travelling companion. As I recollect, this man was a tradesman by profession and I think he showed documents proving he was in touch with a German economics service. Furthermore, he was very angry at this untimely arrest.

Question 13: K 30 and Multon continued on their journey to Paris on 8 June 1943. Do you know what missions they effected in Paris? Did they take part in the arrest of General Delestraint alias Vidal at the place given in the message intercepted at the Dumoulin mailbox, that is, La Muette metro station on 9 June 1943 at 9.00 a.m? And then the arrests of Gastaldo alias Garin alias Galibier and Théobald alias Jacques Terrier, deputies to General Vidal, at about 9.25 a.m. the same day at La Pompe metro station?

Answer: I cannot say for sure if Multon and K 30 went on together to Paris. What is certain is that K 30 reported to Section IVE, Sturmbannführer Kieffer, to make arrangements for the arrest of General Delestraint. I know nothing of the arrangements made for the seizure of this French officer or his deputies. Nor am I familiar with any aspects of the execution of the arrests. I was not in Paris at the time.

Question 14: What do you know about these arrests: 1. through reports by Moog and Multon; 2. through official reports?

Answer: Moog (K 30) told me verbally what happened in Paris and later I read the results of the operation in daily reports from the BDS Frankreich. Moog related to me that in La Muette metro entrance he went up to a man whose general appearance and his wearing of the Légion d'Honneur led him to suppose he was Delestraint alias Vidal. He told him he was there on behalf of Didot who had been prevented from coming, and he suggested to the 'general' that he should get in his car which was close by. The 'general' said all right but also asked that his deputies nearby be told. All these people were asked to get in the car and they were taken to Avenue Foch. Moog gave me no details of what happened afterwards. SS Sturmbannführer Kieffer told me to give instructions.

Question 15: Did Saumande and Doussot called André, whose photos I will now show you, participate 1. in the seizure of Didot-Hardy on the train at Chalon-sur-Saône; 2. in the arrests of General Vidal and his deputies Gastaldo and Théobald?

Answer: I fully recognize these two men you are showing me in the photos. One was a friend of K 30 and was coded K 4; that was Saumande. I know the other one only by the name André. I cannot say whether either or both took part in the arrests we are talking about.

Question 16: In what circumstances and on what date was Didot-Hardy moved to Lyons?

— 275 —

Answer: In my previous evidence I made a mistake by one month; I am sorry, but it was unwitting. These events took place in June and not July 1943. As to the present question, Didot-Hardy was transferred by myself the day after his arrest on 9 June in Lyons. But I might be a day out. What I can say is that, owing to the urgency of the matter, I personally went to Chalon-sur-Saône to fetch Hardy with my car and I was in civilian clothing. My car was a Citroën with French number plates.

Question 17: Tell us in the fullest detail what contacts you had in Lyons, at the HQ of the KDS service, with Didot-Hardy. What was his attitude at first? What statements did he make? Did the idea of offering his services come from you or from him? What documents were found on Didot-Hardy or in his luggage (letters – who were they from? to whom were they addressed?). Have you in your possession any letter addressed to Mademoiselle Lydie Bastien, 113 quai Pierre-Scize in Lyons, which Hardy forgot in a suit pocket? Can you recall the contents? Do you know the domicile of Hardy at 112 Chemin de Saint-Just at Vaize? How did you find that? Did you go there with him or did you send other people, Moog and Multon in particular? What commitment did Hardy make to your service in order to gain his freedom? Did you yourself question Hardy? Let us have details of your interrogations. Was the matter of a French railway sabotage plan discussed? Have you documents relating to this plan? Where did they come from? What about Hardy's luggage? Can you produce documents giving details of where they were seized and the people whose homes they were found at? Are they documents provided by Hardy? Were they documents that you or your aides went to get on tip-offs from Hardy, in his presence or otherwise?

Answer: I first made contact with Hardy at Chalon-sur-Saône prison. I had never seen him before. I greeted him by saying: 'Good-day Monsieur Hardy.' I already knew his real name from Multon and he also told me Hardy wore camouflage glasses with false lenses. When I greeted him by that name, Hardy denied his identity. I let that drop and took him to my car, that is, without using handcuffs. Inside the car we spoke together and I took his glasses off, wanting to show him I knew exactly who he was. I realized that the lenses were indeed false. Hardy then understood that it was no longer any good playing around with me and he said it was Multon alias Lunel who had given him away because he saw him on the train. Then Hardy talked about his fiancée because I found a letter from her on him. I must add that when Hardy and his luggage were searched, nothing of any interest was found on him apart from that letter. He was deeply fond of his fiancée and feared she would be arrested too. I replied that I had nothing against her and he need not worry about her. I had the impression he was pleased about that. We arrived at the École de Santé Militaire where my service was. The standing orders were that all arrested persons should be taken to Fort Montluc. Hardy was not sent there. The laws did not apply to him in the same way. I gave him a room on the first floor in our service. I locked him into the room, telling the guard he was there and saying nobody must speak to him.

The reason I did not send him to Fort Montluc was that, on our way back to Lyons after his arrest, and in the talks we had together in the car, I gained the impression that one could discuss things with him. I did not discuss duty with him, but personal things.

In the afternoon and evening I went with him to his room and interrogated him about his Resistance activities. I was alone with Hardy and he spoke to me very frankly about his work, without reservations of any kind. He said in particular that he was in charge of railway sabotage. I asked him nothing about his comrades and he did not mention them to me. Bur Hardy told me what I already knew about his Paris meeting with General Delestraint.

The initiative for suggesting he offer his services to us came from me. I pointed out to Hardy the privileged treatment he was enjoying. He was aware there was a reason for it. But when I asked him directly to work for me, mentioning the risks he ran, he did not immediately reply in the affirmative; he asked for time to think it over. This key conversation between Hardy and me, occurred the day after his arrest. As I remember it, Hardy gave his consent in the afternoon or evening that same day. At the same time he declared he could render me great service because he was not what could be termed a 'little boss'. He assured me of his loyalty because he realized the risks I myself was taking where he was concerned. He gave me his word of honour and shook my hand.

I cannot remember any document being found either on Hardy or in his luggage. I well remember that letter addressed to Lydie Bastien, but that was a completely private matter.

Before Hardy's arrest we only knew about his maildrop. It was certainly through him that we learned the address of his Vaize domicile. While it is possible that someone in my service went there, I never went there myself. I cannot say now which person might have gone to Hardy's domicile at Vaize.

After he agreed to operate for me, Hardy conveyed to me that he ought to be released very quickly otherwise he might become hot and lose his old contacts, particularly his liaison agent.

Hardy promised me to continue his activities as Resistance network leader and to report to me everything that happened.

I personally interrogated Hardy but I never drew up a report about his interrogation, and that was deliberate because I wanted to use him.

There was never any mention between Hardy and myself of a railway track sabotage plan in France and personally I did not see any documents about that plan. Naturally we discussed sabotage matters but it would be wrong to say a plan was discussed. However, Hardy was to notify me of all orders he might receive regarding his activities in the Resistance.

As I sought to work with Hardy, it would have been dangerous for me to make immediate moves to find either individuals or documents. I cannot remember having obtained documents after Hardy's arrest. Perhaps data collected in Lyons led to the finding of such things in other places, but I am not completely sure about that.

The plan set up by me using Hardy was aimed at carrying out a major operation against this branch of the Resistance, an operation that would have covered the whole of France. This plan was not put into effect, because the Caluire affair took place first and was a more immediate concern; and secondly because Hardy disappeared.

Question 18: Do you know if Moog, Pierre, (K 30) went with Hardy to the parents of Lydie Bastien at 113 quai Pierre-Scize, either before his release or after the arrest of Heilbronn alias Arel alias Hennequin, which occurred on 12 June 1943 around 2.15 p.m.?

Answer: I don't know about that. However I am convinced that Hardy and Moog met later, that is, after Hardy's release.

Question 19: What emerged from the interrogations of Hardy? What were your instructions? What were the pledges made by Hardy?

Answer: I have already answered those questions. I repeat that the questioning of Hardy did not lead to arrests in Lyons itself. Naturally I sent a report to BDS Frankreich, but I do not know what action was taken about the report and what arrests might have been carried out. It is possible that the seizure of Heilbronn in Lyons was linked with the Hardy business, but right now I do not recall any possible connection.

Question 20: On what date was Hardy freed on your orders? Were the terms of his work covered in a request sent to the BDS in Paris? By what means was your request conveyed? What did you request? What reply did you get?

Answer: Hardy was freed on my orders on 11 or 12 June 1943. In any event it could not have been 10 June because I had to wait for the answer to a work-permit application I had made for him.

I sent this authorization request to BDS Paris using a 'Fernschreiben' which was a high-speed telegram, and Paris referred the matter to RSHA Berlin (AMT IV) because it could not assume responsibility for the matter.

In the telegram I asked for permission to release Hardy on the grounds he was willing to work for us. He was already known to my superiors in the hierarchy because I sent Paris a report almost immediately after his arrest. The telegram had to be short and I could not include details of the plan I had for using Hardy, but I wrote another report covering that.

In view of the urgency of the matter, the reply reached KDS Lyons by 'Fernschreiben' direct from Berlin. Berlin gave the go-ahead to employ Hardy under my personal responsibility, and the authorization was signed by Gruppenführer Muller Amtschef IV of the RSHA. The BDS in Paris was simultaneously notified by Berlin.

Question 21: Hardy says he was freed on the evening of 10 June 1943, a Thursday, and that a pass was issued to him. Is that true? Was he not in fact released on 12 June 1943, the Saturday before Whit Sunday?

Answer: As I have already said, I do not think Hardy was let out on the evening of 10 June 1943. I am absolutely sure it was the 11th, but I could be wrong one day either way. I told Hardy he was free to go but I informed him that for the first few days one of my men would be tailing him, and I asked him to report to me every evening in person. Actually for a week after his release Hardy slept in his room at our service in the École de Santé Militaire. He was not guarded at night. The man who was to be Hardy's contact was Unterscharführer Stengritt alias Harry. It was under this last name that I introduced him to Hardy. Stengritt knows Hardy well.

I cannot recall giving Hardy a pass right away, as he claims.

Question 22: In the statement by Hartwig Max Willi, police inspector in the Intervention Commando sent from Berlin, which reached Lyons early in June 1943, and was placed under the command of Kommissar Werth, it emerges that Hardy was questioned on 10 June 1943 by this same Hartwig about Lyons region plans contained in a suitcase. It is said that you ordered Hartwig to conduct this interrogation as he speaks very good French. Do you remember 1. the interrogation; 2. the results; 3. the place where the case was found? Give us all the details. Was it a wicker suitcase?

Answer: Werth, Obersturmführer and Kriminal Kommissar, was the head of the SonderKommando AS directly responsible to RSHA Berlin Section IV E. I was expected to hand over to this SonderKommando anything I might obtain about the Secret Army's activities, whether sabotage or intelligence proper, especially radio transmitters. Naturally Werth knew about the Hardy affair and, as I recall, he asked my permission to have one of his men interrogate Hardy. I agreed of course. I remember there was some business about a suitcase but I am unable to provide details. That subject has completely gone out of my mind, and it is your remarks that are jogging my memory. I cannot therefore give particulars either about the contents of that suitcase or what it was like or where it was found.

Question 23: Under orders from you, Hartwig, it seems, went with Hardy to Paris on 12 June 1943. There, Hardy was to meet his fiancée, Lydie Bastien. This trip is said to have been a very short one. He was back on 13 June 1943. Are these details correct? Do you remember the report Hartwig wrote, or any details about where Hardy went?

Answer: It is true that Hardy had my consent to go to Paris and see Lydie Bastien. I cannot remember who went with him but it is quite possible it was Hartwig. I must add that I do not recognize that person at all from the photo you showed me. Hardy went there and back. I do not recall the date exactly of that trip, or details of the report drawn up by the escort on their return. The journey was essentially for personal reasons.

Question 24: In the period from Hardy's release to 21 June 1943, what contacts did he have with you and your service?
1. Did Lunel return from Paris between 11 and 21 June 1943? Did he meet Hardy in the premises of the Santé Militaire?
2. On what date and why did Hardy come to your offices?
3. Was he obliged to sleep at the École de Santé? How many times did he sleep there? What procedure was followed when he turned up? Did he report to you yourself or to an officer in your service?
4. After his seizure at Chalon, was he held in one of the Lyons prisons, Montluc for example?
5. On 12 June 1943 Heilbronn alias Arel alias Hennequin was arrested near Lyons-Perrache railway station around 2.30 p.m. just after talking with Didot-Hardy. Please tell us how this arrest was carried out. Who ordered it? Did it originate from Hardy?

Answer: During the period from his release to 21 June 1943, apart from his Paris trip, Hardy stayed in Lyons. He was in touch with me daily, either personally or through

Stengritt. For example, around 15 June he came to me himself to tell me about the meeting in Lyons of the Resistance leaders. In his maildrop he had in fact collected the announcement about this meeting, which was to be held after the arrest of General Delestraint. At the same time he was ordered to attend it. Hardy added that at that meeting General Delestraint's successor would be appointed and he further said that Moulin, that's what he called him, would also be there.

It is possible that Multon alias Lunel got back from Paris between 11 and 21 June 1943 but I cannot confirm that. I do not think he met Hardy in the Santé Militaire premises. Since Multon had squealed on Hardy, and Hardy believed he had indeed done that, it is understandable that Multon did not want to meet him. At any rate, I do not know if they met somewhere other than the offices of our service.

As I was responsible for Hardy's movements and actions, I obliged him to sleep at the École de Santé as I said. He came at least five times.

Hardy always reported to me when he came in the evening. The guard knew him and let him come direct.

I say again that Hardy, who had been taken at Chalon, where he was held for a few hours at the prison, was not held subsequently in another prison, either in Lyons or anywhere else. I also solemnly affirm that he was not subjected to any maltreatment. Any allegation on his part to the contrary would be pure invention. Our relationship was always very courteous.

Heilbronn was seized by men from the Sonder-Kommando AS led by Kriminal Kommissar Werth on information supplied by Hardy. I do not know the details of this affair, which was handled by a service other than mine, but it is certain that Hardy designated him for the arrest, having fixed a rendezvous for Heilbronn and knowing he was being followed by Werth's men. If I remember correctly, Werth had obtained evidence of Heilbronn's activity in the Resistance.

Question 25: Under questioning Heilbronn has said that in the course of his interrogation he was taken for Didot-Hardy for a long time. Was this deliberate or not, because there is no possible physical resemblance between the two? Heilbronn had left Hardy just before being arrested, and moreover you yourself and your service had full information about Didot-Hardy, whom you had released.

When Hennequin was seized, this being the alias under which Heilbronn was arrested, an admission card to the War Ministry was found on him in the name of Engineer-Captain Heilbronn, including his photo. Confusion with Didot was thereafter no longer possible. Give a full explanation on that subject.

Meanwhile, in a letter dated 18 June 1943 and sent to the Police Inspector, you referred to the apartment of 'the Jew Marc Heilbronn' arrested 12 June 1943 for 'black market activities and anti-German scheming', and domiciled at 23 rue Jean-Marc Bernard in Lyons. Kindly give detailed information about Heilbronn and tell us the purpose and origin of the confusion with Didot after his arrest.

Answer: I again state that Heilbronn alias Hennequin was arrested by men of the SonderKommando AS led by Werth, and that I had nothing to do with his interrogation. There was no confusion in the minds of the interrogators about the person of Didot-Hardy. I can only suppose that Werth, knowing both Hardy and Heilbronn, whom he had arrested, appeared to be making a mistake all the time about the identity of Didot-Hardy to make Heilbronn think his arrest was fortuitous and was not due to denunciation by Hardy. In short, it was a camouflage trick, very likely. Because Werth knew I was concerned to spread it around that Hardy was free of all restraints and that he was still being sought.

Question 26: What is the exact nature of the information you asked Hardy to get? Did it relate to a meeting of the Resistance leaders? What information did Hardy give you about that, and how soon ahead of the meeting: date of meeting, venue, those who were to attend?

Answer: I have already supplied answers to that question. I repeat that Hardy was supposed to give me details about the Resistance organisations and more specially tell me of any orders he received from superiors. The Resistance leaders' meeting came up only after Hardy's trip to Paris, as I have said. The date of the meeting was mentioned on the document Hardy found in his mailbox, but the place and people to take part were not given.

Question 27: Did you know a certain Aubry alias Thomas? Were you nearby when Hardy and Aubry met on Sunday 20 June 1943 at 11.30 a.m. at Pont Morand? Were you the civilian sitting on the bench near Pont Morand reading a newspaper?
   Give us precise details as to the circumstances in which you knew of the Didot-Aubry meeting on 20 June 1943 at Pont Morand. Did Hardy himself tell you, or was it through the Dumoulin maildrop?

Answer: A mistake as to identity caused me to say earlier that Aubry was caught at the same time as General Delestraint in Paris. I mixed him up with Gastaldo. I did not know Aubry personally, but I knew about him from various service reports from Paris and Marseilles.
   Hardy said he could enable me to identify his liaison agent and Aubry a few days ahead of the planned Resistance leaders' gathering. This would mean I could be sure of getting to the venue. I remember that only the date was set, but not the place or the participants. Hardy had already met Aubry and knew from him that he too was to be there.
   I therefore went to the meeting place at Pont Morand with Stengritt. I was the civilian on the bench reading the paper. Stengritt was beside me but gave no evidence of knowing me. We saw Hardy meet up with two men.

— 285 —

Afterwards, when he came to me in the afternoon, he told me the taller of the two men was Aubry. So it was from Hardy himself that I learned the circumstances of the Pont Morand meeting.

Question 28: Kindly state the arrangements made for the arrest of the Resistance military chiefs on 21 June 1943.
1. Is it true that Didot informed you that a meeting of this kind was to be held on 21 June 1943?
2. On what date did you know about this meeting?
3. What data was given you by Didot-Hardy as to the date, place and time of the meeting; those who were to attend; and the presence of Max, General de Gaulle's delegate?
4. How and through whom did you know the meeting was to be at Caluire at Dr Dugoujon's house?
5. What was the part played by Madame Delétraz alias Delatray alias Madame Deville?

Regarding Madame Delétraz, kindly tell us:
a. The circumstances under which she was reportedly arrested by your service in connection with the Jura affair on 16 April 1943.
b. In what manner she came to work for your service and more especially how she came to be working under orders from K 30 (Moog, Robert, called Pierre, called Bobby) and in the apartment of Monsieur Meffray, Place des Celestins in Lyons.
c. Her exact role in the arrest of Berthie Albrecht, Frenay's secretary at Mâcon.
d. On 21 June 1943 at the École de Santé in Lyons, did she obtain guidance from you and K 30 in order to follow Hardy, who was to attend the meeting and join up with Aubry at 1.45 p.m. at the Croix Paquet funicular railway? Were handcuffs tried out on Hardy, real or doctored, in the presence of Madame Delétraz?
e. At that time did you discuss how Hardy and Madame Delétraz were to recognize each other and what signs they would use to indicate whether the meeting place was around Croix Paquet or if a tram was to be taken?

f. Madame Delétraz followed Hardy and Aubry. Did she take the funicular and then tram number 33?

g. Did she come and meet you at Croix Paquet at the funicular, and did she then lead you directly or after much hesitation to the villa of Dr Dugoujon, and did she at once take tram number 33 again to the École de Santé?

6. How was the arrest of the Resistance leaders set up at Caluire? How was the operation carried out? Did Moog, Pierre (K 30), Multon, Saumande and Doussot alias André, whose photos I am showing you, join in the arrests?

7. Kindly describe exactly how the arrests were effected. What orders did you give about the attitude Hardy was to adopt and how he should behave when you intervened.

8. Describe Hardy's flight. Did the police and people from your service know about your orders?

9. Was Hardy wounded by a bullet fired by one of your men or by himself?

10. Who were the people arrested at Caluire? What did you know about each of them before the arrests? How did you know? Who told you?

Answer: It is correct that Hardy alias Didot told me a Resistance leaders' meeting was scheduled for 21 June 1943 in Lyons, but when he provided that information he did not yet know where or who was to attend. That was four or five days before the date set. As I have said, Hardy learned of the meeting from a document from Paris in his mailbox.

When Hardy supplied this information to me and added that he himself was to be at the gathering also, I judged that the matter was highly important and decided to carry out the arrest of those present. As Hardy was to be included among them, it was necessary to lay down plans for the operation. Every evening before the meeting I saw Hardy, and he produced new facts obtained through his liaison agent. That was how he told me Max was going to be there. Hardy disclosed to me the true identity of Max, saying his real name was Moulin, and he spoke to me about his activity in the Resistance.

Hardy spoke about Aubry as well but before the meeting. He did not mention other people.

On the morning of the day set for the gathering, Hardy still did not know where it would be. Through a meeting with his liaison agent he was to find out the place, and the agent was to take him.

The plan we worked out involved following Hardy. Also in on the planning with Hardy and me were Untersturmführer Wenzel and Stengritt, I myself ordered Wenzel to handle the tailing and establish a system of vans and relay points so that I would have the details early enough. I was in uniform and with my men and two cars, or maybe it was three, I waited on the banks of the Rhône, where we were to learn what the venue was. Moog, Pierre (K 30), Saumande (K 4) and Doussot took part in tailing Hardy but not the arrest. For that I designated men in uniform. Multon was out of the whole operation.

I remember clearly that a woman took part in the tailing, but I cannot say what her name was. Let me add that I ordered Wenzel to deal with that.

It was Multon who dealt with the arrest of Madame Delétraz alias Deville. I have forgotten what work she did for our service and the exact way in which she joined in the arrest of Berthie Albrecht at Mâcon.

There is another detail which I gave at my previous questioning: at Wenzel's suggestion Hardy used yellow chalk to mark his progress; on the garden gate, the stairs and the door of the meeting room on the first floor at the Caluire villa. In that way we were absolutely sure that the meeting was at Dr Dugoujon's house and I could put into effect the arrest procedure.

With that information, I went to Caluire with my men and had the villa surrounded, which was not difficult, the house being on its own. And I issued the instruction that people could be allowed in but no one was to leave the building.

I went inside the house myself, and followed the crosses straight to the meeting room, followed by Wenzel and Stengritt. I opened the door and to obtain a surprise effect I fired up into a wall. All those in the room dived and I saw Hardy right away. I summarily questioned all those present as to their identity, and had them searched. Naturally they all gave their cover names. After that I interrogated them separately. Eventually it was Hardy's turn. He himself gave me the true identities of those present, and Stengritt noted them right away.

Then Hardy told me we had got there too early, that the meeting had not started and that they were still waiting for Moulin, adding that he might be in the waiting-room. It is certain that, unless Hardy had given me that tip, Moulin might have eluded me, because the people in the doctor's waiting-room did not interest me. I had them brought up, without knowing who exactly they were. I resumed the summary questioning. Hardy came to me again and pointed out Moulin and the other two men.

There was no special arrangement for Hardy, who was to be arrested along with the others. However, he had worked out a plan for his escape with Stengritt.

The detained persons were taken to the cars. Stengritt took Hardy, and when they got near the car, Stengritt released the twist, there was a scuffle and Hardy got away in accordance with the agreed plan. All the Germans with me knew Hardy was to escape. I had warned them at the planning stage of the operation.

Hardy ran off and, as planned, my men fired into the air. But my driver Barthel forgot the warning and ran after Hardy, fired but missed. My men put him right on that and the chase ended. At that moment I myself was still in the meeting room and I watched Hardy's get-away through the window. I saw my driver making a mess of things and severely reprimanded him.

Later Hardy told me he hid in a ditch and wounded himself with the small pistol I had given him some days previously to protect himself, and I think what Hardy told me was correct because Barthel had a 12 mm Colt and would have seriously wounded Hardy.

I forget the names of the people we caught at Caluire, except for Moulin and Aubry and Dr Dugoujon. I knew nothing about these people before the arrest. I personally interrogated Moulin. The others were probably questioned by men of the SonderKommando under Werth.

By 'Fernschreiben' I informed BDS Paris of the operation's success thanks to tips from Hardy, listing the names of those detained, particularly Moulin alias Max. Next day, 22 June, BDS Paris instructed me to transfer Moulin at once to Paris.

Question 29: Of those held at Caluire, who was it who made statements directly implicating certain or all the persons seized or gave details of their jobs?

At what stage were the true identities of Jacques Martel and Ermelin Claude known?

Answer: I cannot answer that question, as I myself did not carry out interrogations of the detained persons. I simply effected the arrests and conducted Moulin's initial interrogations. I also know that this Caluire operation led to a number of arrests in other parts of France on BDS orders to local KDS.

Question 30: Were you familiar with all the documents concerning the AS discovered by the Germans in 1942–3? Give full details on their discovery.

Answer: Personally I acquired numerous documents about Resistance matters but I cannot claim to have known them all. These items were sent to Paris where they were summarised and despatched to Berlin. Locally we used only data that was useful locally. The AS side as a whole could only be handled in Paris.

Question 31: German documents that fell into French hands

indicate the extent of the results your service obtained against the Secret Army. Do you know those documents?

Answer: I do not know of those documents' existence. I should say here that at RSHA there was an *'Auswertungabteilung West'* which exploited documents received from the western territories. This section drew up main reports for RSHA, as well as for the top echelons, military and civil, of the Reich.

Items relating more specially to the Secret Army in France and repressing it, especially after the Caluire affair, were supplied either by BDS Frankreich Section IV or, in the case of affairs in Lyons, after the arrest of Hardy alias Didot by the SonderKommando AS headed by Kriminal Kommissar Werth, and I would remind you that this worked directly under the RSHA Berlin IV E.

Werth knew all the details, either by examining the files or by questioning detainees. This allowed the compiling of the envisaged overall documents.

I want to say again, to clear up matters of detail which you are putting to me about the main German documents, that I did not undertake interrogations of persons arrested at Caluire, except Moulin.

It is possible I saw Aubry, but I did not produce a report about him. Nor can I say whether those arrested, especially Aubry, volunteered information or gave it as a result of maltreatment.

Question 32: You have just been given extracts from the Kaltenbrunner document (extracts read to witness and questions put on various relevant points). Is this in accordance with the facts known to the German SD service in Lyons at 23 or 24 June 1943?

Answer: Yes, this document generally conforms to the facts known by the SD Lyons service, including the Werth SonderKommando because they played the most significant part in the AS repression and carried out the exploiting of material.

Question 33: Kindly state how and at what date you informed BDS Paris and the Berlin chief of the RSHA of the following facts: a. the arrest of Hardy-Didot, and your use of him in your service
b. the arrest of Heilbronn.
c. the Caluire arrests.

Answer: Regarding the arrest of Didot-Hardy I notified BDS Paris the same day by *'Fernschreiben'* and a few days later in a detailed report.

As to Heilbronn's arrest, Werth handled it and it is possible that he sent a report to Berlin but I cannot give any details. BDS Paris was naturally kept informed of this arrest.

The Caluire detentions were notified to BDS Paris by *Fernschreiben* the same day, that was the rule, and a few days later in a detailed report.

Question 34: At what stage did you notify these same recipients of the identities of Jacques Martel (Jean Moulin) the Ermelin (Aubrac).

Answer: The telegram to BDS Paris announcing the success of the Caluire swoop mentioned the name Moulin, Jean, alias Max. Jean Moulin was immediately identified. I cannot say as regards Ermelin, I did not do the interrogating. I can add that Hardy gave us the precise identities of the people who were at the Caluire gathering.

Question 35: Kindly describe what led up to your personal detention of Madame Madeleine Raisin on the morning of 22 June 1943 at the domicile of Monsieur Cornu, where Aubry lodged.

Answer: I myself did not question Aubry. I cannot recall personally (as you allege) arresting Madame Raisin. The day after her arrest, 22 June, I interrogated Jean Moulin.

I do not know what might have been discovered either at Madame Raisin's place or at Monsieur Cornu's.

Question 36: At Madame Raisin's home did you find seven copies of a rail sabotage plan for the south zone, that is, the former Free Zone, the regions being identified by the codes R1, R2, R3, R4, R5 and R6?

Answer: A plan of that sort may have been found, but I cannot confirm it. Anyhow, it was not I who found the plan. I would remember that.

Question 37: Is it correct that, for the German services, Hardy drew up the rail sabotage plan. When would that have been?

Answer: It was just after his arrest that Hardy drew up the plan. He may have done the plan on his own, I cannot be sure. I provided him with writing materials and I think this plan was his token of good will towards us.

Question 38: Do you know about the so-called 'Green Plan', and at what stage did you hear of its existence?

Answer: Yes I do. The 'Green Plan', which was the sabotage programme for the railways throughout France, was drawn up by Hardy. It was Hardy himself who spoke to me about it, but I never knew the details of the plan.

Question 39: Which documents did Hardy work on to reproduce the sabotage plan which he had drawn up previously, and which he may have utilized? Were these captured documents? Captured at his place? At a tailor's place? Who was he? Where did he live? Was it at Hardy's domicile? On that point, did you know of his domicile with Monsieur Bessiron, 112 Chemin de St Just at Vaize? This domicile is mentioned on a data sheet drawn up by the Abwehr with regard to Hardy.

Answer: Hardy reconstituted the programme in question from memory. He did not work from captured documents.

Question 40: On what date was this programme sent to BDS Paris by your service?

Answer: I've forgotten. But, in view of the importance of the matter, the delay was not very great.

Question 41: On what exact date was Hardy released by you: in the morning of 10, 11 or 12 June 1943? Was he constantly followed? Did you know of the contacts he re-established with Resistance members between 12 and 21 June 1943? State persons and places if possible. Say why those people were not arrested by you or your service. Was there agreement between you and Hardy not to seize certain persons? Who were they? Where did Hardy sleep at that time?

Answer: I have already answered those questions. Personally, I think Hardy was freed on 11 June 1943. For two or three days he was escorted by Stengritt, except for the Paris trip. Then for several days he slept at our service premises. On 20 June 1943 he also slept at my service. Nobody stopped him going to his domicile. Hardy informed me of contacts he was making again with Resistance members between 12 and 21 June.

First he met his fiancée Lydie Bastien in Paris, and brought her back to Lyons. Then he met his liaison agent whom he revealed to me at the same time as Aubry, though of course not face to face, and finally Heilbronn. If he met others, he did not tell me.

These persons were arrested by my service, except Heilbronn so as not to spoil it for Hardy. In any case Heilbronn was held by Werth's men and on that point I would remind you of the confusion over Heilbronn's identity, and his being mistaken for Didot-Hardy.

Hardy and I had agreed these people should not be caught, in particular Lydie Bastien and the liaison agent. Furthermore, when he told me about Aubry, we agreed that he should not be detained.

Question 42: After Hardy was taken by the French police in Lyons, how did you know he was held in Antiquaille Hospital: from the French police? State the names of the policemen who told you that, or whether you intervened at the French police services and more particularly with police officer Cussonac and Commissaires Petiot and Kubler.

Answer: The French police arrived at the Caluire premises after shots were fired. I don't know who told them. Hardy was arrested by the French police. Hardy was to have come to see me during the evening of 21 June 1943, to collect money and fill me in on the details. He failed to turn up and I worried about him.

Two days later I was on the phone to officer Cussonac, who asked me if my service had carried out the Caluire arrests. I said it was my service and I took the opportunity of asking him for a copy of the French police report on the incident. When I looked through this report I learned that Hardy had been detained by the French police, that he was wounded and was in Antiquaille. I then told the service run by Cussonac that Hardy had been arrested by ourselves and that he had managed to get away. I asked the French police to hand him over and they agreed to that. I rather think it was Commissaire Petiot who brought Hardy to my offices. I thanked the French police warmly for their gesture, in an attempt to protect Hardy.

Question 43: Hardy was in Antiquaille from 21 to 28 June 1943. During that time he was interrogated by you or your people. Tell us about that fully.

Answer: I did not question Hardy during the period you mention. Nor do I believe he was questioned by any German service, but I can't be certain of that. After all, it is even possible I questioned him as part of the cover for him.

Question 44: When he quit Antiquaille, was Hardy taken to the École de Santé and interrogated by you? What was his demeanour? Did he give data about his attributions and functions and those of others sought or arrested by you either in Paris (Vidal, Gastaldo, Terrier) or in Lyons or Caluire (Heilbronn, Aubry, Lacaze, Lassagne, Parisot (Xavier), Schwarzfeld, Dugoujon, Jacques Martel (Jean Moulin), Ermelin (Aubrac) concerning the rail sabotage plan?

Answer: When he left Antiquaille, Hardy was brought to my service at the École de Santé Militaire. Alone with me, Hardy narrated his get-away after the Caluire swoop. He said he wounded himself to show his Resistance comrades that he had managed to escape. His idea was to go back home and get treatment from a doctor. The fortuitous arrest by the French police spoiled that plan for him. Hardy was in my office for two hours and he gave me some tip-offs. But the wound was hurting him and he was feverish, so I had him taken to the Croix Rousse German hospital. I told the hospital director to take good care of him.

Question 45: On what date was Hardy transferred to Croix Rousse German hospital? Why was he taken there?

Answer: I have already told you. It was on 28 June 1943 that Hardy was admitted to the German hospital.

Question 46: While he was in Croix Rousse hospital, did you send Kommissar Werth and the interpreter Inspector Hartwig to find out his medical condition?

Answer: Werth may have gone to see Hardy, but he did it on his own. I could not give orders to Werth, or send him to Hardy. It is very likely he told me he intended to call on Hardy.

Question 47: What was Hardy's behaviour and demeanour while in that hospital? Was he taken to the École de Santé for questioning? Say what he was asked. In that period was he active in your service? Could he go out freely sometimes? In what circumstances? Where did he go?

Answer: Hardy was free while in the German hospital, I mean by that, that he was not cared for like a detainee. The head of the hospital knew about Hardy. While there, he never came to the École de Santé for questioning. If we had questions to put to him, either Werth or Stengritt or I went to the hospital. While he was there he was not active for us. In any case he had to have treatment for his condition. He did not leave the hospital because, in the eyes of the French police, he was under arrest.

Question 48: In fact, did Hardy escape from Croix Rousse or was his escape staged by your service with the agreement of the hospital medical people?

Answer: Hardy stayed in the German hospital for treatment for about a month and a half. When he was better, the chief doctor there advised me of the fact. So I called on him and told him I would come and fetch my 'friend Hardy' during the night. Around 11.00 p.m. to midnight I did indeed fetch Hardy in a car, with the consent of the doctor. That too was a mock escape. I took Hardy to Lyons near the domicile of Lydie Bastien, whom he wanted to see first. Next day he wanted to try contacting his liaison agent. That was late July/early August 1943. Two days after he 'escaped' from hospital I met Hardy in Lyons with Stengritt. I cannot recall where, but I well remember that I handed him some money and a forged French identity card. I cannot remember the name on the card.

Question 49: Do you know Lydie Bastien? Did she go and see Hardy at the École de Santé or in Croix Rousse hospital?

Did Hardy have the chance to see her when he was in hospital there?

Answer: I had no personal contact with Lydie Bastien. She was in touch with Stengritt, and he went at least twice to her place. This woman did not visit Hardy when he was on our premises. I cannot say whether she went to see Hardy in the German hospital; maybe she went with Stengritt. Hardy used to write letters and gave them to me, asking me to get them to Lydie Bastien. I cannot remember whether she used the same method.

Question 50: Why were Madame and Monsieur Bastien, of 113 quai Pierre-Scize, Lyons, arrested on 2 September 1943 and kept in Montluc prison until 30 September or 1 October 1943?

Answer: I am unable to answer that question, as I left Lyons for Paris at the end of August 1943. I was in Paris until 5 December 1943, when I returned to my post in Lyons. During that period I went to Germany and to North Italy to deal with the Rote Kapelle business. To be precise I was absent from Lyons from 31 August to 5 December 1943. During that lapse of time I was not concerned with things in Lyons.

Question 51: After they were arrested, Madame and Monsieur Bastien were questioned by Lutjens, whose photo we will now show you, concerning Hardy's hide-out and the domicile of their daughter, Lydie Bastien. What was the point of these interrogations?

Answer: When I gave Hardy the identity card I mentioned, I arranged a meeting with Hardy for a week later. He failed to turn up, and I lost touch with him thereafter. I have never seen him since and nor has he shown up at all. I myself never cancelled the search for Hardy, and if it was abandoned, it happened during my absence. So I reply negatively to your question, not being aware of the arrest of Lydie Bastien's parents which I have learned from you.

Question 52: Did you know that Hardy was arrested on 21 June 1943 by the French police at the home of Madame Damas, Quai de Serin, Caluire?
Did you know what the relationship was between Hardy and the Damas couple? Did you know that after his genuine or supposed escape Hardy sought refuge with Madame Damas again?

Answer: I do not know those details.

Question 53: Did you have any contact with Hardy after he got away from the Croix Rousse? Details please.

Answer: I have already dealt with that. As I said, there was just one meeting between us.

Question 54: On 25 and 26 June 1943, did you yourself supervize the first transfer from Lyons to Paris Fresnes prison of the people arrested at Caluire, namely: Dugoujon, Lassagne, Aubry, Schwarzfeld, Madame Raisin and Lacaze?

Answer: No, I do not think I took those people myself.

Question 55: Did you issue orders that some of them should be treated better? Which ones? For what reasons?

Answer: It was not I who conducted the questioning of those people, as I already explained. But I do recall that Aubry revealed plenty, and it is quite possible that, at the request of Werth or someone in his Kommando, the accused was given privileged treatment. But I could not confirm that.

Question 56: Why was Jean Moulin transferred later on and accompanied by yourself? State the date of transfer. Why was Aubrac kept back at Montluc prison?

Answer: I remember the BDS asking for the urgent transfer of Moulin to them. I took Moulin myself by car. I cannot state the exact transfer date, which might have been at the same time as the other detained were moved. I do not know why Aubrac remained in Lyons. The interrogations were conducted by Werth.

Question 57: In the service run by Kieffer, head of the Paris BDS Section IV E, did you know Misselwitz, Ernst, and Meiners, Heinrich? In the presence of either or both at the BDS Paris, 74, later 86, Avenue Foch, did you relate the events surrounding the arrest of Didot-Hardy, his behaviour after his arrest, the part he played in the Caluire arrests, the reconstitution of the rail sabotage plan for the German services in June or July 1943, either during the transfer of the detainees or when on mission to Paris?

Answer: I do not recollect knowing those two men with Kieffer, whom you mention. I took Moulin to Paris and handed him over to Sturmbannführer Boemelberg, as he had requested, but it was Service IV E, headed by Kieffer, who took delivery. It may be that during talks among comrades in Kieffer's service I expanded on the Hardy affair, but I would not have gone into details as your question suggests. Perhaps Misselwitz and Meiners, junior officers in Service IV E, saw the reports I sent. That is the only way I can explain it.

Question 58: Did you know of the summary compiled in September 1943 by Captain Gegauf alias Kramer alias Monsieur Eugene of the Abwehr, a copy of which I am about to show you, concerning the parts played by these officials in Paris of the Dijon SR base: K 30 (Moog, Pierre,

Robert, alias Bobby) and K 4 (Saumande), in the following matters:
1. Jura (arrest of Berthie Albrecht); 2. Arrest of Didot-Hardy on 8 June 1943 at Chalon-sur-Saône; 3. Arrest of General Delestraint alias Vidal? Give full details about this subject.

Answer: I was not familiar with this summary by Gegauf about agents K 30 and K 4. It was dated September 1943 and I had already left Lyons as I said before.

Question 59: Have you anything to say about the questions I have been asking you? Can you recall any details we have not raised that could shed light on the matter in hand?

Answer: No, I have nothing to add. I may have been mistaken as to dates, as these things happened more than five years ago. But in principle this is what happened.
   Even so I should like to make it clear that Hardy worked for me of his own free will and not under constraint. He had several chances to give us the slip. He did not do so. What is more, he enabled us to carry out several operations against Resistance networks, which shows he wanted to work for us. Hardy took money from me, and he therefore received his wages. Hardy was very ambitious too. I do not know what his job was in the Resistance after he broke away from me, but looking back I imagine he wanted a more important role and he stopped at nothing to achieve that, because he betrayed his comrades and even his leaders. That is my personal opinion, of course, and I have nothing more to declare.
   Evidence read to witness, who confirmed and signed with us.

      Klaus Barbie   Chapuis
      Whiteway   Bibes
   This being the record of evidence comprising thirty sheets terminated seventeenth July one thousand nine

hundred and forty-eight, for submission to the Commander of Military Justice Gonnot, Examining Magistrate of the Permanent Military Court, Paris, with his Rogatory Commission of 23 June 1948 and documents returned herewith.

The Commissioner
Bibes

Bibliography

Alexandrov, Victor *La Mafia des SS*, Stock 1978

Amouroux, Henri *L'Impitoyable Guerre Civile*, Robert Laffont 1983

Basse, Martin and Jo *Histoire de Caluire et Cuire*, Editions Fot, Lyon 1976

Bénouville, Guillain de *Le Sacrifice du Matin*, Robert Laffont 1946

Calef, Henri *Jean Moulin, une Vie*, Plon 1980

Chambon, Albert *Mais Que Font Donc Ces Diplomates . . .* , A. Pedone 1983

Cordier, Daniel *Jean Moulin et le C.N.R.*, CNRS 1983

Dantas Ferreira, Ewaldo *O Depoimento do SS Altmann-Barbie*, José Olympio, Rio 1972

Devigny, André *Je Fus Ce Condamné*, Presses de la Cité 1978

Fest, Joachim *Hitler*, 2 vols Gallimard 1973

Frenay, Henri *La Nuit Finira*, Robert Laffont 1973

Frossard, André, *La Maison des Otages*, Fayard 1960

Fuchs, Gottlieb *Le Renard*, Albin Michel 1973

Harzer, Philippe *Klaus Barbie et la Gestapo en France*, Le Carrousel-FN 1983

Höhne, Heinz *L'Ordre Noir*, Casterman 1968

Klarsfeld, Beate *Partout Où Ils Seront*, Edition Spéciale 1972

Klarsfeld, Serge *Vichy-Auschwitz*, Fayard 1983

Michel, Henri *Jean Moulin l'Unificateur*, Hachette 1971

Moulin, Jean *Premier Combat*, les Editions de Minuit, réédition 1983

Moulin, Laure *Jean Moulin*, Presses de la Cité 1982

Murphy, Brendan *The Butcher of Lyons*, Empire Books 1983

Noguères, Henri *Histoire de la Résistance en France*, vol. 3, Robert Laffont 1972

Paillole, Paul *Services Spéciaux 1935–1945*, Robert Laffont 1975

Ponchardier, Dominique *La Mort du Condor*, Gallimard 1976
Ruby, Marcel *La Résistance et la Contre-Résistance à Lyons*, 'Klaus Barbie, de Montluc à Montluc', L'Hermès 1979, 1981, 1983
Speer, Albert, *Journal de Spandau*, Robert Laffont 1975
Thorndike, Guillermo, *El Caso Banchero*, Mosca Azul (Lima) 1980
Vergès, Jacques *Pour En Finir Avec Ponce Pilate*, Le Pré aux Clercs 1983
Vergès, Jacques and Étienne Bloch, *La Face Cachée du Procès Barbie* Samuel Tastet 1983
Wiesenthal, Simon, *Les Assassins Sont Parmi Nous*, Stock 1967
'*La Gestapo en France*', Historia hors série no. 27, Paris 1972
'*Klaus Barbie and the United States Government*' Report and Exhibits [submitted by Allan A. Ryan, Jr] US Department of Justice 1983

Index

Albrecht, B. (Resistance) 69, 286
Altmann, *see* Barbie
Amouroux, H. 37, 257
André, F. ('Crooked Jaw')
(collaborator) 39–41, 73, 109,
120, 129
Armistice Commission 30
Aubrac, L. (alias 'Ghislaine de
Barbentanne') 95–8 *passim*
Aubrac, R., aliases 64, 66; and
Barbie 97, 215, 300; and
Caluire meeting 71–2, 77–87
passim, 92, 95–8 *passim*
Aubry, H. (alias 'Thomas
Avricourt') (Resistance) 65,
66; and Caluire meeting 72,
77–81 *passim*, 85, 91, 93, 285,
290–2; tortured 87

Badinter, R. 240, 258–9
Banzer, Gen. H. 188, 203, 205,
217, 223
Barbie, Klaus, aliases 23, 25,
34, 110, 130, 138, 141, 147–54
passim, 163; as Altmann
165–215 *passim*; Altmann
unmasked 215, 249;
antecedents 4–5, father
(Klaus) 4–6, mother (Anna
Hees) 4, 146–7, 163, 174–5,
181; arrest of 249; author's
interviews with 209–16
passim; children of (Ute and
Klaus-Georg) 13–14, 151,
166, 172, 175–6, 181, 184–9
passim, 196, 201, 224–7, 231,
261–5 *passim*; daughter-in-
law (Françoise) 180, 183–7,
224, 227, 232; crimes against
humanity 16, 22, 49, 99–100,
109–12 *passim*, 248, 260;
early years 3–8; extradition
demands for, French 136,
160, 189, 201, 205, 217, 235,
247, German 106, 235, 237,
241–2, 272; and the French
6, 146, 182, 218; and Hardy
('Didot') 69–83 *passim*, 141,
180, 270–301 *passim*;
interrogations of 16–17,
133–6, 140, 158, 221,
269–302; and the Jews 2, 16,
146, 180, Bron massacre
116–20, deportations of
16–19, 20–4 *passim*, 32–3,
43–58 *passim*, and final
solution 48; in Lyons SS
30–126 *passim*, *see* individual
events; in Lyons jail 251–68
passim; marriage 9, 12–13;
mistresses 24, 40–1, 130; and
Moulin 25, 62–3, 265,
admiration for 86, 134, 180,
183, 226, 231, Caluire
capture of 67–84, torture of
87–94 *passim*; physical
appearance 1, 8, 10–11,
17–18, 34, 47, 58, 103, 107,
138, 148, 198; postwar
activities (in Europe) 141–2,
147–54 *passim*, *see also*
United States; postwar
searches for 127–133, 146–7,
151–4, 174–6, 185–6, 196–209
passim; and Resistance
(French) 25, 28–33 *passim*,

— 305 —

crimes against humanity 43–4, 235, 247–8; concept of 49, 260, *see also* Barbie
CROWCASS 132, 153

Dabringhaus, E. 156–7
Debray, R. 185–6, 203, 217–18, 223, 233–8 *passim*
Deferre, G. (alias 'Elie') (Resistance) 72, 74–5
Delestraint, Gen. C. (aliases 'Mars' 'Vidal') (Resistance) 66, 68, 70–1, 80, 91–4 *passim*, 272–5
Delétraz, E. 73, 76–7, 80, 286–8
Dollar, J. 132–3
Doussot (collaborator) 73, 76, 105, 108, 140, 275, 287–8
Draganovich, Prof. K. 167–8
Dugoujon, Dr F. (Resistance) 65–6, 73, 81, 84–91 *passim*, 215, 286–7, 290
Duhail, J. (alias 'Vallin') (Resistance) 103–5
Dumoulin, Mme 70, 271–2

Favet, J. 53–5
Ferreira, E-D. 6, 18, 218, 221
Forced Labour Service 30
France, counter-espionage service 136–44 *passim*, 174–6, 196; extradition demands by 136, 160–2 *passim*, 189, 201, 205, 217, 247; and Operation Barbie 235–53; and US 136–9, 140, 157–8, 160
Frenay, H. (alias 'Charvet') (Resistance) 28, 63, 65, 69
Frossard, A. 98, 112
Fuchs, G. 89–90

Garçon,•Maître M. 71, 73, 82, 84, 161
Gastaldo (Resistance) 66, 71, 274
Gaulle, Gen. de 49, 63, 67, 136, 177, 180, 187; and Debray 217–18, and Moulin 25, 28; and Resistance 25, 28, 31
Gerlier, Cardinal 59, 114, 122–3, 125
Germany postwar, *see* West Germany
Germans in South America 184, 189, 202, 204–7
Gestapo, *see* SS
Giraud, H. 35, 128, 132
Glas, A. 107–8
Glasberg, Abbé 58–60
Goldberg-Cojot, M. 226, 235
Graaf, T. de (alias 'Gramont') (Resistance) 29, 77–8
Guesdon, L. 110, 125

Hardy, R. ('Didot') (Resistance) 65, 66, 235, 258; accusations against, by Barbie 71, 73–6 *passim*, 80, 82, *see also* Appendix, by Delétraz 76–7, by Stengritt, 83; acquitted twice 84; and Caluire meeting 72–81 *passim*, escape 82–4; and capture of Delestraint 70–1; and Nazi agents 69–70
Hees, Anna, *see* Barbie
Heilbronn (Resistance) 279, 283–4, 292–4
Hernu, C. 240, 256
Himmler 19, 30, 38–9
Hoffmann, Dr A. 9–11
Hollert, Col. F. (SS) 33, 42, 109, 175